'EXPERT PRIVILEGE' IN CIVIL EVIDENCE

Expert evidence frequently wins or loses cases. The importance of handling that evidence properly is therefore paramount. Fundamental to this is the application of privilege. Indeed, thorny privilege issues relating to expert documents, drafts, communications, instructions, collateral use, joint statements, statements of replaced experts, amongst other issues, come up time and again in practice.

This book approaches 'expert privilege' as a subcategory of privilege of its own. This is not because it is defined by a uniform subset of rules that apply to all situations in which expert material is at issue, but precisely because it is not. Neither can assumptions about privilege in expert evidence be based on other areas of application. Instead, 'expert privilege' is a highly idiosyncratic and problematic area. None of the traditional privilege texts are dedicated to this important subject. A book dealing with 'expert privilege' as a subject area of its own is therefore highly overdue. This is the first such book.

This book provides an overview of the issues, cases and rules that feature in this complex area, with the touchstone of practicality kept very much in mind throughout. The order in which issues are discussed follows the process by which expert evidence is prepared, from instruction through to collateral use. The intended readership is solicitors and counsel practicing in England and Wales in all the areas of civil, commercial litigation that use expert evidence. This book will also be of interest to practitioners in other common law countries and academics who are interested in English procedural law.

'Expert Privilege' in Civil Evidence

PAUL ENGLAND

·HART·
PUBLISHING

OXFORD AND PORTLAND, OREGON
2011

Published in the United Kingdom by Hart Publishing Ltd
16C Worcester Place, Oxford, OX1 2JW
Telephone: +44 (0)1865 517530
Fax: +44 (0)1865 510710
E-mail: mail@hartpub.co.uk
Website: http://www.hartpub.co.uk

Published in North America (US and Canada) by
Hart Publishing
c/o International Specialized Book Services
920 NE 58th Avenue, Suite 300
Portland, OR 97213-3786
USA
Tel: +1 503 287 3093 or toll-free: (1) 800 944 6190
Fax: +1 503 280 8832
E-mail: orders@isbs.com
Website: http://www.isbs.com

British Library Cataloguing in Publication Data
Data Available

ISBN: 978-1-84113-303-4

Typeset by Hope Services, Abingdon
Printed and bound in Great Britain by
TJ International Ltd, Padstow, Cornwall

Preface

This book hopes to demonstrate that 'Expert privilege' should be considered for practical purposes as a subcategory of its own. This is not because it is defined by a uniform subset of rules that apply to all situations in which expert material is at issue, but precisely because it is not. Conclusions about the protection of privilege in expert evidence cannot be made based on any other area of application. Instead, in large part because of the role of Part 35 of the Civil Procedure Rules, 'expert privilege' is a highly idiosyncratic and problematic area. A book dealing with 'expert privilege' as a subject area of its own is therefore highly overdue. This is the first such book to do so.

The idea for the book came from a webinar presentation made to clients, solicitors, external counsel and expert organisations on 17 September 2008, entitled 'Privilege and Experts: Common Problems and the Case-Law'. The intention of the talk was to deliver a guide to the most common privilege issues that arise in the preparation of experts' reports. The subject headings were organised roughly according to the basic chronology of the steps involved in this process and the lifecycle of such evidence, from instruction to use in collateral proceedings. Each of the basic issues identified was followed by a summary of the leading cases and then a tentative summary of the position of the law. Above all, the presentation was intended to provide practical guidance, while not avoiding the nitty-gritty of the case law and procedure. It proved unexpectedly popular, with a large number of participants logging on to listen to the speakers and watch the accompanying slides. However, the webinar format has its limitations. With only 45 minutes available, it was necessary to skip lightly through the key points. However, with the facility for email questions to be sent in during the webinar, it was clear that there was much still to be explored and we were touching on issues of great interest to many. This book is therefore aimed at this same audience but is intended to expand on the issues that were discussed in the webinar in more detail. The book is intended to provide a digest of the issues, cases and rules that assist in what is a complex area. However, the touchstone of practicality is kept very much in mind throughout and so the order in which issues are discussed is kept largely in line with the process by which expert evidence is prepared. New issues are also included, such as the privilege issues raised by experiments and survey evidence and reliance on undisclosed documents. The fascinating question of whether privilege is an absolute right or a matter of policy is also explored. Again, with accessibility and application in mind, every effort has also been made to keep the book short and concise.

Table of Contents

Table of Cases

Table of CPR Provisions

1

Introduction

. . . it is surprising that it is possible in 2002 to have a sustained argument on so apparently basic a point. However, . . . on closer examination the law in this area is not perhaps as clear as we might have expected . . .

Tomlinson J in *Three Rivers (No. 5)* [2002] EWHC 2730 (Comm):

Background

1. It can be helpful to think of privilege as a broad sea, covering, protecting and obscuring the detailed bed of information underneath. It is dense, opaque and notoriously complex in its movements. In some places, depending on the tide, the bed breaks above the surface where it can be seen. It is something to be respected, where failing to have the correct chart before setting sail can result in foundering upon a rock.
2. Marine analogies may not work for everyone, but privilege certainly does have the nature of washing into day-to-day legal matters. Knowing how it behaves is therefore a practical difficulty that will be faced frequently. Nowhere is this more of an issue than in the preparation of evidence and, in particular, expert evidence. Frequently, expert evidence is a critical element, or even the only element, to which the court looks for assistance in coming to a decision. Therefore, in an adversarial environment, knowing how privilege does or does not protect materials at the various stages of preparation and use of expert evidence is critical. However, as this book will illustrate, where expert evidence is concerned, understanding the application of privilege, to echo Tomlinson J's words, is far from as straightforward as might be supposed. In fact, a body of law of its own has grown up about expert evidence, making it a subject in its own right. This has been largely prompted by the introduction of Civil Procedure Rules Part 35 a decade ago. The rules applying to expert evidence in this Rule have a number of effects, direct and indirect, that are unique to privilege in expert evidence. It is the way in which privilege applies to expert evidence that is the subject of this book.

Issues Covered

3. The book begins with a brief outline in chapter 2 of the types of privilege that can apply in English law, in order to set the scene. Within this context it then describes the type of privilege that will apply to the preparation of expert evidence in UK proceedings. Chapter 3 then looks at the underlying way in which privilege applies to the work of an expert and when Part 35 will apply. In particular, it addresses the difficult question of what a Part 35 expert is. It also provides an introduction to the purpose and policy behind Part 35 as described by Lord Woolf in his 'Access to Justice Final Report'.
4. Chapter 4 moves on to examine the first specific area in which Part 35 will normally apply to expert reports—the stage of issuing instructions. It addresses the consequences that the rules of Part 35 may have on the disclosure of instructions, including the production of drafts and other documents included in those instructions. Chapter 5 assesses more broadly what happens when a document is referred to in an expert's report outside the context of the expert's instructions. Chapter 6 continues the theme of documents used to assist in preparing expert evidence by looking at the status of those documents pre-existing litigation. It asks the seemingly counter-intuitive question whether documents that are not privileged can become privileged, and what the status is of copies.
5. Chapter 7 turns to the issue of the single joint expert. Specifically, it discusses the privilege status of instructions by each party to a joint expert and the effect of joint experts' meetings. This chapter also deals with discussions that take place between unilaterally appointed experts and the joint written statements that may result.
6. Chapter 8 returns to general privilege themes by asking whether earlier drafts of expert reports are privileged. Chapter 9 follows this by addressing the vexed question of what happens to the privilege status of an expert report when the party instructing that expert decides to change one or more of its experts. Chapter 10 takes the focus off experts themselves and looks at the related subject of experiments. It sets out the rules on privilege that apply to experiments, and considers whether there is a wider application of these rules and their relationship to expert evidence.
7. When an expert report has been served, what further use may be made of it? This question is addressed in chapters 11 and 12. Chapter 11 looks specifically at the use an expert report can be put to by other parties to the same proceedings for which it was produced. Chapter 12 considers whether the expert evidence from one set of proceedings may be used in collateral proceedings.
8. Chapter 13 steps back and reflects on the nature of the relationship between privilege and public policy and how this has a bearing on expert evidence issues both in theory and in practice, as borne out by the various situations

discussed in this book. Finally, in chapter 14, practical observations are made that may need to be considered when preparing expert evidence in order to avoid privilege problems.

2

What Type of Privilege?

Introduction

9. In order to provide a context for the discussions in later chapters, this chapter describes in brief outline the types of privilege that can apply in English law: 'legal advice privilege'; 'litigation privilege'; 'without prejudice privilege' and, 'common interest privilege'. The chapter looks at which of these forms of privilege is relevant to the preparation of expert evidence in English proceedings.[1]

Legal Advice Privilege

10. Legal advice privilege covers confidential communications[2] between a lawyer and the lawyer's client which come into existence for the purpose of giving or obtaining legal advice. It comes into existence without regard for whether litigation is contemplated or pending. Legal advice privilege protects such documents against a demand from a third party for disclosure. Legal advice privilege also comes into being for communications between client and solicitor made directly or through an agent.

Qualifying Communications

11. To attract legal advice privilege the communication must have the dominant purpose[3] of the giving or receiving of legal advice. Legal advice is broader than advice on the state of the law:[4]

> . . . legal advice is not confined to telling the client the law; it must include advice as to what should prudently and sensibly be done in the relevant legal context.

[1] Privilege against self-incrimination and the privilege issues relating to EC proceedings arising from the Court of First Instance (CFI) decision in joined cases *T-125/03 & T-253/03 Akzo Nobel Chemicals Ltd and Akcros Chemicals Ltd v Commission* are not within the scope of this book.

[2] See also documents evidencing such communications—*Three Rivers (No 5)* [2002] EWHC 2730 (Comm).

[3] ibid.

[4] See *Balabel v Air India* [1988] 2 All ER 246.

However, there are limitations:

> . . . to extend privilege without limit to all solicitor and client communication upon matters within the ordinary business of a solicitor and referable to that relationship are too wide . . ..

12. The leading decision on the extent of legal advice is now that of the House of Lords in *Three Rivers (No 6)*,[5] in which it was asked do the communications between the Bank of England, their solicitors, Freshfields, and counsel relating to the content and preparation of the so-called overarching statement submitted on behalf of the Bank to the Bingham Inquiry qualify for legal professional privilege? Also, in relation to what sort of communications can legal professional privilege be claimed?
13. Approving statements in the earlier case of *Balabel v Air India*,[6] the Lords had the following to say about what communications would qualify, per Lord Scott:

> This remark is, in my respectful opinion, plainly correct. If a solicitor becomes the client's 'man of business', and some solicitors do, responsible for advising the client on all matters of business, including investment policy, finance policy and other business matters, the advice may lack a relevant legal context. There is, in my opinion, no way of avoiding difficulty in deciding in marginal cases whether the seeking of advice from or the giving of advice by lawyers does or does not take place in a relevant legal context so as to attract legal advice privilege. In cases of doubt the judge called upon to make the decision should ask whether the advice relates to the rights, liabilities, obligations or remedies of the client either under the private law or under public law. If it does not, then, in my opinion, legal advice privilege would not apply. If it does so relate then, in my opinion, the judge should ask himself whether the communication falls within the policy underlying the justification for legal advice privilege in our law. Is the occasion on which the communication takes place and is the purpose for which it takes place such as to make it reasonable to expect the privilege to apply? The criterion must, in my opinion, be an objective one.

14. It appears that the House of Lords' touchstones for the protection of legal advice privilege to arise are that the communications in question should have a 'relevant legal context'. Whether there is a relevant legal context depends on whether the advice relates to the 'rights, liabilities, obligations or remedies of the client either under the private law or under public law'. Providing this is the case, it would appear that the communications must also be such as to objectively expect legal advice privilege to apply by virtue of public policy. One such category of communication is the 'presentational advice' at issue in the *Three Rivers* case:

> The 'relevant legal context' was the Bingham Inquiry and the question whether the Bank had properly discharged its public law duties under the Banking Acts.

[5] *Three Rivers (No.6)* [2004] 3 WLR 1274.
[6] *Balabel* (n 4).

> The presentational advice falls, in my opinion, squarely within the policy reasons underlying legal advice privilege.
>
> I would be of the same opinion in relation to presentational advice sought from lawyers by any individual or company who believed himself, herself or itself to be at risk of criticism by an inquiry, whether a coroner's inquest, a statutory inquiry under the 1921 Act or an ad hoc inquiry such as the Bingham Inquiry. The defence of personal reputation and integrity is at least as important to many individuals and companies as the pursuit or defence of legal rights whether under private law or public law. The skills of professional lawyers when advising a client what evidence to place before an inquiry and how to present the client and his story to the inquiry in the most favourable light are, in my opinion, unquestionably legal skills being applied in a relevant legal context.

Who is the Lawyer?

15. Legal advice privilege protects communications between a lawyer and the lawyer's client. So, who is the lawyer?
16. It is clear that 'lawyer' refers to practising barristers and solicitors:[7]

> . . . in our opinion the privilege should be strictly confined to legal advisers such as solicitors and counsel, who are professionally qualified, who are members of professional bodies, who are subject to the rules and etiquettes of their professions, and who owe a duty to the Court. This is a clearly defined and easily identifiable qualification for the attachment of privilege. To extend the privilege to unqualified advisers such as personnel consultants is in our opinion unnecessary and undesirable . . ..[8]

17. The group barristers and solicitors include those working in-house, provided it is in their capacity as lawyers and not as executives.[9] Foreign lawyers are also protected by legal advice privilege for the purposes of English law. This form of privilege also extends to trainees and paralegals, so long as they are supervised.
18. In *Dadourian Group International Inc v Paul Francis Simms*[10], the issue arose whether legal advice privilege could be claimed for advice given by a solicitor after having been removed from the roll. Restating the position of the law that legal advice privilege does not apply to any relationship with a client outside that of solicitors and barristers, Patten J held that in circumstances where the client knew that the advice was coming from a solicitor who had been struck

[7] In addition, s 280 of the Copyright, Designs and Patents Act 1988 confers privilege on communications relating to the protection of any invention, design, technical information, or trade mark, or as to any matter involving passing off with 'patent agents' as defined by sub-s (3). For 'in-house' patents agents, the relevant part of this sub-s is (a) which applies to registered patents agents (ie those registered in the UK—see s 275) or 'a person who is on the European list'.

[8] *New Victoria Hospital v Ryan* [1993] ICR 201 (Tucker J).

[9] But not in relation to EU competition law—see text to n 1.

[10] *Dadourian Group International Inc v Paul Francis Simms* [2008] EWHC 1784 (Ch).

off, that advice could not be protected by legal advice privilege. However, it does not necessarily follow from this that a client who in good faith instructs someone whom he mistakenly believes to be a qualified solicitor or barrister should forfeit the protection of the legal privilege which he would otherwise obtain in relation to the disclosures he has made or the advice he has received.[11]

The Client and Client Experts

19. In the absence of litigation, communications with third parties are not privileged. Documents prepared by third parties or agents for the purpose of assisting a client to take legal advice are also not privileged. Consequently, advice taken by a client from an expert in the absence of litigation is not privileged and hence is disclosable. The picture may be more complex when the expert is an employee of a corporate client but, since the *Three Rivers* series of cases, the definition of client has narrowed and great care needs to be exercised in determining who exactly the client is.

20. *Three Rivers District Council v The Governor and Company of the Bank of England (No 5)*[12] *Three Rivers (No 5)*[13] concerned the inquiry into the supervision of BCCI after its collapse by certain UK authorities, including the Bank of England. To assist in the inquiry, the Bank of England appointed a committee of three Bank officials (the 'Bingham Inquiry Unit' or 'BIU') to deal with communications arising between the Bank and its solicitors, Freshfields, in relation to the inquiry and between the Bank and the inquiry. The claimants in the ongoing litigation sought disclosure of documents created by employees of the Bank, other than the BIU, during the course of the inquiry.

21. The Court of Appeal in *Three Rivers (No 5)* held that, for the purposes of the inquiry, the BIU was Freshfield's 'client' and that other Bank employees were third parties to that relationship. Any documentation prepared by other Bank employees, regardless of whether it was at the request of Freshfields or not, would be treated the same as documents prepared by independent third parties and therefore not protected by legal advice privilege.

    Only those at the client engaged in the seeking and receiving of advice from external lawyers are entitled to legal advice privilege. Internal communications made by other employees that contributed to the seeking of that advice were not so protected.

22. As a result of *Three Rivers (No 5)*, when proceedings are not underway and not in reasonable prospect (for which see the following section), great care should

[11] See, for example, *Calley v Richards* (1854) 19 Beav 40.

[12] *Three Rivers District Council v The Governor and Company of the Bank of England (No 5)* [2003] QB 1556.

[13] *Three Rivers (No 5)* (n 2). This decision is not to be confused with the *Three Rivers (No 6)* (n 5) decision of the House of Lords, which concerned the application of legal advice privilege to the 'presentation' of advice.

be taken when communicating with both third parties and internal employee experts, and in the creation of documents by these parties.

Litigation Privilege

Basic Principles

23. Communications between parties or their solicitors and third parties for the purpose of obtaining information or advice in connection with existing or contemplated litigation are privileged, but only when the following conditions are satisfied: (a) litigation must be in progress or in contemplation; (b) the communications must have been made for the sole or dominant purpose of conducting that litigation; (c) the litigation must be adversarial, not investigative or inquisitorial.[14]
24. Thus, there is a distinction between legal advice privilege and litigation privilege as they relate to expert evidence. The former attaches to communications between solicitor and client only, but the latter can protect reports by third parties prepared on the instructions of a client for the purposes of litigation. In the former case the privilege attaches to all communications whether related to litigation or not, but in the latter case it attaches only to documents or other written communications prepared with a view to litigation.

Adversarial Proceedings

25. Proceedings must be adversarial in nature. In *Re L (A Minor) (Police Investigation: Privilege)*,[15] L had been admitted to hospital after ingesting methadone. Her mother, who was a drug addict, claimed the child had taken it accidentally. The local authority instigated care proceedings under Part IV of the Children Act 1989 in respect of L and her brother. During these proceedings, the parents' solicitor, with leave of the Court, commissioned a report from a chemical pathologist which cast doubt on the mother's explanation that L had taken the drug accidentally. The police, who wished to investigate whether a criminal offence had been committed, sought disclosure of this report. The High Court judge ordered its disclosure, and this ruling was upheld by the Court of Appeal. The mother appealed to the House of Lords, contending that the report was confidential, being protected by legal professional privilege.

[14] Summarised, obiter, by Lord Carswell in *Three Rivers (No 6)* (n 5).
[15] *Re L (A Minor) (Police Investigation: Privilege)* [1997] AC 16.

26. In *Re L* the majority of the House of Lords held that care proceedings under the Children Act 1989 Part IV were inquisitorial rather than adversarial and placed the welfare of the child as the primary consideration; litigation privilege was by necessary implication excluded from the terms and overall purpose of the Act. Hence, the mother could not rely upon litigation privilege in the report.

27. It is not clear from *Re L* how widely the concept of proceedings of an adversarial nature is to be construed, because the particular consideration in this case was the welfare of a child. The approach of the Lords seems to have been that there is a distinction to be made between cases in which the parties have control over what is put in front of the Court and in which the Court must decide which case it prefers, and cases in which the onus is on the Court to protect one particular party, as Lord Jauncey commented:

> . . . in these proceedings, which are primarily non-adversarial and investigative as opposed to adversarial, the notion of a fair trial between opposing parties assumes far less importance. In the latter case the judge must decide the case in favour of one or other party upon such evidence as they choose to adduce, however much he might wish for further evidence on any point. In the former case the judge is concerned to make a decision which is in the best interest of the child in question.

In this case, care proceedings:

> are so far removed from normal actions that litigation privilege has no place in relation to reports obtained by a party thereto which could not have been prepared without the leave of the court to disclose documents already filed or to examine the child.

28. The facts of this case, concerning as they do the expert report of a chemical pathologist, demonstrate that privilege protection is unlikely to be available to expert evidence in circumstances where the proceedings are non-adversarial.

Dominant Purpose

29. Litigation privilege protects communications with third parties providing that they come into existence with the dominant purpose of gathering evidence in circumstances where legal proceedings are in existence or in reasonable prospect. Use in litigation need not be the sole purpose but, where there are other purposes, use in or in connection with litigation must be the dominant purpose for the creation of the document; the test was formulated by the House of Lords in *Waugh v British Railways Board.*[16] *Waugh* concerned an action for negligence . The plaintiff's husband died as a result of injuries sustained in a railway accident involving the collision between locomotives, one of which he was driving. As happened in this case, after an accident

[16] *Waugh v British Railways Board* [1980] AC 521.

occurred it was the practice of his employer, the defendant railways board, to make a brief report to the railway inspectorate about an accident on the day it happened. Soon afterwards a joint internal report ('the joint inquiry report') was prepared. This incorporated statements of witnesses and was also sent to the inspectorate. In due course a report was also made by the inspectorate for the Department of the Environment. The heading of the joint inquiry report stated that it had finally to be sent to the board's solicitor for the purpose of enabling him to advise the board.

To assist with her action, the plaintiff sought discovery of, inter alia, the joint inquiry report. The board refused to disclose the report on the basis that one of the principal purposes of preparing it had been so that it could be passed to their chief solicitor to enable him to advise the board on its legal liability and, if necessary, conduct their defence to the proceedings. Accordingly, the defendant said, it was subject to legal professional privilege.

30. It was held to be clear on the evidence that the report was prepared for a dual purpose: railway operation and safety purposes on the one hand, and for the purpose of obtaining legal advice in anticipation of litigation, on the other. The first purpose was more immediate than the second, but both were of equal rank or weight. So the question was whether the second purpose was enough to support a claim of privilege, or whether it had to be the sole purpose, or the dominant or main purpose. Lord Wilberforce commented:

> It appears to me that unless the purpose of submission to the legal adviser in view of litigation is at least the dominant purpose for which the relevant document was prepared, the reasons which require privilege to be extended to it cannot apply. On the other hand to hold that the purpose, as above, must be the sole purpose would, apart from difficulties of proof, in my opinion, be too strict a requirement, and would confine the privilege too narrowly: . . .

Lord Simon of Glaisdale also stated:

> I would certainly deny a claim to privilege when litigation was merely one of several purposes of equal or similar importance intended to be served by the material sought to be withheld from disclosure, and a fortiori where it was merely a minor purpose. On the other hand, I consider that it would be going too far to adopt the '*sole* purpose' test applied by the majority in *Grant v. Downs*,[17] which has been adopted in no United Kingdom decision nor, as far as we are aware, elsewhere in the Commonwealth. Its adoption would deny privilege even to material whose outstanding purpose is to serve litigation, simply because another and very minor purpose was also being served. But, inasmuch as the *only* basis of the claim to privilege in such cases as the present one is that the material in question was brought into existence for use in legal proceedings, it is surely right to insist that, before the claim is conceded or upheld, such a purpose must be shown to have played a paramount part. Which phrase or epithet should be selected to designate this is a matter of individual judgment. Lord Denning M.R., as we have

[17] *Grant v Downs* 135 CLR 674.

seen, favoured adoption of the phrase employed in the Law Reform Committee's Sixteenth Report, viz., 'material which came into existence . . . *wholly or mainly*' for the purpose of litigation (para. 17). 'Wholly' I personally would reject for the same reason as I dislike 'solely', but 'mainly' is nearer what I regard as the preferable test. Even so, it lacks the element of clear paramountcy which should, as I think, be the touchstone. After considerable deliberation, I have finally come down in favour of the test propounded by Barwick C.J. in *Grant v. Downs*, . . . in the following words, at p 677:

'Having considered the decisions, the writings and the various aspects of the public interest which claim attention, I have come to the conclusion that the court should state the relevant principle as follows: a document which was produced or brought into existence either with the *dominant* purpose of its author, or of the person or authority under whose direction, whether particular or general, it was produced or brought into existence, of using it or its contents in order to obtain legal advice or to conduct or aid in the conduct of litigation, at the time of its production in reasonable prospect, should be privileged and excluded from inspection.' (Italics added.)[18]

31. The test is thus definitively one of dominant purpose. In deciding whether a communication is subject to 'litigation privilege', the court has to consider objectively the purpose of the person or authority that directed the creation of the communication on the basis of the evidence.[19]

Statutory Obligations

32. Complications may arise in the context of statutory and regulatory obligations. In *West London Pipeline and Storage Ltd v Total UK Ltd*[20] it was held that where a report is prepared pursuant to a statutory obligation, the purposes of those instigating the report are irrelevant.[21] The same principle should apply where the obligation is a regulatory one. However, in this case the defendants' claim for privilege in reports and communications could not be rejected on the ground that they were produced pursuant to regulatory duties, because while there might be an implied duty to investigate under the regulations at issue, there was no duty to report. Similarly, in *Re Barings Plc*,[22] it was held that where a report is prepared pursuant to a statutory obligation, the purposes of the instigator of the report are irrelevant.

[18] The earlier Court of Appeal authority of *Ankin v London & North Eastern Railway Co* [1930] 1 KB 527 was expressly overruled by the Lords.

[19] *Guinness Peat Properties Ltd v Fitzroy Robinson Partnership* [1987] 1 WLR 1027.

[20] *West London Pipeline and Storage Ltd v Total UK Ltd* [2008] *EWHC 1729.*

[21] Pursuant to the Control of Major Hazard Regulations 1999.

[22] *Re Barings Plc* [1998] 1 All ER 673, concerning administrators' reports to the Secretary of State pursuant to the Company Directors Disqualification Act 1986 s 7(3).

Contemplated Litigation

32. A party must be aware of circumstances rendering litigation between itself and a person or class of persons a reasonable prospect. *USA v Philip Morris Inc and British American Tobacco (Investments) Ltd*[23] concerned a claim by the United States against a number of tobacco companies alleging that since 1953 the tobacco companies had engaged in an unlawful enterprise to deceive and defraud the American public, and consumers of cigarettes, about the health risks of smoking and about their knowledge and attitude to them. In support of litigation in the United States, letters of request were issued seeking evidence for use at trial from F, a partner in a firm of London solicitors. These were issued on the basis that F's evidence was necessary because he had played a central role in the creation and implementation of document destruction policies to protect one of the defendants, British American Tobacco (BAT) and its affiliates, including the UK company BATCo. BATCo and F resisted on grounds of, amongst other things, litigation privilege as covering all communications passing between F and BATCo and other members of the BAT group. An issue that arose for consideration was the extent to which litigation must be in contemplation in order to claim privilege in respect of confidential communications.

34. In *Philip Morris* the Court of Appeal cited to their own established authority in *Re Highgrade Traders*[24] that litigation privilege may be claimed in respect of documents brought into being at a time when litigation is 'reasonably in prospect'. Earlier, explaining the policy behind this test at first instance in *Philip Morris*, Moore-Bick J had given further guidance on what the measure of 'reasonably in prospect' should be:

> It has been recognised on many occasions that there is a conflict between the need to enable clients to communicate freely with their legal advisers in relation to litigation and the need to ensure that all relevant material is before the court… The point at which litigation should be regarded as sufficiently likely for confidential communications between client and his lawyer to attract privilege on this ground therefore involves striking an appropriate balance between these two factors. The requirement that litigation be 'reasonably in prospect' is not in my view satisfied unless the party seeking to claim privilege can show that he was aware of circumstances which rendered litigation between himself and a particular person or class of persons a real likelihood rather than a mere possibility.

The judge added that it would not be enough that there was a general apprehension of future litigation, nor was it sufficient that there was a 'distinct possibility that sooner or later someone might make a claim'. In the Court of Appeal, otherwise stating that Moore-Bick J was correct in his approach, Brooke LJ sought only to take the emphasis away from 'real likelihood'. It was,

[23] *USA v Philip Morris Inc and British American Tobacco (Investments) Ltd* [2004] 1 CLC 811.
[24] *Re Highgrade Traders* [1984] BCLC 151.

Brooke LJ said, merely a counterpoint to a 'mere possibility'—the judge had not, he concluded, intended to suggest that there must be a greater than 50 per cent chance of litigation.[25]

Production of Documents to Third Parties

Relationship with Confidentiality

35. Privilege should not be confused with confidentiality—a document can be confidential without being privileged. However, the right to withhold production of a document on the grounds of privilege is lost in a document once it ceases to be confidential. Hence, a client may without restrictions consent to privileged documents being produced to another party, but in this case the right to withhold production of the documents is lost. Alternatively, a client may agree to produce privileged documents for a limited purpose only. If this happens, the client can assert the right not to produce the same documents for any purpose outside the limited purpose for which it was agreed to produce them. Furthermore, it appears that if documents are produced to a party on the express basis that privilege is not to be waived, then that party may not retain those documents when consent is withdrawn. In *B v Auckland District Law Society*,[26] the Privy Council explains that the privileged nature of documents should not be confused with the rights that attach to them. In this case, which is an appeal from the Court of Appeal of New Zealand, but which deals with the UK approach to privilege, states:

> The society argued that, once the documents were produced to Mr Ennor, they ceased to be privileged. Their Lordships consider that this is playing with words. It confuses the nature of the documents with the rights to which the arrangements with Mr Ennor gave rise. The documents are privileged because they were created for the purpose of giving or receiving legal advice. If they are not produced voluntarily, production cannot be compelled. If they are produced voluntarily, the right to withhold production no longer attaches to them. In that sense the privilege may be said to be lost. But they are the same documents, and it is not inappropriate to describe them as privileged. Their inherent characteristics are the same. The policy which protected them from unauthorised disclosure is the same. The cat is still a cat. It can be put back in the bag.

However, as the propositions above indicate, the documents must have a right of recovery attaching to them:

[25] Particular considerations will apply in certain circumstances, for example, see s 413 of the Financial Services and Markets Act 2000 in relation to regulatory investigations. Such individual considerations are outside the scope of this book.

[26] *B v Auckland District Law Society* [2003] 2 AC 736 (Privy Council, New Zealand); see also, *British Coal Corporation v Dennis Rye Ltd (No2)* [1988] 1 WLR 1113.

> There is another confusion also. The appellants want to recover the documents because they are privileged. But they do not rely on privilege to found their cause of action. A party who has parted with possession of documents may have a right to recover possession on any one of a number of grounds. He may reclaim them because they belong to him; or because he has a contractual right to recover them; or because they are confidential; or because he has parted with them for a limited purpose and equity will not permit the recipient to retain them once that purpose is fulfilled. In the present case the documents are both privileged and confidential, but the appellants do not rely on privilege or confidentiality to found their claim to recover them. They rely on the terms of the arrangements under which they were supplied and the limited purpose for which they permitted use to be made of them.

Obligations of confidentiality over disclosed documents can be implied in the absence of an express agreement in circumstances where it would be expected to be assumed by those involved, and it was a plain inference, that the communications about the advice received by a third party were intended to be confidential between them.[27] Thus, for example, documents that are accidentally produced to another party are confidential and must be returned without being read. The correct approach is to examine the relevant acts of waiver and put them in their context. Whether privilege has been waived depends on what was said and the purpose for which it was said.[28]

Common Interest Privilege

36. Common interest privilege is not actually a type of legal professional privilege of its own. It instead describes the principle under which documents already protected by privilege may be shared by parties with a common interest without losing the right to protection from production. As Brightman LJ in *Buttes Gas & Oil Company v Hammer (No 3)*[29] commented:

> . . . if two parties with a common interest and a common solicitor exchange information for the dominant purpose of informing each other of the facts, or the issues, or advice received, or of obtaining legal advice in respect of contemplated or pending litigation, the documents or copies containing that information are privileged from production in the hands of each. . . .
>
> The parties must therefore share a common solicitor and the information must itself be privileged from disclosure in the hands of the communicating or primary party. The privilege can be either legal advice privilege or litigation privilege. The second party obtains the same protection in respect of the shared material by establishing that it was disclosed to him in recognition of his shared or common interest in the subject matter of the communication.

[27] *Gotha City v Sotheby's* [1998] 1WLR 114.
[28] *Susan Yvonne Dore v Leicestershire County Council* [2010] EWHC 34 (Ch).
[29] *Buttes Gas & Oil Company v Hammer (No 3)* [1981] 1 QB 223.

37. In more recent authorities, a somewhat broader approach is taken as to the nature of the relationship that constitutes a community of interest. For example, in *Svenska Handelsbanken v Sun Alliance and London Insurance Plc*,[30] Rix J considered that insurers and reinsurers may well have a common interest analogous to that between an assured and his liability insurers, despite the absence of any particular and relevant provisions in a reinsurance contract. In this case, the evidence was only that the insurers felt obliged to communicate the advice at issue to the reinsurers. This, the judge held, was a recognition of a de facto obligation in the absence of any clear legal obligation.

In *Formica Ltd v ECGD*,[31] Colman J expressed the view that the essential notion behind common interest privilege is that the parties have a common interest in the confidentiality of the advice at issue. The fact that differences may arise between parties of whatever closeness of interest, such as to prevent them from at all times using the same lawyers, or such as may indeed even cause them to find themselves ultimately on opposite sides of litigation, does not necessarily mean that they cannot be parties with a common interest for the purpose of this concept.[32]

38. Ultimately, the courts will not be prescriptive about the circumstances in which the two parties will have a sufficient 'common interest' in the particular communications concerned. The issue has to be decided on the facts of the individual case.[33]

Without Prejudice Communications

39. Without prejudice is a narrower category of privilege to those so far discussed. It is different in kind to legal advice privilege and litigation privilege as it does not protect communications between the lawyer and the client. Instead, it protects communications between parties to a dispute from being generally admissible in evidence if they are made for the purpose of a genuine attempt to resolve that dispute. As such, it is founded on the public policy of encouraging the settlement of disputes, even though this may conflict with the policy of providing the court with the best evidence.[34] Public policy also requires those negotiations to be protected from disclosure to third parties.[35] A 'dispute' does not require litigation to have been commenced or threatened.[36] Nor does it depend on temporal conditions. Instead, the test is whether the parties might

[30] *Svenska Handelsbanken v Sun Alliance and London Insurance Plc* [1995] 2 Lloyd's Rep 84.
[31] *Formica Ltd v ECGD* [1995] 1 Lloyd's Rep 692.
[32] See also, *The World Era* [1993] 1 Lloyd's Rep 363.
[33] *Winterthur Swiss Insurance Company v AG (Manchester) Ltd (in liquidation)* [2006] EWHC 839 (Comm).
[34] *Oceanbulk Shipping & Trading SA v TMT Asia Ltd* [2010] EWCA Civ 79.
[35] *Rush & Tompkins Ltd v Greater London Council* [1989] AC 1280.
[36] See, for example, *Bradford & Bingley Plc v Rashid* [2006] 1 WLR 2066.

reasonably have contemplated that litigation would result if they could not agree, as Auld LJ commented in *Barnetson v Framlington Group Ltd*:[37]

> The critical feature of proximity for this purpose, it seems to me, is one of the subject matter of the dispute rather than how long before the threat, or start, of litigation it was aired in negotiations between the parties. Would they have respectively lowered their guards at that time and in the circumstances, if they had not thought or hoped or contemplated that, by doing so, they could avoid the need to go to court over the very same dispute? On that approach, which I would commend, the crucial consideration would be whether in the course of negotiations the parties contemplated or might reasonably have contemplated litigation if they could not agree.

40. Without prejudice privilege does not apply to apparently open communications designed only to discuss the repayment of an admitted liability rather than to negotiate and compromise a disputed liability; for example, letters offering a sum in settlement of a shortfall owing to a mortgagee after a possession order was granted to the offeror.[38]
41. It is trite law that the use or non-use of the words 'without prejudice' in negotiations to settle a dispute may indicate whether the communications at issue attract privilege, but these words are not necessarily determinative of the point.[39]
42. Documents disclosed to demonstrate that an agreed settlement has concluded negotiations are generally not protected by without prejudice privilege. In E*nglish and American Insurance Co Ltd v Axa Re SA*,[40] settlement discussions and a without prejudice meeting took place. Following the meeting, one of the parties confirmed its position in a letter marked 'without prejudice'. Later, the other party sought to rely on this letter in evidence. It was held that the purpose of the letter was to put a statement on the record of the position, which implicitly was to be an open statement. It was therefore not 'without prejudice'.
43. Without prejudice privilege cannot be used to cloak 'unambiguous impropriety' such as blackmail and perjury. However, the public interest in the without prejudice rule is great and should not be sacrificed save in truly exceptional and needy circumstances. For example, a mere inconsistency between an admission and a pleaded case, with the mere possibility that such a case may lead to perjury, is not enough to exclude the privilege; it is the fact that the privilege itself is being abused that does so.[41]

[37] *Barnetson v Framlington Group Ltd* [2007] 1 WLR 2443.
[38] *Bradford & Bingley* (n 36).
[39] *Barnetson v Framlington Group* (n 37) and *Rush Tompkins GLL* [1989] LAC 1280
[40] *English and American Insurance Co Ltd v Axa Re SA* [2007] 1 CLC 1.
[41] *Savings & Investment Bank Ltd (in liquidation) v Fincken* [2004] 1 WLR 667; see also *Robin Jeanne Williams v Anthony Steven Hull* [2009] EWHC 2844 (Ch).

Chapter Summary

44. Legal advice privilege should be treated warily in expert matters. Advice given by an expert before proceedings were in existence or contemplation by a third party will not be covered by legal advice privilege, and will thus be disclosable. Following *Three Rivers (No 5)*, even the communications and work product of experts within the client's own organisation are unlikely to be protected unless they are one of the team of individuals seeking and receiving advice from external counsel. Great caution should therefore be exercised when considering the creation of such material.
45. The great majority of expert privilege issues will fall within the scope of litigation privilege. This is because litigation privilege will protect communications with and documents prepared by third parties. The limitation, however, is that these must have been prepared for the sole or dominant purpose of conducting litigation. Such litigation must be in progress or in contemplation, such that it is reasonably in prospect, although it does not necessarily need to be more likely than not. When considering whether such privilege will apply, awareness must also be had to whether the proceedings are truly adversarial, rather than investigative or inquisitorial.
46. Normally, the right to refuse production of documents on the basis of privilege will be lost when confidentiality is lost. However, restrictions may be agreed on the purpose for which privileged material is disclosed. The right to refuse production on the basis of privilege will not be lost for material that is shared with a party with which the producer has a common interest in that advice. However, the scope of what amounts to a common interest in these circumstances is as yet unsettled.

3

Part 35

Introduction

47. Chapter 2 outlines the principal three categories of privilege in English law and explains that the form of privilege relevant to an enquiry about expert evidence will, in the great majority of cases, be litigation privilege.[1] This chapter begins by looking briefly at the underlying way in which this privilege[2] applies to the work of an expert. It then introduces the relationship between the rules of Part 35 of the Civil Procedure Rules (CPR)—Experts and Assessors—and the activities of an expert that might be subject to privilege. The starting point for tracing this relationship is to ask: when is an expert a Part 35 expert and what if they are not?

48. Before embarking on the detailed discussion of provisions of Part 35 in the following chapters of this book, in order to understand the objectives that Part 35 was designed to achieve, this chapter also reviews the policy elements behind its drafting as discussed in Lord Woolf's Access to Justice Final Report.[3]

To Whom Does Part 35 Apply?

'Behind the Scenes' Experts

49. Who, or what, is the expert? In the course of proceedings, one or more individuals outside the client and legal team need to be included to advise or give evidence on facts or issues which fall within an area of professional expertise on which they are qualified to speak. Typically, in order to find such a person, at an early stage of litigation, and as soon as it becomes apparent that some expert assistance may be needed, a number of initial expert candidates may be consulted. Ideally, the expert of choice is someone who is willing and able to give favourable evidence for a party and be cross-examined about it in

[1] In some circumstances expert material will be without prejudice—see chapter 7.

[2] Unless stated otherwise, 'privilege' is used as short-hand in this book to mean litigation privilege.

[3] The Right Honourable the Lord Woolf, Master of the Rolls, July 1996. http://www.dca.gov.uk/civil/final/index.htm

court. However, not all candidates will be suitable to act as testifying experts. Some may have unhelpful views from the beginning and some may be helpful at first but later turn out to be unfavourable or unwilling to give evidence. The expert may also merely be useful to act as a technical 'interpreter' for the lawyers. In the latter two cases, it is not uncommon for such experts to continue their assistance as 'behind the scenes' or 'advisory' experts by giving partisan help in identifying the strengths and weaknesses of a case and providing technical advice on arguments for a party, without producing evidence.

'Part 35' experts

50. Is there such a thing as a 'Part 35 expert' as a defined and immutable character? Certainly, a Part 35 expert may be considered as a third party who is instructed as defined in CPR 35.2:

> A reference to an 'expert' in this Part is a reference to an expert who has been instructed to give or prepare evidence for the purpose of court proceedings.

Part 35 as a whole applies to such experts. However, despite this definition, there is no single point at which the expert obviously becomes a Part 35 expert with any practical consequences. Nor does it appear that the Part 35 status is irrevocable. A plain example is the expert described above who, initially having been instructed with the purpose and intention of giving evidence in proceedings, later appears unfit for the purpose and does not give evidence. As will be explained in chapter 9, if the expert has not been named and the report of the expert has not been served, this person could helpfully remain as a 'behind the scenes' expert, without Part 35 ever being applied. The reason for this is that an expert is only truly a Part 35 expert if and when an action is undertaken or an event occurs to which a rule in Part 35 applies.[4] A Part 35 expert is therefore an expert to whom a rule applies—more a matter of practical status than principle.

The Effect of Expert Status on Privilege

51. The effect on privilege of the various actions and events which trigger the rules of Part 35 is the subject of the following chapters of this book. Before addressing these issues it is first necessary to ask what is the privilege status of a behind the scenes expert's work, to whom none of the provisions of Part

[4] Although there are signs, as explained in chapter 9, that some events governed by Civil Procedure Rule (CPR) 35 could have consequences that reach back to affect expert work that was not even prepared pursuant to CPR 35.2.

35 apply. In other words, what is the underlying foundation upon which the rules of Part 35 must stand—the default position?

Carlson v Townsend

52. The underlying rule is that work prepared by an expert for the sole or dominant purpose of proceedings or contemplated proceedings is protected by litigation privilege. This is illustrated by the Court of Appeal in *Carlson v Townsend*.[5] *Carlson v Townsend* was a personal injury case concerning a report prepared by an expert named as Mr Trevett and instructed under the personal injury pre-action protocol, before proceedings were issued.[6] The party who instructed Mr Trevett later disavowed him and sought to rely on another expert. Aside from considering whether the pre-action protocol had been breached, it was held by the Court of Appeal that one sanction not available to it would be to override the claimant's privilege in Mr Trevett's report. The report was protected by privilege and disclosure could not be sought.

    The *Carlson* appeal was argued in the context of the pre-action protocol and there was no discussion of behind the scenes advice or Part 35. The decision thus stands as authority for the general principle that expert advice obtained in the circumstances described in chapter 2 is privileged. However, when considering changing an expert, consideration must be given to the complications that are discussed in chapter 9.

53. Behind the scenes expert advice is therefore subject to the general rules of litigation privilege. However, as will be described in later chapters, privilege does not merely apply to behind the scenes advice, it also seems to apply to earlier draft reports, whether or not the final report was actually served as a Part 35 expert report. The general rules of litigation privilege actually appear to apply to all expert work, until overridden by a rule of Part 35 or effectively waived by production. Thus, to return to the marine analogy of chapter 1, litigation privilege has the quality of an opaque, liquid layer of protection. It covers all but the exceptions arising directly or indirectly from certain rules of Part 35. These break through the surface as described in later chapters. In fact, it is these exceptions which prove the general rule.

The Rationale for Part 35

54. Why might some rules of Part 35[7] have the effect of overriding a general rule as important and as entrenched as that of litigation privilege? The answer lies

[5] *Carlson v Townsend* [2001] EWCA Civ 511.

[6] The case is discussed further in chapter 8.

[7] In order to avoid confusion, all quotes from the CPR throughout this book use the CPR as amended in October 2009. This applies to cases that have been decided on extracts of the CPR that have since been amended. If such subsequent amendments are material to that the decision at issue then this is noted.

in why the CPR as a whole was introduced. In July 1996, the Access to Justice Final Report of Lord Woolf, Master of the Rolls, was published. The Report was accompanied by a draft of the general rules forming the basis of a new code of civil procedure; what became the CPR. Commissioned by the Lord Chancellor, the Report arose from concerns that the process of the civil courts was too expensive, too slow and too complex. This placed many litigants at the disadvantage of their opponents, particularly where there was an imbalance in resources. The experience of many litigants was consequently of inadequate access to justice and an inefficient and insufficient procedural system. The Report covered a whole spread of procedural matters, but chapter 13 of the Report (see Appendix A) dealt specifically with issues of expert instruction and evidence.

The purpose of this discussion is not to examine the failings of the pre-CPR system, but to look at the concerns of Lord Woolf and how they fed into Part 35 of the CPR. Doing so provides an insight into the spirit of Part 35 and hence a feel for some of the later decisions that have been made pursuant to its rules. The primary concerns of Lord Woolf are described at the beginning of chapter 13 of the Report:

> 1. It was a basic contention of my interim report that two major generators of unnecessary cost in civil litigation were uncontrolled discovery and expert evidence. No-one has seriously challenged that contention.
>
> 2. A large litigation support industry, generating a multi-million pound fee income, has grown up among professions such as accountants, architects and others, and new professions have developed such as accident reconstruction and care experts. This goes against all principles of proportionality and access to justice. In my view, its most damaging effect is that it has created an ethos of what is acceptable which has in turn filtered down to smaller cases. Many potential litigants do not even start litigation because of the advice they are given about costs, and in my view this is as great a social ill as the actual cost of pursuing litigation.
>
> 5. There is widespread agreement with the criticisms I made in the interim report of the way in which expert evidence is used at present, especially the point that experts sometimes take on the role of partisan advocates instead of neutral fact finders or opinion givers.

55. In essence, Lord Woolf's principal concerns with regard to experts were, first, the excessive cost of experts and, secondly, an often perceived lack of impartiality and transparency. Too often, these aspects of litigation could be used by some parties to abuse the system, as Lord Woolf continues in chapter 13:

> 7. The purpose of the adversarial system is to achieve just results. All too often it is used by one party or the other to achieve something which is inconsistent with justice by taking advantage of the other side's lack of resources or ignorance of relevant facts or opinions. Expert evidence is one of the principal weapons used by litigators who adopt this approach. The present system allows them to withhold from their opponents material which may be damaging to their own case

or advantageous to their opponents'. This practice of non-disclosure cannot be justified, because it inevitably leads to unnecessary cost and delay, and in some cases to an unfair result.

Hence, a fundamental aim of the new rules was to safeguard impartiality by enshrining the existing principle that the expert's duty is to the court and not to those giving the instructions.[8] However, in chapter 13, Lord Woolf also sets out a number of other recommendations that he intends to implement with the new CPR to meet the dual challenges of costs and impartiality.

56. The recommendations begin with the control of expert evidence by the court. First and foremost is the need for parties to apply for leave to adduce such evidence:

> Court control of expert evidence: a flexible approach
>
> 13. Under the system of case management which I proposed in the interim report, the court will have complete control over the use of evidence, including expert evidence. The new rules will say that no expert evidence may be adduced without the leave of the court, which may be given as part of its own directions or specifically on application. There will be a range of options which the court will have a discretion to apply according to the type of case, or to the circumstances of an individual case.

This power is now reflected in CPR 35.4:

> 35.4 Court's power to restrict expert evidence
>
> (1) No party may call an expert or put in evidence an expert's report without the court's permission.
> (2) When parties apply for permission they must identify –
>
> (a) the field in which expert evidence is required; and
> (b) where practicable, the name of the proposed expert.
>
> (3) If permission is granted it shall be in relation only to the expert named or the field identified under paragraph (2).
> (3A) Where a claim has been allocated to the small claims track or the fast track, if permission is given for expert evidence, it will normally be given for evidence from only one expert on a particular issue.
> (Paragraph 7 of practice direction 35 sets out some of the circumstances the court will consider when deciding whether expert evidence should be given by a single joint expert.)
> (4) The court may limit the amount of a party's fees and expenses that may be recovered from any other party.

In fact, the court has not restricted the conditions it can impose to those matters set out in the sub-paragraphs. The consequences that this rule has for privilege are therefore potentially profound, particularly in respect of earlier draft reports when changing experts. These issues are discussed in chapter 9.

[8] *National Justice Compania v Prudential Assurance* [1993] 2 Lloyd's Rep 68 (*The Ikarian Reefer*) and *Cala Homes (South) Ltd v Alfred McAlpine Homes East Ltd* [1995] FSR 818 (Ch).

57. To supplement the court's existing power to direct expert meetings, Lord Woolf put forward the requirement that experts must produce a report stating those issues upon which they are agreed and on those on which they differ. The purpose of this measure would be to ensure the reduction of the time and cost spent in preparing rival expert evidence on issues which are not in dispute:

> Narrowing the issues: experts' meetings
>
> 42. Among the criticisms I made in my interim report was that the present system does not encourage narrowing of issues between opposing experts, or the elimination of peripheral issues. There has been widespread support for my suggestion that experts' meetings were a useful approach to narrowing the issues. In areas of litigation (such as Official Referees' business) where experts' meetings are already the usual practice, there is general agreement that they are helpful. In areas where they are not at present widely used, including medical negligence, the majority of respondents accept that they could be helpful. (This is not, however, the view of the Intellectual Property Working Group, which believes that sequential disclosure of reports may be a better way of narrowing the issues in some cases, or that each expert might usefully be asked to take the opposite side's report and underline the passages with which he or she disagrees.)

However, whilst urging the wider application of expert meetings, Lord Woolf sees the need to ensure that such meetings are not subverted by instructing lawyers:

> 43. Two principal reservations have been expressed, even by those who support experts' meetings in principle. The first (mentioned in my interim report) is that meetings can be futile because the experts are instructed not to agree anything; or, alternatively, are told that any points of agreement must be referred back to their instructing lawyers for ratification. This subverts the judge's intention in directing the experts to meet, because the decision as to what to agree becomes a matter for the lawyers rather than the experts. I recommend in the interim report that it should be unprofessional conduct for an expert to be given or to accept instructions not to agree, and this has been widely supported.
>
> 44. On the basis of the consultation I have carried out, it is far from clear whether these are widespread problems, although there is certainly clear evidence that they do happen on occasions. The solution lies in a clear requirement that the experts must produce for the court, at the end of their meeting, a written list of agreed matters of professional opinion and issues still in dispute. It must be made clear that the discussion is to cover only matters within the experts' professional competence, and that it is for the parties and their legal advisers to consider the effect of any agreement or disagreement on the future conduct of the case.

These recommendations for experts' discussions are embodied in CPR 35.12:

> 35.12 Discussions between experts
>
> (1) The court may, at any stage, direct a discussion between experts for the purpose of requiring the experts to –

(a) identify and discuss the expert issues in the proceedings; and
(b) where possible, reach an agreed opinion on those issues.

(2) The court may specify the issues which the experts must discuss.
(3) The court may direct that following a discussion between the experts they must prepare a statement for the court setting out those issues on which –

(a) they agree; and
(b) they disagree, with a summary of their reasons for disagreeing.

(4) The content of the discussion between the experts shall not be referred to at the trial unless the parties agree.
(5) Where experts reach agreement on an issue during their discussions, the agreement shall not bind the parties unless the parties expressly agree to be bound by the agreement.

The effect that the provisions of this rule have on the privilege of the expert discussions, and the material produced from them, is discussed in chapter 7.

58. A further measure arising from the recommendations in the Final Report is the power of the court to direct that evidence is given by a single joint expert. The aim of this power is to control the amount of expert evidence being produced in circumstances where a single expert is appropriate rather than two or more rival experts. Again, it is to help ensure cost efficiency as well as impartiality:

Single experts
22. It has been suggested to me that by the stage at which case management starts, it will be too late for the court to control the scope of expert evidence because parties will already have appointed their own experts. There are of course circumstances in which a party will need to consult an expert before proceedings have started, sometimes even before legal action is in contemplation. It does not, however, follow that each party is entitled to rely on its own expert evidence for the purposes of litigation. Once litigation appears likely, the use of experts will be subject to different considerations: impartiality is of paramount importance, and because of the costs shifting rule, parties need to be protected against the extravagant use of experts by their opponents.

Single experts are provided for in CPR 35.7 and CPR 35.8:

35.7 Court's power to direct that evidence is to be given by a single joint expert

(1) Where two or more parties wish to submit expert evidence on a particular issue, the court may direct that the evidence on that issue is to be given by a single joint expert.
(2) Where the parties who wish to submit the evidence ('the relevant parties') cannot agree who should be the single joint expert, the court may –

(a) select the expert from a list prepared or identified by the relevant parties; or
(b) direct that the expert be selected in such other manner as the court may direct.

35.8 Instructions to a single joint expert

(1) Where the court gives a direction under rule 35.7 for a single joint expert to be used, any relevant party may give instructions to the expert.
(2) When a party gives instructions to the expert that party must, at the same time, send a copy to the other relevant parties.
(3) The court may give directions about –

(a) the payment of the expert's fees and expenses; and
(b) any inspection, examination or experiments which the expert wishes to carry out.

(4) The court may, before an expert is instructed –

(a) limit the amount that can be paid by way of fees and expenses to the expert; and
(b) direct that some or all of the relevant parties pay that amount into court.

(5) Unless the court otherwise directs, the relevant parties are jointly and severally liable for the payment of the expert's fees and expenses.

The very direct impact of these rules on the privilege of instructions, in particular the exchange of instructions between parties in CPR 35.8(2), and on the evidence obtained is also discussed in chapter 7.

59. The recommendations discussed above were intended to be practical measures that the court could adopt to control evidence for the purpose of saving cost and ensuring impartiality. As will be discussed later, all of these measures have a potential impact on the privilege protection afforded to expert evidence, although the way in which they do so is not immediately apparent in all cases from what Lord Woolf says or the way it is implemented in the CPR. However, when dealing directly with the issue of impartiality it is readily apparent that changes to privilege protection were both contemplated and desired by Lord Woolf in his Final Report:

Impartiality

25. There is wide agreement that the expert's role should be that of an independent adviser to the court, and that lack of objectivity can be a serious problem. This may sometimes arise because of improper pressure on experts from solicitors, . . .
26. The present system has the effect of exaggerating the adversarial role of experts, and this helps neither the court nor the parties. As the Court of Appeal has recently remarked:

'For whatever reason, and whether consciously or unconsciously, the fact is that expert witnesses instructed on behalf of parties to litigation often tend . . . to espouse the cause of those instructing them to a greater or lesser extent, on occasion becoming more partisan than the parties.'[9]

31. One of the recommendations in my interim report was that, once an expert had been instructed to prepare a report for the use of a court, any communication between the expert and the client or his advisers should no longer be the subject of legal privilege. My intention was to prevent the suppression of relevant opinions or factual material which did not support the case put forward by the party instructing

[9] *Abbey National Mortgages Plc v Key Surveyors Nationwide Ltd* [1996] EGCS 23.

the expert. There is, I believe, no disagreement with that intention, but it has been put to me very strongly that waiver of legal privilege is not the way to achieve it. The point has been made that experts must be free to submit drafts to clients and their legal advisers, so that factual misconceptions can be corrected. A further objection is that a great deal of time could be wasted if all these documents were disclosable, because the opposing party would have to comb through the various versions of a report to identify any changes, the reasons for which would not always be clear in any event. Another possibility is that lawyers and experts might begin to subvert the system by avoiding written communication in favour of off the record conversations.

32. I accept, in the light of these arguments, that it would not be realistic to make experts' reports disclosable. I do not, however, consider that privilege should apply to the instructions given to experts. The Chancery Working Group has pointed out that major problems can arise when opposing experts are working from different instructions, which leads to reports that are hard to compare and use. Joint or agreed instructions would meet this specific point, but even a single expert's report may be unclear or open to misinterpretation unless the instructions on which it is based are known.

33. Under the new system, transparency of instructions to experts will be particularly important. The effectiveness of pre-action protocols will depend on it. On the fast track, in cases where there are diverging opinions in two reports, it will be absolutely essential for the parties and the judge to know the basis on which the experts have been instructed. I therefore recommend that expert evidence should not be admissible unless all written instructions (including letters subsequent upon the original instructions) and a note of any oral instructions are included as an annex to the expert's report.

34. A further recommendation in the interim report was that any expert's report prepared for the purpose of giving evidence to a court should end with a declaration that it includes everything which the expert regards as being relevant to the opinion which he has expressed in his report and that he has drawn to the attention of the court any matter which would affect the validity of that opinion. That recommendation was widely supported on consultation, and I have come to the conclusion that a declaration along the lines I have proposed, coupled with the requirement for instructions to be disclosed, should be sufficient to meet my concerns about the disclosure of all relevant material.

Clearly, Lord Woolf had the intention, at the time of his Interim Report, of removing the protection of privilege from all communications between the instructing solicitors and the expert. The dramatic nature of this original proposal indicates the degree of concern about matters of impartiality of expert evidence. As it is, this proposal was only scaled back because of the greater evil of its costs implications and impracticality. The settled position on how privilege in instructions to experts should be treated thus became that now embodied in the current versions of CPR 35.10(3) and (4):

35.10 Contents of report

(3) The expert's report must state the substance of all material instructions, whether written or oral, on the basis of which the report was written.

(4) The instructions referred to in paragraph (3) shall not be privileged against disclosure but the court will not, in relation to those instructions –

(a) order disclosure of any specific document; or

(b) permit any questioning in court, other than by the party who instructed the expert,

unless it is satisfied that there are reasonable grounds to consider the statement of instructions given under paragraph (3) to be inaccurate or incomplete.

Despite the fact that these rules are not as far reaching as had originally been proposed by Lord Woolf, their effect is extremely important—an importance that is matched by its complexity. This difficult subject is discussed in chapters 4 and 7.

60. Further rules that will be discussed, which facilitate the court's power to control evidence and attempt to ensure a level playing field between the parties, are CPR 35.1, 35.9 and 35.11:

35.1 Duty to restrict expert evidence

Expert evidence shall be restricted to that which is reasonably required to resolve the proceedings.

35.9 Power of court to direct a party to provide information

Where a party has access to information which is not reasonably available to another party, the court may direct the party who has access to the information to –

(a) prepare and file a document recording the information; and

(b) serve a copy of that document on the other party.

35.11 Use by one party of expert's report disclosed by another

Where a party has disclosed an expert's report, any party may use that expert's report as evidence at the trial.

Jackson LJ's Review of Civil Litigation Costs

61. In November 2008, Lord Clarke, then Master of the Rolls, appointed Jackson LJ to conduct a fresh review of civil litigation costs in the courts of England and Wales. Following a Preliminary Report in May 2009,[10] Jackson LJ published his 'Review of Civil Litigation Costs: Final Report' on 14 January 2010.[11] The judge's terms of reference for the conduct of his review required him to review the rules and principles governing the costs of civil litigation and to make recommendations in order to promote access to justice at proportionate cost. Although there was no expectation that sweeping reforms would be recommended, of the kind made by Lord Woolf, there was the possibility that changes would be proposed to the CPR, including Part 35, in order to bring Jackson LJ's recommendations into effect.

[10] Jackson LJ, 'Review of Civil Litigation Costs: Preliminary Report' (The Stationery Office, 2010).
[11] Jackson LJ, 'Review of Civil Litigation Costs: Final Report' (The Stationery Office, 2010).

62. As regards expert evidence, however, Jackson LJ is cautious. He broadly concludes that there is nothing fundamentally wrong with the manner in which expert evidence is currently adduced in civil litigation and that there are sufficient rules governing the use of such evidence already in place:

> There is now a wealth of guidance on the use of expert evidence: CPR Part 35 (as recently amended); practice direction 35; the Protocol for the Instruction of Experts to give evidence in Civil Claims; the Model Form of Expert's Report published by the Academy of Experts; and also a wealth of judicial decisions on what experts should or should not do, when single joint experts might be appropriate, and so forth. It is doubtful whether either lawyers or litigants or experts will welcome yet another raft of rules about expert evidence emerging from this review.

63. The substantial problem identified in the Report is that in some cases litigation costs are unnecessarily increased by unduly long expert reports. Jackson LJ concentrates his discussion on four key areas by which this problem might be addressed:

(a) Case Management

First, the judge notes that a well drawn order for expert evidence will not only identify the expert or the expert discipline, but also identify the issues which the expert will address.

However, he also suggests that judges might in future make greater use of their powers under CPR 35.4(4) to restrict recoverable costs in respect of expert evidence. To this end, he says he recommends the amendment of Part 35 or its accompanying practice direction to require that a party seeking permission to adduce expert evidence provides an estimate of the costs estimate for that evidence to the court.

Presently, there is a presumption in the small claims track and the fast track of the use of one expert witness (who may or may not be a single joint expert) on any particular issue:[12] On the other hand, the judge observes, in multi-track cases new section 7 of Practice Direction 35 gives guidance as to the factors which the court should take into account, when deciding whether to make an order for a single joint expert.

(b) One Size Does Not Fit All

The judge acknowledges that the requirements for effective expert evidence in personal injury cases, commercial cases, construction cases, clinical negligence cases, valuation disputes, insurance disputes, tree root claims and so forth are all 'totally different'. Consequently, he explains, a web of differing practices in relation to expert evidence has been created by practitioners and judges

[12] CPR 35.4(3A).

in different specialities, which the rules in Part 35, Practice Direction 35 and the personal injury claims pre-action protocol are wide enough to embrace. These rules could not realistically be expected to spell out what forms of order are conventional in all types of litigation.

(c) Costs Sanctions

In cases where expert evidence 'strays materially beyond the issues in the case', Jackson LJ notes that the judge already has power to impose costs sanctions. However, he recommends that judges be more willing to exercise this power in cases where prolix or irrelevant expert evidence has led to wastage of costs.

(d) Concurrent Evidence ('Hot Tubbing')

Having considered submissions made to him about the possible benefits of adopting the Australian system of concurrent evidence, dubbed 'hot tubbing', Jackson LJ recommends that a pilot study is adopted. This should be evaluated to ascertain: (a) the types of case in which concurrent evidence is successful; (b) what costs are saved; and (c) whether the parties and their advisers perceive the process as enabling each side's case to be properly considered. The judge then says, somewhat tentatively, that if the results of this assessment are positive, then consideration should be given to amending Part 35, so that it expressly enables the judge to direct that the concurrent evidence procedure be used in appropriate cases.

64. As a result of his considerations of (a) to (b) above, Jackson LJ ultimately makes two recommendations that will, or potentially will, have an effect on the provisions on Part 35. These are:

(i) CPR Part 35 or its accompanying practice direction should be amended in order to require that a party seeking permission to adduce expert evidence furnishes an estimate of the costs of that evidence to the court.
(ii) The procedure developed in Australia, known as 'concurrent evidence' should be piloted in cases where all parties consent. If the results of the pilot are positive, consideration should be given to amending CPR Part 35 to provide for use of that procedure in appropriate cases.

Of these two recommendations, it is potentially the second, concurrent evidence, or 'hot tubbing' as it is known colloquially, which may have implications for privilege. Although it is too early to speculate how this recommendation may be implemented, if it follows the Australian example, it will involve experts giving testimony concurrently in court—open to question by the court and each other, coming to agreement on some issues and disagreement on others. On the face of it, an approach broadly similar to this would seem to leave little scope for privilege to protect any instructions between those experts, or indeed the discussions between the experts themselves. In this respect it may prove to be more onerous in its effect on privilege than any of the existing rules on instructions or discussions between experts (see chapters 4 and 7, respectively).

Chapter Summary

65. Some distinction can be drawn between those experts who assist a party from 'behind the scenes' throughout the lifetime of proceedings and those who are 'Part 35 experts'. However, although defined as an expert who has been instructed to give or prepare evidence for the purpose of court proceedings, the label does not have any general implications—an expert is only truly a 'Part 35' expert when a rule in that part applies to them. Hence, the behind the scenes expert can broadly be thought of as an expert who will remain untouched by Part 35 because it is not the intention to use their evidence at any stage in the actual proceedings (subject to the concerns discussed in chapter 9).
66. The underlying rule is that, where the conditions in chapter 2 are fulfilled, litigation privilege will protect behind the scenes expert evidence. As *Carlson* demonstrates, a layer of litigation privilege will also cover Part 35 expert evidence until a provision of Part 35 forces features of that evidence above the surface.
67. In his Access to Justice Final Report, Lord Woolf expressed the concern that a large litigation support industry had developed in which huge costs were being generated across all types of litigation. One facet of this was the way in which experts were being used. In addition, Lord Woolf was critical of the way in which experts were sometimes prone to take on the role of partisan advocates for the party instructing them. Although all the rules introduced by Part 35 are not novel with respect to the earlier Rules of the Supreme Court, a number of its provisions are intended to bring new means to cure, or at least mitigate, the problems identified by Lord Woolf. Some of these rules have a direct impact on privilege, such as the rules relating to instructions. Others, which are designed to increase the court's control over evidence and to restrict the amount of evidence produced, have an indirect effect, as will be seen in the following chapters of this book.
68. The costs of expert evidence continue to be an issue in the Review of Civil Litigation Costs by Jackson LJ. However, this Report recommends nothing like the substantial changes recommended by Lord Woolf. The key proposal as regards expert evidence that may have an effect on privilege in future is that of 'hot tubbing'.

4

Instructions

Introduction

69. In the previous chapter the general rules of litigation privilege were discussed as they apply to the work of 'behind the scenes' experts. That chapter also discusses how the work and activities of an expert could generally be said to come within the application of Part 35 of the Civil Procedure Rules (CPR) such as to make the expert a 'Part 35' expert. This chapter now starts to look at the specific provisions of Part 35 that affect the general application of privilege by addressing instructions to experts.
70. Regardless of whether an expert begins his or her involvement as a behind the scenes expert or not, the effect of Part 35 must be addressed at an early stage of that expert's involvement. The solicitor instructing the expert needs to address Part 35 before the solicitor can even consider whether the expert will be used as a fully testifying 'Part 35' expert at some later date. This is because Part 35 directs the way in which expert evidence must be prepared from the very beginning, at the stage of issuing instructions. As we shall see in this chapter, if evidence is later given, a failure to adhere to the directions of Part 35 on instructions may result in an order for disclosure of instructions, and the disclosure and production of drafts and other documents for which privilege might otherwise have been maintained. If this happens, it will be regardless of whether the expert was contemplated as a CPR 'Part 35' expert at the time the expert was first interviewed and given instructions. Hence, the solicitor who prepares the evidence of an expert needs to consider the status of the tasks and questions set to the expert, the communications in which correspondence with the expert is documented and the other documents and drafts supplied to the expert.
71. To examine the effect of Part 35 on expert instructions, it is necessary to turn to the regime provided in CPR 35.10(3) and (4).

CPR 35.10

Objectives

72. As discussed in chapter 3, it is a fundamental tenet of the rules provided by Part 35 that expert evidence should assist the court and that an expert's duty is to the court and not to the instructing party. More specifically, the Lord Woolf's Access to Justice Final Report states the importance of ensuring that instructions to experts are transparent. A recommendation for ensuring this was that the court and all the parties should know what the expert has been asked to do, so that as far as possible there can be no question of the expert preparing evidence on the basis of hidden objectives, leading instructions, or undeclared opinions of other parties. Part 35 seeks to achieve this in CPR35.10(3):

CPR 35.10(3)—What the Report Must Contain

73. CPR 35.10(3) states:

> The expert's report must state the substance of all material instructions, whether written or oral, on the basis of which the report was written.

This rule is echoed by Practice Direction, paragraph 3.2(3) which provides that it applies not only to instructions, but also to facts:

> . . . a statement setting out the substance of all facts and instructions which are material to the opinions expressed in the report or upon which those opinions are based.

74. The purpose of CPR 35.10(3) and its supporting Practice Direction is therefore to ensure that transparency is maintained in dealings between an expert and the expert's instructing solicitors from the very beginning. This is achieved by the direction that the 'material instructions' to the expert must be set out in the report so that the court and the other parties can see them.[1] In less complex cases where instructions are provided to the expert in a single letter of instructions, the statement of instructions may be conveniently provided by annexing this letter to the back of the report. Alternatively, for example, where instructions are given cumulatively, over a period of time, a list summarising the solicitor's instructions is provided in the formal paragraphs at the start of the report.[2]

[1] See the Protocol for the Instruction of Experts to give Evidence in Civil Claims para 13.15: 'The mandatory statement of the substance of all material instructions should not be incomplete or otherwise tend to mislead. The imperative is transparency.'

[2] Practices differ depending on the applicable court and practice area of litigation. The formalities and practices of presentation of the expert report are outside the scope of this book and practitioners are referred to the guides and conventions of the courts in their respective practice areas.

75. CPR 35.10(3) raises two key questions: (a) what are material instructions; and (b) what is the privilege status of the instructions that are stated in the report? The answer to both questions is answered to some extent by the very next provision of the CPR, CPR35.10(4).

CPR 35.10(4)—Material Instructions and their Status

76. CPR 35.10(4) states:

> The instructions referred to in paragraph (3) shall not be privileged against disclosure but the court will not, in relation to those instructions—(a) order disclosure of any specific document; or
>
> (b) permit any questioning in court, other than by the party who instructed the expert, unless it is satisfied that there are reasonable grounds to consider the statement of instructions given under paragraph (3) to be inaccurate or incomplete.

77. As regards privilege, the rule clearly says that the statement of material instructions is not privileged against disclosure. This seems obvious, since a statement of material instructions is disclosed by virtue of its inclusion in the expert report, once that report itself has been served. However, the rule then imposes a limitation on the extent and consequences of disclosure by providing that 'in relation to' those instructions it will not order the disclosure of specific documents or allow the cross-examination of the expert by a party other than the instructing party. It seems that the words 'in relation to' are intended to encompass those matters relevant to the instructions that fall outside the ambit of 'material', whether they are matters recorded in a document, or otherwise matters that are cross-examinable in general.

78. There is a condition that must be satisfied for the limitation in CPR 35.10(4) to apply. The condition is that if the court is satisfied that there are reasonable grounds to consider that the statement of material instructions given in the report, pursuant to CPR 35.10(3), is 'inaccurate or incomplete', the limitation does not apply and the court may go behind the statement of material instructions. It may do so by ordering disclosure of those documents relating to the material instructions stated or allowing the expert to be cross-examined on those instructions. In other words the cost of failing to provide a complete and accurate statement of material instructions will be that the CPR 35.10(4) limitation no longer applies and potentially all matters in relation to the material instructions lose privilege.

The difficulty for the solicitor who wishes to provide a complete and accurate statement of the instructions, is determining what CPR 35.10(3) means by 'the substance of material instructions'. Moreover, what are instructions in this context? Clearly, given the consequences of failing to provide a complete and accurate statement of instructions, this is a matter of some importance. Some matters will obviously be instructions, for example, directing the expert to determine the cause of a fire in a warehouse, or to examine the extent of a spinal injury suffered by a person involved in an accident. However, what about other factual information provided to the expert to support the expert in preparing the report? What, for example, is the privilege status of documents provided to the expert to provide the background information necessary to form an opinion? The rest of this chapter looks at how CPR 35.10(3) and (4) have been applied to these issues.

Instructions and Inaccurate or Incomplete Statements

Undisclosed Basis of Discussion—Morris v Bank of India

Application under CPR 35.10(3)

The application in *Christopher Morris v Bank of India*[3] concerned matters underlying an expert's instructions. It arose from the collapse of Bank of Credit and Commerce International. Before Hart J, the applicants complained, amongst other matters, that the respondent's banking expert, Mr Wragge, had failed to identify in his report all the instructions upon which his report was based. In his report, Mr Wragge identified the documents that he had considered in the course of its preparation, namely: an amended 'points claim' and amended defence in the action, and the documents disclosed by the defendant/respondent, Bank of India. However, the applicants noticed that there were parts of the report in which Mr Wragge referred to matters that were not contained in the pleadings or in the documents disclosed by Bank of India. Mr Wragge had not identified the source of his information in respect of those latter matters and, moreover, they appeared to raise new factual allegations that had not been pleaded. In the circumstances of this action, where statements of fact had not yet been exchanged, the applicants complained that this left them unaware of whether the outstanding issues would be covered by the witness statements to be exchanged, and thus open to cross-examination, or whether the Court was to have only the benefit of an expert report based on unsubstantiated facts.

It seems to have emerged in correspondence from Bank of India's solicitors that the outstanding matters referred to derived from draft witness statements. At the time of preparing Mr Wragge's report it had been assumed that these would be exchanged before expert evidence. However, when it later became clear that this would not happen, express references to the witness statements as such were removed. However, evidence derived from those statements nonetheless remained. Not content to wait for statements of fact to be served, the applicants sought an order that copies of the documents referred to in the expert report be produced.

[3] *Christopher Morris v Bank of India* (Ch D 15 November 2001).

The application asked that the following be served on the applicants:

> (a) . . . a document recording the information, including details of all the facts and/ or assumptions which underlie the information, referred to and/or relied upon in Mr. Wragge's above expert report; and
> (b) copies of the documents mentioned in Mr. Wragge's expert report, . . .

79. In *Morris v Bank of India*, Hart J agreed that Mr Wragge's report was defective. It did not contain a 'statement of the substance of all material instructions, whether written or oral, on the basis of which the report was written', as required by CPR 35.10(3). Because the report did not contain such a complete statement, the Judge was satisfied that it was 'incomplete and inaccurate' for the purposes of CPR 35.10(4) and it was therefore open to the Court to order disclosure of the instructions given to Mr Wragge in relation to the evidence derived from the witness statements.

Consequences of Inaccurate or Incomplete Statement

80. Having found the statement of instructions incomplete and inaccurate in *Morris v Bank of India*, the question was then one of what exactly should be disclosed. This was difficult because it was unclear to the Court in what form the factual evidence had been supplied to Mr Wragge. For their part, Bank of India tried to avoid giving disclosure of any draft witness statement itself by offering to give a statement of the further matters that formed part of Mr Wragge's instructions. However, Hart J considered this beside the point—what should be disclosed would depend on what had happened:

> (a) If Mr Wragge had been instructed by providing him with the draft witness statements, used the information supplied in them in his report, but then simply removed references to those statements in his report, then the statements themselves would lose their status as privileged from disclosure because they were part of the instructions under CPR 35.10(3); but
> (b) If when instructed, Mr Wragge was told to put out of his mind any confidential material he had seen earlier, including witness statements, and instead had been supplied with certain assumptions of fact for the purposes of his report, then only those assumptions of fact would be instructions falling within CPR 35(3) and (4).

81. In *Morris v Bank of India*, Hart J concluded that the draft witness statements themselves would lose their character as being privileged from disclosure, if they formed part of the instructions referred to in paragraph (3) of CPR 35.10. However, in the latter case, only the assumptions of fact would be disclosable as matters falling within the instructions. The 'fruits of the order', as Hart J put it, would depend on what had been supplied to Mr Wragge.

Avoiding Disclosure under CPR 35.10(4)

82. Could the order for disclosure have been avoided in *Morris v Bank of India*? It seems from the following statement of Hart J that it could have been:

> . . . it would appear that the report would have so complied [with CPR 35.10(3)] had it said that it was based on, inter alia, in addition to the matters that are referred to in the report, the matters confirmed to him by [the defendant's solicitor] as being factual matters that are referred to in the report, and had then stated what the substance of that factual information was. That would have been done by reference to a document if the confirmation had been contained in a document, or by a summary of the oral communication if it had been by oral communication.

Hence, even if draft witness statements had been supplied to Mr Wragge, disclosure of the statements themselves could have been avoided if the report had simply pointed out in the instructions that they were being relied upon.

83. *Morris v Bank of India* is a warning of what can happen if the requirements of CPR35.10(3) are unfulfilled and how seriously the courts will treat it. It can be seen from this that the consequences for non-disclosure of the substance of material instructions on the basis of which the report is written can go further than the original disclosure requirement. If the draft witness statement itself had been supplied then its disclosure would be required by the order of Hart J. If the report had simply stated the substance of the matters contained in the statement on which Mr Wragge had based the relevant parts of his report, this would have been unnecessary. It is not clear from the decision whether this 'extra disclosure' was supposed to serve as a penalty for non-disclosure, but it does appear to go further than might have been expected.

Documents Provided for Instruction—Lucas v Barking

84. *Morris v Bank of India* illustrates a situation in which matters are discussed in an expert report for which the instructions underlying those discussions are not given. It was not established in that case whether the instructions were given by the provision of a draft witness statement itself, or whether the information was provided by the solicitors from the witness statement indirectly, in a digested form. There was no reference to the witness statement itself in the report. However, is there any guidance in the case law on the circumstances in which specific documents that are referred to in an expert's report can be obtained, because they are not stated as part of the substance of material instructions? Can documents be considered instructions at all? The Court of Appeal had to consider these issues in a case arising from circumstances far removed from those of *Morris v Bank of India*—the personal injury case *Lucas v Barking, Havering and Redbridge Hospitals NHS Trust*.[4,5]

4 *Lucas v Barking, Havering and Redbridge Hospitals NHS Trust* [2004] 1 WLR 220.

5 See also *Expandable Ltd v Rubin* [2008] EWCA Civ 59, where this case was considered.

Application under CPR 31.14(2) at First Instance

85. *Lucas v Barking* concerns a claim against the defendant, NHS Trust, for personal injury arising as a result of negligence. The claimant, Mr Lucas, served with his particulars of claim two experts' reports discussing his injuries. Both these reports referred to a witness statement of Mr Lucas that had been provided to the experts. One of the reports, Dr Mason's, also referred to an earlier expert report which had not been served on the defendant. This earlier report was by Dr Durdey. There is nothing to suggest that these documents would not have been served at the due time but, before this could happen, the defendant applied for an order for inspection of the draft witness statement and Dr Durdey's report. In this case, the application was made under CPR 31.14(2):

> Subject to rule 35.10(4), a party may apply for an order for inspection of any document mentioned in an expert's report which has not already been disclosed in the proceedings.

Mr Lucas was reluctant to provide these documents and resisted the application on the basis that the documents were instructions and fell within the CPR 35.10(4) exception to disclosure. However, the defendant was successful before Master Ungley at first instance. Master Ungley based his decision on the authority of Morland J in a case called *Taylor v Bolton HA*, which concerned similar facts.[6] In ordering disclosure of the documents, the Master considered that documents were not included within the meaning of 'instructions' referred to in CPR 35.10(3).

Can 'Instructions' Include Documents?—Lucas v Barking in the Court of Appeal

86. The Court of Appeal in *Lucas v Barking* considered whether it should adopt the narrower construction of '*instructions*' in *Taylor v Bolton*, which had

[6] It is held by the Court of Appeal in *Lucas v Barking* that *Taylor v Bolton* is no longer good authority on this issue. *Taylor v Bolton HA* [2000] CLY 310 was itself based on an earlier version of Civil Procedure Rule (CPR) 31 which did not include CPR 31.14(2), but instead included a sub-para (1)(e) which added 'experts reports' to the list of documents in which documents referred to might be inspected (although this was still expressed to be subject to CPR 35.10(4)). There was some discussion in *Lucas v Barking* about the distinction between the old rule CPR 31.14(1) containing para (e) and the new rule in which this had been deleted. The particular issue was whether there was formerly a prima facie right to inspect documents referred to in expert reports. This was not fully argued and the Court of Appeal did not have a concluded view. However, Laws LJ felt it difficult to accept that this could confer an absolute right to inspect documents referred to in abrogation of the inherent privilege of such documents. Particularly since this would be 'quixotic if documents whose privilege is expressly withdrawn (CPR, r.35.10(4)) were subject only to limited rights of disclosure but those (CPR, r.35.14(1)) whose privilege is only impliedly withdrawn were liable to be inspected without restriction'. As a result of *Lucas v Barking*, this issue would appear to be academic in the field of instructions in expert evidence, but see *Expandable Ltd v Rubin* [2008] EWCA Civ 59 for a discussion of this issue in a more general context and chapter 5, where this issue is explored.

excluded medical reports provided to the expert, or whether instead a wider interpretation should be adopted.[7] In *Taylor v Bolton*, Morland J had said:

> In my judgement instructions are what an expert is told to do. What answers he is asked to give to specific questions. This is illustrated, in my judgement, by the first paragraph of Dr Wazou's report dated 18 August 1997, in which he says: 'I have been instructed to examine Donna Taylor and provide a report on her development from birth, her present neurological and general health state, prognosis for the future and estimation of life expectancy.' In my judgement, those in very form are the instructions given by the claimant through her solicitors to Dr Wazou. Dr Wazou then goes on to say: 'Donna was seen in the presence of her parents. I had available to me at the time of preparing this report documentary medical evidence supplied to me by instructing solicitors,. . .' and then he sets out those reports, including medical reports. . . In my judgement, the material upon which an expert is asked to comply with his instruction to answer questions, give a prognosis, etc are not part of the instructions, but the basic material upon which the expert is asked to reach his conclusions in accordance with his instructions, and therefore, in my judgement, the material, the basic material supplied to the expert is not part of the instructions.

The Court of Appeal in *Lucas v Barking* did not agree with Morland J's narrow approach. It had no difficulty finding that Mr Lucas' statement was supplied to the expert as part of the instructions given to prepare the expert's report. Similarly, the draft report of Dr Durdey, supplied to Dr Mason, was part of her instructions. It had been given to her to instruct her about what Dr Durdey had been saying.[8]

Laws LJ in *Lucas v Barking* is clear about the rationale for this broad understanding of instructions:

> . . . the aim of CPR 35.10(3) and (4) is broadly to ensure that the factual basis on which the expert has prepared his report is patent. That approach demands a wide reading of the term 'instructions', and would be frustrated by the approach taken by Morland J in Taylor ('instructions are what an expert is told to do').

The Relationship between CPR 35.10 and CPR 31.14

87. Although the application in *Lucas v Barking* had been made under CPR 31.14, the Court of Appeal stated its view that even if CPR 31.14 gave an absolute

[7] Note also that the Court of Appeal was referred to an earlier Court of Appeal authority, *Bennett v Compass Group UK & Ireland Ltd* [2002] EWCA Civ 642, which came to a similar conclusion to Morland J in *Taylor v Bolton*. That is, the Court thought that CPR 35.10(4) was not relevant because 'instructions' do not cover documents and the old CPR 31.14(e) specifically provided for the disclosure of documents referred to in an expert's report. The Court in *Lucas v Barking* declined to follow this, apparently on the basis that the provision for expert reports had since been deleted from the rule.

[8] The Protocol for the Instruction of Experts to give Evidence in Civil Claims para 13.15 also provides useful guidance on what is meant by 'instructions': 'The term "instructions" includes all material which solicitors place in front of experts in order to gain advice. The omission from the statement of "off-the-record" oral instructions is not permitted. . . .'

right to inspection, the position in relation to experts' reports is separately dealt with.[9] Furthermore, the Court explained that it had to consider CPR 35.10 when considering expert reports. Specifically, CPR 35.10(4) is designed primarily to give protection to a party that would otherwise have waived privilege by being compelled to set out matters in an expert's report under CPR 35.10(3). Substantial parts of Mr Lucas' statement had been set out in the expert report as 'material instructions' pursuant to CPR 35.10(3).[10] CPR 35.10(4) is intended to prevent such compliance with CPR 35.10(3) from rendering a statement such as that of Mr Lucas from being disclosable, unless there are grounds for believing that the statement given in the expert's report is 'inaccurate or incomplete'. It is thus also designed to prevent, as far as possible, lengthy arguments about whether there has been a waiver of privilege entitling further disclosure.

'Substance of all Material Instructions'

88. In *Lucas v Barking*, the defendant argued that if the draft witness statement and draft expert report form part of the instructions, as the Court held, then it must follow that 'the substance of all material instructions...' had not been set out, because the whole of the statement and report were not provided. The Court of Appeal was not impressed by this argument. CPR 35.10(3) only required the substance of material instructions. There is no requirement to supply all the information or instructions supplied to the expert.[11] Furthermore, the protection of CPR 35.10(4) was worded to apply to specific documents and particular questions on an area specifically because of the risk that reference to part of privileged material may waive privilege to the whole.

The Court of Appeal would not order disclosure of the draft witness statement and draft report, but there was little further guidance in the case on what constitutes a material instruction. The substantial parts of Mr Lucas' statement that had been set out appear to have been considered as material instructions. However, in respect of Mr Durdey's report, it is not clear whether the reference to this document provided a sufficiently complete and accurate statement of the substance of material instructions for the purpose of CPR 35.10(3) and 35.10(4), or simply that the document itself was not material. The Court said that there was no basis at the stage at which they heard the case for suggesting that the material instructions were in any way inaccurate or incomplete.

[9] Although it was not specific about why—see the discussion in chapter 5.

[10] See chapter 5 for a discussion of deployment by reliance on content, outside the context of instructions.

[11] See *Salt & Consignia Plc* [2002] CLY 420, for an example of how CPR 35.10(3) and (4) have been applied by the County Court. In this case Salt provided Consignia with edited versions of letters from Salt to Salt's expert. The Court found that the statement of instructions was incomplete and was prepared to order disclosure of the letters as far as they contained material instructions.

'Inaccurate and Incomplete'?

89. The cautious approach to the statement of instructions was reflected in the short supporting judgment of Laws LJ in *Lucas v Barking*, who took a step back to comment on where the overall balance between CPR 35.10(3) and CPR 35.10(4) should lie:

> I think it a premise of the arrangements constituted by 35.10(3) and (4) that in the ordinary way the expert is to be trusted to comply with 35.10(3): the effect of the 35.10(4) restrictions is that the party on the other side may not as a matter of course call for disclosure of documents constituting the expert's instructions as a check to see that 35.10(3) has been fulfilled. There must be some concrete fact giving rise to 'reasonable grounds' within the closing words of 35.10(4). It is unsurprising that the expert is thus to be trusted; it is a piece with his overriding duty to help the court (CPR 35.3). Overall, 35.10(4) in my view strikes an important balance between on the one hand the protection of the party whose privilege is lost, and on the other the vindication of 35.10(3) where there is a real question-mark as to its fulfilment.

In the absence of a 'concrete fact' giving rise to reasonable grounds to consider that the statement of instructions is inaccurate or incomplete, the Court will give the expert the 'benefit of the doubt' and be reluctant to look behind the statement of instructions provided in the expert's report.

Chapter Summary

90. In order to achieve the policy objective of transparency, the general rules of litigation privilege are to a certain extent overridden by the regime provided for by CPR 35.10(3): the 'substance of all material instructions' must be stated in an expert report. CPR 35.10(4) confirms that these will not be protected by privilege. However, there is a balance that is struck by CPR 35.10(4), providing the statement of the substance of all material instructions is not 'inaccurate or incomplete' and the court will not order the disclosure of the documents relating to those instructions nor permit another party to cross-examine the expert on them.
91. The cases of *Morris v Bank of India* and *Lucas v Barking* illustrate situations where the instructions fall either side of the complete and accurate line. In *Morris v Bank of India*, the manner in which the instructions were provided is not revealed, but it was apparent that the expert had prepared evidence based on matters put to him that had not been disclosed in his instructions. The failure to mention these matters rendered the instructions inaccurate and incomplete and the judge ordered those matters to be disclosed in whatever form they had been supplied to the expert.

It is clear from *Lucas v Barking* that the Court of Appeal has put a wide interpretation on the word 'instructions', which it deems to include matters provided to the expert by way of background to assist in the preparation of the expert report and not just those directions that tell the expert what to do. So in *Lucas v Barking*, a draft witness statement and a draft report of another expert provided to the expert were considered instructions and therefore protected from disclosure by CPR 35.10(4), providing the statement of the substance of the material instructions was accurate and complete. In this case there was no requirement to disclose the entirety of the draft report and draft witness statement in circumstances where reference had been made to them in the expert's report. However, it is not clear whether this is because the drafts themselves did not amount to material instructions, or because the reference in itself was sufficient to count as the substance of those instructions. The wider definition of instructions in *Lucas v Barking* suggests that the day-to-day communications, such as emails and telephone attendance notes, including documents supplied, made in relation to expert instructions and during the progress of the preparation of evidence, are covered. Therefore, in many circumstances this material may be 'off-limits' to production, provided the statement of the substance of material instructions is complete and accurate.[12]

92. The Court of Appeal has indicated in *Lucas v Barking* that it will be slow, certainly at an interlocutory stage, to find that instructions are inaccurate and incomplete, and will require a concrete reason to do so. Although *Morris v Bank of India* was decided before *Lucas v Barking*, the decision to order disclosure in that case would appear to be consistent with the *Lucas v Barking* approach—the concrete reason being that tracts of the report evidently discussed matters entirely omitted from the instructions.
93. In *Lucas v Barking*, disclosure of the referenced draft expert report was not ordered, despite the fact that substantial parts of that draft report were apparently set out in the final report in which it was referenced. This result is seemingly inconsistent with the provisions regarding documents referred to in CPR 31.14 (for which see chapter 5). This result was apparently recognised by the Court but dealt with on the basis that expert reports are separately dealt with under the CPR 35.10(3) and (4) regime.
94. The combined effect of CPR 35.10(3) and (4) should be considered by the instructing solicitor from the solicitor's very first interview with an expert; even if those discussions initially occur on a behind the scenes basis only, the expert will later become subject to these provisions if his or her evidence is to be relied upon (the expert becomes a 'Part 35' expert).

[12] See chapter 5 in relation to documents referred to outside the context of instructions.

5

Documents Generally Referred to in the Report

Introduction

95. *Lucas v Barking, Havering and Redbridge Hospitals NHS Trust,*[1] discussed in the last chapter, concerns a situation in which a witness statement and a draft expert report had been supplied to an expert as part of the expert's 'instructions'. Reference to the draft report and the recital of parts of its contents were made, so it was held by the Court, in furtherance of the expert's obligation under Civil Procedure Rule (CPR) 35.10(3) to set out 'the substance of all material instructions'. The Court would not order disclosure of the specific documents itself because there was no concrete reason why the instructions were not accurate and complete pursuant to CPR 35.10(4). However, *Lucas v Barking* and CPR 35.10(3) and 35.10(4) are concerned only with instructions. What happens when a document is referred to outside the context of the expert's instructions? As stated in the last chapter, the decision of the Court of Appeal in *Lucas v Barking* indicates that expert reports are dealt with differently to the other documents listed in CPR 31.14.[2] However, could it also be said that within the context of expert reports, there is a distinction in the privilege regime to be applied to documents which are used under the broad heading of instructions and documents which are referred to in an expert report outside the context of instructions? The words in CPR35.10(4): '. . . the court will not, in relation to those instructions—(a) order disclosure of any specific document', certainly suggests that this rule only applies to documents related to the instructions. The different approach applying between documents referred to in the instructions and documents referred to generally in an expert report is advanced by Rix LJ in *Expandable Ltd v Rubin*:[3]

> . . . the detailed provisions in relation to privilege in relation to an expert's report in any event needed to be separately addressed, requiring cross-reference to CPR 35.10, since that is where this issue in the case of experts' reports is dealt with. Even so, CPR 35.10 deals only with the role of privilege in relation to 'instructions'. It does not deal with the role of privilege in relation to documents mentioned in an

[1] *Lucas v Barking, Havering and Redbridge Hospitals NHS Trust* [2004] 1 WLR 220.

[2] A matter now made clear by the present, revised drafting of CPR 31.14(2).

[3] *Expandable Ltd v Rubin* [2008] EWCA Civ 59.

expert's report wholly generally. Therefore, outside the scope of CPR 35.10, the position of documents mentioned in an expert's report is the same as in the case of documents mentioned in a statement of case, a witness statement, a witness summary or an affidavit.

96. So, the treatment of documents mentioned in an expert's report wholly generally is different to that described in chapter 4, as regards privilege. Instead, the same rules apply to these documents as apply to the other documents listed by Rix LJ. Outside the context of instructions, expert reports are just another document on the CPR 31.14 list:

> (1) A party may inspect a document mentioned in –
>
> (a) a statement of case;
> (b) a witness statement;
> (c) a witness summary; or
> (d) an affidavit.
> (e) Revoked.
>
> (2) Subject to rule 35.10(4), a party may apply for an order for inspection of any document mentioned in an expert's report which has not already been disclosed in the proceedings.
> (Rule 35.10(4) makes provision in relation to instructions referred to in an expert's report.)

In other words, where instructions are not concerned, it is as if the words 'Subject to rule 35.10(4)' and the final section in brackets were removed from this rule. This chapter explores the application of privilege to documents under this rule, as it applies to documents mentioned in an expert report outside the context of instructions.

Documents 'Mentioned'—Expandable v Rubin

Background

97. CPR 31.14 applies to documents 'mentioned', so the first issue to be addressed is what it means for a document to be mentioned in an expert report. This issue is addressed in depth by the Court of Appeal in *Expandable v Rubin.* In short, this case concerned a section 363 application under the Insolvency Act 1986. The application arose from a claim over monies that the claimant applicants said should be transferred by the respondent supervisor of a failed Individual Voluntary Arrangement, Mr Rubin. The effect of CPR 31.14 was addressed in this application in the context of a witness statement prepared by Mr Rubin. The statement made reference to an interview conducted by Mr Rubin's solicitor of the debtor under the IVA, Mr Clarke. Mr Rubin's solicitor subsequently sent the notes of this interview to Mr Rubin under cover

of a letter which drew attention to discrepancies between what Mr Clarke said in the interview and what he had said in an earlier note to Mr Rubin. This was reflected in Mr Rubin's witness statement like this:

> . . . In particular it will be noted that there are several inconsistencies between Mr Clarke's note to me and what he told Mr Zaidi . . . I think it right I draw the Court's attention to the fact that after Mr Zaidi had interviewed Mr Clarke he [Mr Zaidi] wrote to me enclosing a copy of his note of the meeting and drawing my attention to the discrepancies (which, by the way, I did not think in any way assisted Prime/Expandable Trust with their claim).

First Instance and Appeal

98. On the basis of the words '. . . wrote to me enclosing a copy of his note of the meeting and drawing my attention to the discrepancies . . .', the claimant companies sought disclosure of the covering letter, so they could judge for themselves what the inconsistencies were. Whilst all the parties agreed that the letter would normally be privileged, it was argued that this privilege had been waived pursuant to CPR 31.14 on the basis that the letter had been mentioned in Mr Rubin's witness statement.

At first instance before Registrar Simmonds, and then on appeal to Patten J, it was held that there was no mention of the letter. As Registrar Simmonds put it:

> The communication is imprecise. It does not say whether it is a letter or an email. It is not mentioned by date. The wording is explanatory of process rather than being mentioned in a specific and direct form.

Second Appeal

99. On a second appeal, the Court of Appeal addressed this issue by first looking, for comparison, at the text of RSC Ord 24 r 10(1) under the old regime:

> (1) Any party to a cause or matter shall be entitled at any time to serve a notice on any party in whose pleadings, affidavits or witness statements reference is made to any document requiring him to produce that document for the inspection of the party giving notice and to permit him to take copies thereof.

Rix LJ then looked at how this rule with its use of the language 'reference is made' had been applied by the Court of Appeal in *Dubai Bank Ltd v Galadari (No 3)*.[4]

[4] *Dubai Bank Ltd v Galadari (No 3)* [1990] 1 WLR 731.

Comparing the Old Rules—Dubai Bank

100. In *Dubai Bank*, the Court had to consider whether the following three pieces of language referred to documents for the purpose of RSC Ord 24 r 10:

(a) 'instrumental in setting up a discretionary trust';
(b) 'with a guarantee'; and
(c) 'by virtue of a mandate from the account holders'.

The Court held that the phrase in (a) merely referred to the setting up of a trust, not a document as such. However, phrases (b) and (c) did refer to documents by way of guarantee and mandate, respectively. In order to explain this, in his judgment for the court in *Dubai Bank*, Slade LJ contrasted two situations: first, a situation in which a transaction is referred to and, secondly, a situation in which a document is specifically mentioned. So, for example, in the former case in the expression 'the property Blackacre was conveyed by A and B', no document had been referred to even though it may be more or less certain that a document had been used to effect the transaction. The Court rejected the argument that a reference to a transaction that on the balance of probabilities will have required a document was a reference to that document in itself:

> It seems to us to involve reading the phrase "reference is made to any document" as including reference by inference. This we do not regard as the natural and ordinary meaning of the phrase. To our minds, the phrase imports the meaning of a direct allusion to a document or documents.

The test preferred by Slade LJ in *Dubai Bank* was whether there was a 'direct allusion' to a document. The Court also considered that a reference to a document may be compendious rather than to an individual document.[5] Furthermore, Slade LJ seemed to draw a line between a reference to the *effect* of a document and the *contents* of the document, the latter apparently coming within the rule, the former not (this is discussed later in the chapter in the section entitled 'Reliance on "Effect" or "Contents"?').

'Direct Allusion' and 'Specifically Mentioned'

101. Having considered *Dubai Bank*, the Court of Appeal in *Expandable v Rubin* was content to assume that there is no effective or substantive difference in the meaning of RSC Ord 24 r 11 and the present CPR 31.14 and adopted Slade LJ's test of 'direct allusion' as an elucidation of the word 'mentioned'.[6] The Court also confirmed that this should mean the document had been

[5] See also *Smith v Harris* (1883) 48 LT 869.

[6] See also *Vardinoyannis v Ansol Ltd* (Unreported High Court, 23 May 2001), Blackburne J held that he did not think there was any material difference between the words '*reference is made to a document*' in RCS Ord 24 r 10, and '*a document mentioned*' in CPR 31.14.

'specifically mentioned' to use a further gloss of Slade LJ in *Dubai Bank*. The Court in *Expandable v Rubin* also held that the document does not have to be relied on, or referred to in any particular way or for any particular purpose, in order to be mentioned.

102. It is clear from the decision made about the words 'he wrote to me' in Mr Rubin's witness statement in *Expandable v Rubin* that this is not intended to be a narrow interpretation of the word 'mentioned'. The words 'he wrote to me' were held to be no different to saying 'he wrote a writing', a direct allusion to making a document and therefore a mention of it for the purpose of CPR 31.14. What seemed to matter to the Court in coming to this conclusion was that the document itself should be the direct subject matter of the reference. Furthermore, the Court did not appear to be concerned that it was unknown whether the writing had been in an email or a letter. All that mattered to the Court was that there should be a document of some description.

The Effect of Mentioning a Document

103. If the above discussion is not to be a dry discourse on the meaning of 'mentioned', it is necessary to look at what effect establishing that a document has been mentioned has on privilege. Having dealt with the meaning of 'mentioned', the Court in *Expandable v Rubin* went on to deal with this issue:

The Old Rule

Buttes Gas and Oil Co v Hammer (No 3)[7]

104. Again, looking to authorities under the old RSC regime for guidance, Rix LJ in *Expandable v Rubin* turned to the case of *Buttes Gas and Oil Co v Hammer (No 3)*. In *Buttes Gas*, inspection was sought of documents referred to in the plaintiff's pleadings. The plaintiff contested production of these documents on the basis of privilege. It was held that a mere reference to the documents was not a waiver of privilege. Lord Denning MR put it like this:

> In general, it is clear that if a party refers in his pleading to a document, the other side are entitled to require it to be produced, see RSC, Ord. 24, r.10(1) and (2); but it is open to the pleader to object to its production, see RSC, Ord. 24, r.11(1)(a).

Brightman LJ also said:

> So far as waiver by pleading is concerned, I agree with the judge that reference to a document or to its contents in a pleading does not waive any legal professional privilege attached to it.

[7] *Buttes Gas and Oil Co v Hammer (No 3)* [1981] 1 QB 223.

So, to the judges in *Buttes Gas*, the words of the RSC showed that reference to a document was not intended to be an automatic waiver of privilege and a party asked to produce a document for inspection on the basis of a mere reference could object to that production. However, what is the position under CPR 31.14?

Under the CPR—Prima Facie Right to Inspection?

Lucas v Barking

105. There is some discussion in the decision of *Lucas v Barking* about whether there is a prima facie right to inspect documents referred to in expert reports, or whether an application must be made to obtain inspection. Laws LJ felt it difficult to accept that CPR 31.14 could confer an absolute right to inspect documents referred to in abrogation of their inherent privilege. Particularly since this would be:

> quixotic if documents whose privilege is expressly withdrawn (35.10(4)) were subject only to limited rights of disclosure but those (35.14(1)) whose privilege is only impliedly withdrawn were liable to be inspected without restriction.

The CPR Rules Considered in Expandable v Rubin

This was not fully argued and the Court of Appeal did not have a concluded view. In *Expandable v Rubin*, on the other hand, Rix LJ looked at the issue exhaustively by reference, in addition to CPR 31.14, to the following rules:

> CPR 31.3:
>
> (1) A party to whom a document has been disclosed has a right to inspect that document except where –
>
> (a) the document is no longer in the control of the party who disclosed it;
> (b) the party disclosing the document has a right or a duty to withhold inspection of it; or
> (c) paragraph (2) applies.
>
> (Rule 31.8 sets out when a document is in the control of a party)
> (Rule 31.19 sets out the procedure for claiming a right or duty to withhold inspection)
> (2) Where a party considers that it would be disproportionate to the issues in the case to permit inspection of documents within a category or class of document disclosed under rule 31.6(b) –
>
> (a) he is not required to permit inspection of documents within that category or class; but
> (b) he must state in his disclosure statement that inspection of those documents will not be permitted on the grounds that to do so would be disproportionate.
>
> (Rule 31.6 provides for standard disclosure)

(Rule 31.10 makes provision for a disclosure statement)
(Rule 31.12 provides for a party to apply for an order for specific inspection of documents).

CPR 31.15:

Where a party has a right to inspect a document –
(a) that party must give the party who disclosed the document written notice of his wish to inspect it;
(b) the party who disclosed the document must permit inspection not more than 7 days after the date on which he received the notice; and
(c) that party may request a copy of the document and, if he also undertakes to pay reasonable copying costs, the party who disclosed the document must supply him with a copy not more than 7 days after the date on which he received the request.

(Rule 31.3 and 31.14 deal with the right of a party to inspect a document).'

and, CPR 31.19

(1) A person may apply, without notice, for an order permitting him to withhold disclosure of a document on the ground that disclosure would damage the public interest.
(2) Unless the court orders otherwise, an order of the court under paragraph (1) –

(a) must not be served on any other person; and
(b) must not be open to inspection by any person.

(3) A person who wishes to claim that he has a right or a duty to withhold inspection of a document, or part of a document, must state in writing –

(a) that he has such a right or duty; and
(b) the grounds on which he claims that right or duty.

(4) The statement referred to in paragraph (3) must be made –

(a) in the list in which the document is disclosed; or
(b) if there is no list, to the person wishing to inspect the document.

(5) A party may apply to the court to decide whether a claim made under paragraph (3) should be upheld.
(6) For the purpose of deciding an application under paragraph (1) (application to withhold disclosure) or paragraph (3) (claim to withhold inspection) the court may –

(a) require the person seeking to withhold disclosure or inspection of a document to produce that document to the court; and
(b) invite any person, whether or not a party, to make representations.

(7) An application under paragraph (1) or paragraph (5) must be supported by evidence.
(8) This Part does not affect any rule of law which permits or requires a document to be withheld from disclosure or inspection on the ground that its disclosure or inspection would damage the public interest.

Six Reasons Why the Buttes Gas Regime is Good Law

106. Considering the above rules, Rix LJ gave six reasons why the regime under CPR 31.14 should not be taken to have changed the position as set out in *Buttes Gas* under the old rules. These reasons can be summarised as follows:

1. There was no solid reason, if any, why the drafters of the CPR, in contra-distinction to the previous law, should have decided to require the automatic and absolute waiver of privilege as the price for the mere mention of documents in statements of case and the like.
2. There is nothing in Part 31 itself to explain such a change of philosophy.
3. Such a change in philosophy would have the effect, apparently for the first time in the history of English litigation, that the fundamental protection of privilege is automatically abandoned by the mere mentioning of documents.[8]
4. There is no reason why CPR 31.19 should not be read as having general application, whether or not a previous rule within Part 31 should have referred expressly to a right to object to inspection or should have expressly cross-referred to it. In particular, CPR 31.19(4)(b) appears to be well designed for the situation where disclosure is made by mentioning a document within CPR 31.14. Though CPR 31.15 appears to be absolute in terms ('must permit inspection') it is not, as demonstrated by the cross-reference to CPR 31.3, which allows for claims of privilege.
5. A possible reason why CPR 31.14 does not expressly cross-refer to CPR 31.19 is that CPR 31.14 is merely an adjunct to CPR 31.3, making further cross-reference unnecessary. CPR 31.3 is a rule of general application whenever 'a document has been disclosed'. Although disclosure generally takes place by list under CPR 31.10, it also takes place by virtue of the mention of documents in CPR 31.14. The latter form is merely a species of disclosure and comes within the general CPR 31.3 rule.[9]
6. For these reasons the qualified rights of privilege in CPR 35.10(4) and 31.14(2) throw no light on the role of the principles of privilege in relation to documents mentioned otherwise than in an expert's report. Even so, CPR 35.10 deals only with the role of privilege in relation to 'instructions'.[10]

Mere Mention does not Automatically Waive Privilege

107. The answer was therefore clear in the mind of Rix LJ and his fellow judges—the mere mention of a document in a statement of case or other document as specified in CPR 31.14 does not automatically waive the protection of privilege in it. In principle, objection can be made against production of that document for inspection. The same applies to documents in an expert's

[8] Rix LJ refers to *R v Derby Magistrates' Court, ex p B* [1996] 1 AC 487; *General Mediterranean Holidays SA v Patel* [2000] 1 WLR 272; *R v Secretary of State for the Home Department, ex p Simms* [2000] 2 AC 115.

[9] See *Smithkline Beecham Plc v Generics (UK) Ltd* [2004] 1 WLR 1479.

[10] See chapter 4.

report, providing reference is not made in relation to instructions so as to bring the reference under the separate considerations of CPR35.10(4).

Waiver of Privilege by Deployment

What is Required?

Reliance?

108. If the mention of a document is not enough to waive privilege in it, so as to entitle inspection, then in what circumstances will privilege be waived? It has been suggested that there must at least be reliance, to some extent. This is supported by the following statement of Brightman LJ in *Buttes Gas:*

> It is to my mind equally clear that a party cannot rely on a privileged document so pleaded without thereby waiving privilege. Therefore sooner or later Buttes will have to decide whether to forego privilege in respect of a privileged document which is pleaded, or to abandon reliance on it. If they sit on the fence until the trial (if any) begins or is in actual progress, they will do so at their own risk.

Difficulty comes in determining quite the extent and nature of the reliance that will give rise to a waiver of privilege, as Donaldson LJ put it, also in *Buttes Gas*:

> It must be right that a bare reference to a document in a pleading does not waive any privilege attaching to it as otherwise there would be no scope for taking objections under RSC Ord. 24, r.11(1), when a notice was served under r.10(1). If, on the other hand, a document is reproduced in full in the pleading, its confidentiality is gone and no question of privilege could arise. Where the line is drawn between these two extremes may be a matter of some nicety, . . .

Limitations on Reliance Test

109. The judges in *Buttes Gas* did not need to determine where the line should be drawn, but this issue came up again a few years later in *Marubeni Corporation v Lal Fouzof.*[11] This decision concerned the status of an indirect reference made to Japanese legal advice in an affidavit. Under the RSC discovery was sought of the documents containing that Japanese advice. At first instance it was held that there had been a waiver of privilege in relation to the advice, on the basis that the plaintiff was placing reliance upon it. However, in the Court of Appeal, Lloyd LJ stated that he believed using a test of reliance was

[11] *Marubeni Corporation v Lal Fouzof* (CA, 16 November 1986).

an incorrect approach. The reason for this was that there could not be a case in which a document referred to in an affidavit in interlocutory proceedings was not being relied upon. So, to use reliance alone as the test would have far reaching consequences and there would be no practical scope for the claim of privilege at all.[12] Instead, it must be asked, reliance on what?

Reliance on 'Effect' or 'Contents'?

The Importance of Telling the Difference

110. As did Donaldson LJ in *Buttes Gas*, the Court of Appeal in *Marubeni* thought there was a contrast to be drawn between a mere reference to a document and the quotation of its contents. In this case it was argued that the reference to the Japanese advice was a reference to its contents, and as such there was a waiver of privilege. However, the Court of Appeal did not agree. It held that there was merely a reference to the *effect* of the document, not a reference to its contents and that these were different things, albeit that in certain circumstances it might be difficult to determine the difference. A reference to the effect of the advice was not enough to waive privilege. A similar conclusion was reached in *Government Trading Corporation v Tate & Lyle*[13] in which an affidavit sworn by a solicitor contained the statement:

> The information contained in this paragraph is derived from a firm of lawyers practising in Tehran whom my firm has consulted, and I believe it to be correct.

The Court refused the application in *Tate & Lyle* for production of the document containing the Iranian lawyers' advice. In the judgment of Robert Goff LJ there was not a waiver of the document, because the deponent was merely setting out the substance of a matter and giving the source of his information on it. In his view, this was nothing like a waiver of privilege:

> [the deponent] of the affidavit was referring to a certain matter, he was setting out the substance of it and he was (I fear inadequately) giving the source of information. I do not read that, in the context of the interlocutory application then before the Commercial Judge, as amounting to anything like a waiver of privilege.[14]

[12] The judge gave as an example, under the old rules, the waiver of privilege that would result in counsel's advice being referred to in support of a good defence to a claim in Order 14 summary judgment proceedings. Under Order 14, the test was 'no triable issue', but there seems to be no reason why the judge's comments should not be equally applicable under Part 24 and the test of 'no reasonable prospect of success'.

[13] *Government Trading Corporation v Tate & Lyle* (1984) 81 LSG 3341.

[14] See also *Infields Ltd v P Rosen & Son* [1938] 3 All ER 591.

Effect

110.1 In *Bourns Inc v Raychem Corp*,[15] Aldous LJ commented on *Marubeni*, the reasoning of which he closely followed. He said that all the deponent was doing in *Marubeni* was saying:

> I am being frank with the court. I have received certain information from Japan and I believe it provides no defence to the defendants.[16]

In other words, as Aldous LJ continued to explain, there was not reliance on the contents of the document, there was reliance only on the effect of the document. The reference was made to the Japanese lawyers because there was a duty for the deponent to give his source of information and this could only be done by referring to what he had been told.

111. The principle that emerges from these authorities, therefore, is that a document which would normally be privileged will not lose its privileged status merely because it has been referred to in an expert report,[17] witness statement, affidavit or statement of case.[18] Reliance on the document alone is also not the test, if this reliance is on the effect of the document only.

Contents

112. Instead of reliance on effect, waiver of privilege requires reliance on the content of the document.[19] This brings the discussion back to a consideration of the spectrum of activity that lies between reliance on a summary of a small amount of content on one side, to a verbatim quotation of most or all of a document on the other side.

[15] *Bourns Inc v Raychem Corp* [1999] 3 All ER 154.

[16] *cf Clough v Thameside and Gloucester Health Authority* [1998] 2 All ER 971, which was disapproved in part by Aldous LJ in *Bourns*.

[17] In Bourns it was also argued before the Court of Appeal that Marubeni was not concerned with expert evidence, which was subject to its own duties (referring to *National Justice Compania Naviera SA v Prudential Assurance Co Ltd (The Ikarian Reefer) (No 1)* [1993] 2 Lloyds Rep 68, but now formalised in Part 35). An essential element of expert evidence being that the court and parties should know of the information supplied to the expert so that the basis of this opinion could be tested. However, Aldous LJ was not impressed: 'The principles of law are clear. Service of a witness statement, whether it be a statement of an expert or a witness of fact, waives privilege in that statement. As stated in the *Marubeni Corp* case, mere reference to a document does not waive privilege in that document; there must at least be reference to the contents and reliance.' (emphasis supplied.)

[18] In *Marubeni* it was argued that the case of *Buttes Gas* and the old, nineteenth-century authority of *Roberts v Oppenheim* (1884) LR 26 Ch D 724 were only relevant to pleadings on the basis that pleadings merely put forward contentions, whereas affidavits were a category apart because they put forward evidence. It was held that this could not be correct following what was said by the Court of Appeal in *Infields* where a summons stated: 'There has furthermore been disclosed by the plaintiffs a bundle of documents for which privilege has been claimed by them, which trace the history of the development of the various clip designs supplied by the firm of Karl Veith to the plaintiffs and which are quite inconsistent with the defendants' said allegations.' This was held not to waive privilege in the documents mentioned by mere reference.

[19] *Bourns* [1999] 3 All ER 154 (Aldous LJ); see also Digicel *(St Lucia) Ltd v Cable & Wireless Plc* [2009] EWHC 1437 (Ch).

Clearly, as Donaldson LJ suggested in *Buttes Gas*, a verbatim quotation of a whole document must be a waiver of privilege, both in principle and also as a matter of practical effect. More difficulty will be encountered in determining the effect on privilege of relying on more minor content. In *Bucknell v British Transport Commission*,[20] the production of an entire statement was ordered on the basis of the defendant's witness admitting in cross-examination that he had made a signed statement and said certain things in it. In agreement with the other members of the Court, Denning LJ said:

> it seems to me that the judge was correct, because although this statement may well have been privileged from production and discovery in the hands of the Transport Commission at one stage, nevertheless when it was used by cross-examining counsel in this way, he waived the privilege, certainly for that part which was used; and in a case of this kind, if the privilege is waived as to the part, it must, I think, be waived also as to the whole. It would be most unfair that cross-examining counsel should use part of the document which was to his advantage and not allow anyone, not even the judge or the opposing counsel, a sight of the rest of the document, much of which might have been against him.

'Cherry-Picking' Content—Nea Karteria

Background

113. The concern in *Bucknell* that unfairness should not result from allowing reliance only on parts of the content of a document that are to a party's advantage, were developed further in *Nea Karteria Maritime Co Ltd v Atlantic and Great Lakes Steamship Corporation*.[21] This case concerned a claim for losses against two defendants following an explosion on a coal-carrying vessel shipped by the second defendant (Devco). The explosion resulted from the ignition of gas emitted by the cargo and there was an issue as to whether this had been caused by the crew smoking. A seaman gave a statement for Devco that a match had been struck prior to the explosion. In turn, the boatswain gave a statement for the plaintiff that there had been no smoking. Some three years later the seaman who had given the statement gave answers to a Greek lawyer in response to a list of questions put by English solicitors for the plaintiffs. The answers were compiled into a document called 'P35' on which the seaman was cross-examined at trial because of inconsistencies with his earlier statement. In particular, attention focussed on a passage of P35 that referred to a part of the boatswain's statement.

[20] *Bucknell v British Transport Commission* [1956] 1 QB 187.

[21] *Nea Karteria Maritime Co Ltd v Atlantic and Great Lakes Steamship Corporation* (22 June 1981, CLR).

First Issue—Plucking Out of Context

114. Devco called on the boatswain's statement to be produced, but the plaintiffs refused, claiming it was privileged. Mustill J thought the application of *Bucknell* clear to this situation. He said that the principle underlying the rule of practice in that case was that where a party was deploying in court material that would otherwise be privileged, the opposite party and the court must have the opportunity of satisfying themselves that what the party has chosen to release from privilege represents all the material relevant to the issue. To allow a part to be plucked out of context would be to risk injustice through its true meaning and weight being misunderstood.

In this case, however, in reasoning that is not transparent, the plaintiff was held not to have made the boatswain's statement part of the evidence of the action. The seaman's latter statement merely assented to something the boatswain's statement said, it did not mean that the Court was being asked to actually take into account anything the boatswain had said. It was, instead, found that only the seaman's earlier statement had been put in evidence by pointing to inconsistencies with it.

Second Issue—Satisfaction that the Evidence is Accurate

115. A second question arose in *Nea Karteria* as to whether privilege had been waived in the list of questions which had been used by the Greek lawyer, in his interview with the seaman. In evidence, the seaman had claimed that he gave his answers in P35 'just to be rid of the lawyers'. The plaintiff called the Greek lawyer to explain the background to and nature of the interview and Devco responded by submitting that the list of questions that had formed the basis of that interview should be produced. Again, Mustill J reiterated that he could:

> see a rule of positive law being stated in the interests of justice, that where a party chooses to deploy evidence which would otherwise be privileged the court and the opposition must, in relation to the issue in question, be given the opportunity to satisfy themselves that they have the whole of the material and not merely a fragment.

On the facts of *Nea Karteria*, this meant asking in what circumstances the seaman had given an account of events which differed from the account he had given in his earlier statement. This required looking at whether he did give the answers recorded in P35, whether P35 was a complete record of what happened, and of what Mustill J referred to as 'the general atmosphere of the meeting', given the seaman's evidence that he signed the statement to be rid of the lawyers. It was the judge's view that the whole of the substance of the meeting was a 'legitimate subject for disclosure and for cross-examination'.

As regards the list of questions, Mustill J considered that these were part of the meeting and were in a sense an agenda for the meeting. As one-half of the exchange between the lawyer and the seaman, privilege must have been waived in them:

> the interests of justice, which I believe to underlie the authorities on this part of the case, demand that the opposition and the court should have an opportunity to satisfy itself as to the accuracy of the evidence given by the lawyer as to the way in which he conducted the interview.

Support for Nea Karteria

Rigg v Associated Newspapers[22]

116. There are cases at odds with *Nea Karteria*, for example, the first instance case of *Rigg v Associated Newspapers*, which concerned CPR 31.14. Gray J held in *Rigg* that a defence containing a lengthy quotation from the contents of an interview which a journalist had conducted with the claimant were not a 'direct allusion' (adopting Slade LJ's test[23]) to the notes themselves, such that the notes should not be disclosed. It is difficult to reconcile Slade LJ's view that reference to the content of a document is enough for RSC Ord 24 r 10, and Gray J's view that it is not enough to constitute a direct allusion for the purpose of CPR 31.14. It is perhaps important that the judge apparently was not referred to *Nea Karteria* in the *Rigg* case. Having discussed *Rigg* in *Expandable v Rubin*, Rix LJ commented only that 'As often in this area, some fine distinctions may arise.'

Great Atlantic Insurance

117. Although it is a first instance decision, support for the approach taken in *Nea Karteria* as a principle has nonetheless come at Court of Appeal level. *Great Atlantic Insurance Co v Home Insurance Co*[24] was an application brought mid-trial. It concerned a memorandum, of which the plaintiff's solicitors intended to give discovery of the first two paragraphs only. The plaintiffs' solicitors duly provided to the defendants, for use in the trial, copies of the memorandum limited to the first two paragraphs and excluded the additional matter, for which privilege was claimed. In the course of opening at trial, the plaintiffs' counsel read out the two disclosed paragraphs of the memorandum. Later on, the third defendant discovered that the memorandum as read to the judge was incomplete.

[22] *Rigg v Associated Newspapers* [2003] All ER (D) 97.
[23] See earlier section entitled 'Second Appeal'.
[24] *Great Atlantic Insurance Co v Home Insurance Co* [1981] 2 All ER 485.

The third defendant asked for disclosure of the additional matter on the basis that only part of the document had been put before the Court. The third defendant claimed to be entitled to see the whole document, regardless of whether it was originally privileged or not. The Court of Appeal held that the whole of the memorandum had been privileged and was not capable of being divided into two separate and distinct parts. Accordingly, privilege could not be waived in part and asserted as to the remainder. The introduction of the first two paragraphs into the trial record therefore waived privilege over the whole memorandum.

In making this decision, Templeman LJ reiterated the statement of Mustill J in *Nea Karteria*—cherry-picking should not be permitted as a matter of principle:

> I believe that the principle underlying the rule of practice exemplified by *Burnell v British Transport Commission* is that where a party is deploying in court material which would otherwise be privileged, the opposite party and the court must have an opportunity of satisfying themselves that what the party has chosen to release from privilege represents the whole of the material relevant to the issue in question. To allow an individual item to be plucked out of context would be to risk injustice through its real weight or meaning being misunderstood.[25]

Joe Bloggs Sports

118. The issue of cherry-picking was again revisited by the Court of Appeal in *Dunlop Slazenger International Ltd v Joe Bloggs Sports Ltd.*[26] This case concerned whether an option had been exercised or not. In particular, there was an issue as to whether a letter purported to exercise that option had been created on a computer on the date that the defendant claimed. The defendant instructed an expert to look at the hard drive of the computer on which the letter was thought to have been created, but no report was produced. However, in the course of proceedings, statements were produced by the defendant upon which the claimant argued there was a partial disclosure of privileged communications between the defendant and this expert. For example, two paragraphs from a statement of Miss Ahmed:

> On 18 February 2003 JBSL's forensic IT expert reported that it had carried out further investigations on the hard drive from Mr Tariq's computer, and that the 17 June 2002 letter may have been created on a different computer.
>
> JBSL also discovered that there were two versions of the 17 June letter: the difference between the two being the tenth word in line 1, and that Mr Tariq's computer contained, or had contained, two electronic files with similar names: DSIL 17-06-02 and SSIL 17-06-02. In addition, JBSL's forensic expert advised that the internal clock of Mr Tariq's may have been turned back.

[25] See also *George Doland Ltd v Blackburn, Robson Coates & Co* [1972] 1 WLR 1338.

[26] *Dunlop Slazenger International Ltd v Joe Bloggs Sports Ltd* [2003] EWCA Civ 901.

119. The question in *Joe Bloggs Sports* was whether the defendant had waived privilege in at least part of the communications between the defendant and its expert. If so, had they waived privilege by implication in the full communications? To answer this, the Court of Appeal looked again at Mustill J's statement in *Nea Karteria*: 'To allow an individual item to be plucked out of context would be to risk injustice through its real weight or meaning being misunderstood.'

Waller LJ approved the distinction between a reference to the effect of the document and reliance on the content, describing the latter as a 'deployment' case. In this case the paragraphs of Miss Ahmed were held to be clearly a deployment, because they were seeking to refer to the contents of the information that was being supplied by the expert in order to persuade the Court that the further evidence should be permitted, and for the purpose of this evidence being material for the Court to consider at trial. Echoing Mustill J in *Nea Karteria*, Waller LJ said:

> A party is not entitled to cherry pick, and a party to whom privileged information is provided is entitled to have the full contents of what has been supplied in order to see that cherry picking is not taking place.

120. What Waller LJ also made clear is that a party is not entitled to preserve its position and wait to see what actually happens at the trial in order to see if deployment then takes place and whether there is a waiver. If deployment takes place at an interlocutory stage, as happened in this case, and waiver of the privileged material has resulted, then the cherry-picking principle applies.[27]

121. The scope of the disclosure ordered in *Joe Bloggs Sports* was to the documents made in or about February 2003 that were material to what the defendant was informed of by its computer expert.

This raises an issue only implicitly dealt with in *Nea Karteria*—what is the scope of the waiver of privilege protection?

Scope of Waiver—Identifying the 'Transaction'

Principles

122. In *Fulham Leisure Holdings Ltd v Nicholson, Graham & Jones*,[28] a question arose as to the scope to which privilege is waived in material as a result of a partial disclosure. In this case, inter alia, the Particulars of Claim and the statements of three witnesses referred to advice given by leading counsel and solicitors. This advice was only part of legal advice given over a four-month period. Should privilege in all that advice be waived, or are there narrower

[27] See *Derby v Weldon* [1991] 1 WLR 660.

[28] *Fulham Leisure Holdings Ltd v Nicholson, Graham & Jones* [2006] PNLR 23.

criteria by which the waiver should be assessed? What are the boundaries of the waiver?

Disclosure was sought in *Fulham Leisure* on the basis that there had been only a partial disclosure or a partial selection of otherwise privileged information in respect of the advice given and therefore that it gave a misleading picture. In his decision, Mann J stated that the starting point was to identify the 'transaction' in question, following Hobhouse J in *General Accident Fire & Life Assurance Corp Ltd v Tanter.*[29] In *General Accident*, Hobhouse J looked, amongst other cases, behind the judgment in *Nea Karteria*:

> . . . by adducing evidence at a trial one does get involved in potential further waiver. The underlying principle is one of fairness in the conduct of the trial and does not go further than that. The fact that this principle does not arise unless you adduce the evidence at the trial is clearly stated in the judgment of Mustill J.[30] and it was clearly raised by the facts in the *Doland* case[31] and it was likewise raised by the facts in the *Great Atlantic*[32] and *Burnell* cases. Further, if the evidence is adduced, then the extent of the waiver relates to the transaction to which that evidence goes. The extent of the transaction has to be examined and where it is what somebody said on a particular occasion, then that is the transaction. It is not the subject matter of those conversations. It does not extend to all matters relating to the subject matter of those conversations.
>
> Furthermore, [Mustill J] applies what for convenience can be called a single transaction test. He looks to see what is the issue in relation to which the material has been deployed. He held that the issue was what was said at the meeting between the lawyer and the Greek seaman, and the correct evaluation of that meeting, but he did not accept that it extended to other matters which did not form part of the transaction . . . Furthermore, it is central to Mustill J's judgment that you must define what is the subject matter with which you are concerned. He did not treat the subject matter as all the things about which the seaman spoke, but he merely treated as the subject matter what had been said on that occasion.

As Auld LJ noted in *R v Secretary of State for Transport, ex p Factortame Ltd (Discovery)*,[33] the most obvious application of this principle is in relation to a single document, where a party waives privilege as to part of it but seeks to withhold the rest of it. However, it also applies to the attempted partial waiver of privilege in respect of one or more documents relating to the same issue or transaction.[34]

[29] *General Accident Fire & Life Assurance Corp Ltd v Tanter* [1984] 1 WLR 100 (reversed in part by the Court of Appeal).

[30] In *Nea Karteria* (n 21).

[31] *George Doland Ltd v Blackburn Robson Coates Co* [1972] 1 WLR 529.

[32] *Great Atlantic Insurance Co v Home Insurance Co* [1981] 1 WLR 529.

[33] See also Auld LJ in *R v Secretary of State for Transport, ex p Factortame Ltd (Discovery)* [1997] 9 Admin.

[34] See for example *Lyell v Kennedy* [1884] 27 ChD1 and *Paragon Finance v Freshfields* [1990] 1 WLR 1183.

The 'Transaction'—Mann J's Four Step Test

Mann J in *Fulham Leisure* thus identified two concepts that should be borne in mind. First, the transaction or act in respect of which disclosure is made. Then, once disclosure is properly made of that transaction, the application of additional principles of fairness may come into play if it is apparent from the disclosure that has been made that it is part of some larger picture (which is not necessarily part of some bigger 'transaction'). Although it was not entirely clear to Mann J how the second concept should relate to the first.

In fact, Mann J in *Fulham Leisure* actually breaks down the process that must be undertaken when addressing the scope of waiver to four steps, based on the above authorities:

> i) One should first identify the 'transaction' in respect of which the disclosure has been made.
> ii) That transaction may be identifiable simply from the nature of the disclosure made—for example, advice given by counsel on a single occasion.
> iii) However, it may be apparent from that material, or from other available material, that the transaction is wider than that which is immediately apparent. If it does, then the whole of the wider transaction must be disclosed.
> iv) When that has been done, further disclosure will be necessary if that is necessary in order to avoid unfairness or misunderstanding of what has been disclosed.

Chapter Summary

123. The underlying problem addressed in this chapter is what the privilege status of documents referred to is in an expert report but not related to the expert instructions. It is apparent from CPR 35.10(4) and Rix LJ in *Expandable v Rubin* that they are to be treated in the same manner as documents referred to in the CPR 31.14 list. What is not clear is where the distinction lies between a document related to instructions and a document referred to 'wholly generally', to use Rix LJ's words. This is a particular problem given the broad definition of instructions discussed in chapter 4. The case law on the treatment of documents under CPR 31.14 scarcely sheds light on this issue, but it is submitted that examples of documents referred to 'wholly generally' would nonetheless likely include references of the kind discussed above. That is, documents, the content or effect of which, is referred to as a *substitute* for the offering of a direct opinion by the expert writing the report, rather than the object of it.

124. In cases of documents referred to wholly generally in an expert report, the first stage in determining whether a document is liable to production as a whole is to establish whether it is mentioned. The discussions and examples given in *Dubai Bank* and *Expandable v Rubin* illustrate that this is a subtle

exercise where the difference between a direct allusion or specific mention of a document and the inference of a document's existence is not abundantly clear. It matters, because in the latter case CPR 31.14 is not triggered.

125. If CPR 31.14 is triggered, *Expandable v Rubin* sets out six specific reasons why *Buttes Gas* is still good law—mention does not necessarily result in a document losing privilege and a prima facie right to inspection. A mere *reference* to the document will not be enough to waive privilege. Furthermore, reference to the *effect* of a document is also insufficient to waive privilege protection in it.

126. Instead, reliance on the *content* of a document is necessary before privilege in it can be waived. In determining how much content must be relied upon, a line must be drawn on the spectrum between a full quotation of a document's contents and a mere reference to it. However, cases such as *Rigg* illustrate that determining where this dividing line lies is difficult and liable to depend greatly on the facts.

127. A strand of guidance does come in the form of the 'cherry-picking' principle in the *Bucknell, Nea Karteria* and *Joe Bloggs* International cases. These cases state that on grounds of fairness and avoiding the risk of injustice, a party should not be allowed to rely on the part of a privileged document that is advantageous to them and deny access to the rest of the document on the basis of that same privilege. Reference to the principles of fairness and justice makes the extent to which waiver is automatic, if a document is relied upon in part, unclear. So far as a judge will use their discretion on whether privilege is to be waived in a document, *Nea Karteria* suggests that in circumstances where there may have been untoward behaviour, for example the need to establish 'the general atmosphere of the meeting', a judge will be quicker to waive privilege.

128. Privilege may not be waived if the content relied on in the privileged document is divisible from the other content of that document, such that it does not form part of the same issue or 'transaction'. In addition, the court may take matters of fairness into play when deciding on further waiver beyond this transaction.

An interesting question that arises when considering documents referred to 'wholly generally' is the comparison with documents referred to in instructions. A comparison of this chapter with chapter 4 will show that the circumstances in which these documents are liable to be produced for inspection differ. The difference in characterisation is therefore important. Difficulties may arise if documents provided as part of the instructions trigger those rules applying to documents wholly generally. Do the general rules in this chapter apply in such cases? The intention of CPR 35.10(4) seems to be to provide a free-standing regime for such documents and so the application of the general rules appears doubtful. But this is by no means clear.

6

Pre-Existing Documents

Introduction

129. Chapters 4 and 5 have addressed, respectively, the status of instructions supplied to an expert and privileged documents that are referred to by the expert generally.

There is a third category of documents to consider—documents pre-existing litigation, such as scientific papers, theses, reports and other technical papers, from the client or third parties. These may be presented to an expert for reading (but ultimately unreferenced in the expert report) or simply used by a solicitor to give advice to the client. Even in circumstances where the original document was not privileged, can it just be assumed that it will remain unprivileged?

The cases discussed below deal with issues of general evidential application, but they will be particularly relevant to the collection of documentary evidence in order to prepare expert reports.

The Status of Original Documents

130. The law regarding privilege in pre-existing, original documents obtained from a third party source would appear to be well-established. It is summarised in the statement of Sir Baliol Brett MR in *Pearce v Foster*[1] in which a former clerk, who had been dismissed for improperly speculating on the Stock Exchange, sued his former employers for wrongful dismissal:

> I do not think that, where documents are already in existence *aliunde*, the mere fact of their being handed to a solicitor for the purpose of the conduct of the action can create a privilege; but, where documents are brought into existence by a solicitor or through a solicitor for the purposes of consultation with such a solicitor, with a view to his giving professional advice or to the conduct of an action, these are in the nature of professional communications, and are as such privileged.[2]

[1] *Pearce v Foster* (1885) 15 QBD 114.

[2] Although it is unclear from the discussion in *Venturis v Mountain* 1991] 1 WLR 607 what the status of the first half of this statement is as precedent.

It was not until *Ventouris v Mountain*[3] that the Court of Appeal had to squarely consider whether privilege attached to original documents which had not previously been in the possession, custody or power of a party to actual or contemplated litigation, and had not come into existence for the purpose of that litigation, but which had subsequently been obtained by the solicitors of a party for the purpose of that litigation. In *Venturis*, Bingham LJ was referred to a number of Commonwealth authorities that supported the statement in *Pearce v Foster*, in particular the underlying distinction between:

> . . . the purpose for which information is obtained and the purpose for which a document recording information is brought into existence. It is the latter with which the law of professional privilege is concerned.[4]

Likewise, the purpose for which a document was 'created' or 'comes into existence' was the focus of attention in *Baker v Campbell*:[5]

> The privilege cannot operate to put beyond the reach of the law documentary or other material which has an existence apart from the process of giving or receiving advice or the conduct of litigation: see *Grant v Downs* (1976) 135 CLR 674.

Bingham LJ accepted in *Ventouris* that although there are difficulties of consistency in respect of the cases on copies (see the next section), the question to be asked of originals obtained by legal advisers was always that posed by Jacob J in the High Court of Australia in *Grant v Downs*:[6]

> does the purpose [i.e., the intended use] of supplying the material to the legal adviser account for the existence of the material?

If yes, the material is privileged; if no, not.

131. Bingham LJ could see no reason why a pre-existing document obtained by a solicitor for the purposes of litigation should be privileged from production and inspection.[7],[8]

[3] *Ventouris v Mountain* [1991] 1 WLR 607.

[4] *National Employers' Mutual General Insurance Association Ltd v Waind* (1979) 141 CLR 648 (Mason J).

[5] *Baker v Campbell* (1983) 153 CLR 32.

[6] *Grant v Downs* (1977) 135 CLR 674 (but note that this case was overruled by the High Court in Australia in *Esso Australia Resources Ltd v Commissioner of Taxation* 2 ITL Rep 429).

[7] Except perhaps, he acknowledges in the *Lyell v Kennedy (No 3)* (1884) 27 Ch D situation (see the next section).

[8] The other judges of the Court of Appeal agreed with Bingham LJ. The principle has since been applied in *Sumitomo Corporation v Credit Lyonnais Rouse Ltd* [2002] 1 WLR 479.

The Status of Copies

An Old View—The Palermo

132. The background to this area of the law provides some apparently conflicting decisions. Take the case of *The Palermo.*[9] In this case a British ship, the Rivoli, collided with another ship called the Palermo. The master and crew of the Rivoli gave depositions to the 'Receiver of the Wreck', on behalf of a panel called the Board of Trade. Copies of these documents were obtained by solicitors acting for the owners of the Rivoli for the purposes of a separate action between them and the owners of the Palermo. However, the Board of Trade refused to supply copies to the owners of the Palermo. The depositions had not been taken for the purposes of the action between the owners, and so were privileged in the hands of the Rivoli's owners. However, what about the *copies* supplied to the Rivoli's owners, were they privileged?

The Court of Appeal upheld the decision of Butt J at first instance that the copies were privileged. The reasoning for this is not recorded in detail, except that it was said that the copies of the depositions were created for the purpose of the action between the owners of the Palermo and the Rivoli, even if the original depositions were not.

A Different View—Ventouris v Mountain

133. In *Ventouris,* the Court of Appeal cited a number of old authorities, including *The Palermo.*[10] The Court thought questionable the decision in *The Palermo* that copies should be entitled to privilege in circumstances where the original depositions were not entitled to privilege in the hands of the Board of Trade.[11] This view was obiter, because the focus of *Ventouris* was on the status of originals. Nevertheless, as well as doubting the *The Palermo* on the issue, the Court also commented on a further case in which non-privileged third party documents were copied for the purposes of litigation, *Chadwick v Bowman.*[12] In this case copies were held not to be privileged and Bingham LJ comments that this decision does suggest a general rule that non-privileged documents do not, without more, acquire privilege simply because they are copied by a solicitor for the purposes of an action.

[9] *The Palermo* (1884) LR 9 PD 6.

[10] *Anderson v Bank of British Columbia* (1876) 2 Ch D 644; Southwark and *Vauxhall Water Co v Quick* (1878) 3 QBD 315; *Wheeler v Le Marchant* (1881) 17 Ch D 675.

[11] See *Buttes Gas and Oil Co v Hammer (No 3)* [1981] QB 223; and Law Reform Committee, 'Sixteenth Report on Privilege in Civil Proceedings' (1967) (Cmnd 3472).

[12] *Chadwick v Bowman* (1886) 16 QBD 561.

134. In *Ventouris*, the Court of Appeal also looked unfavourably on their earlier decision in *Watson v Cammell Laird & Co (Shipbuilders and Engineers) Ltd*[13] which had distinguished *Chadwick* and instead considered itself bound by *The Palermo*. Bingham LJ felt this authority 'ripe for authoritative reconsideration'.[14]

Copies Reconsidered—Sumitomo Corporation

135. *Sumitomo Corporation v Credit Lyonnais Rouse Ltd*[15] is primarily concerned with the status of translations, which are dealt with in the next section. However, it begins by considering the law of privilege in respect of copies. In *Sumitomo Corporation* an application was made for the inspection of some 700 English translations of Japanese originals. The Japanese originals were in the control of Sumitomo and unprivileged and the translations having been made to assist Sumitomo's US lawyers and, in small part (about 20 documents), their English Lawyers. Andrew Smith J summarised the position under the authorities:

> Legal professional privilege attaches to documents which come into existence for the purposes of obtaining confidential legal advice. In the field of litigation, confidential communications between a party to litigation or his legal adviser and third parties are also protected from inspection. It makes no difference, as [the English solicitors] accept, that here, as far as most of the documents are concerned, the legal advisers are US attorneys and not English lawyers. However, privilege does not extend to documents obtained by a party or his adviser for the purpose of litigation if the document did not come into existence for that purpose: [*Ventouris v Mountain*].
>
> Where a document comes into existence for the purpose of obtaining or giving legal advice or for the purpose of litigation, the position is this. If the original document is not and has not been in the control of the party to the litigation, the copy which he has obtained is privileged; it is taken to 'form part of the brief'[16] . . . However, if the original document is in his control, he cannot, subject to an important qualification to which I shall refer and upon which Sumitomo rely, claim privilege in the copy[17]. . .The same is true if the original document has been, but is no longer, in the party's control . . .[18] As it was put by Lord Evershed in *Watson* [*v Cammell Laird*] 'these copies, the mere replacements of something which he would have had to produce himself, must be produced'.

13 *Watson v Cammell Laird & Co (Shipbuilders and Engineers) Ltd* [1959] 1 WLR 702.

14 *cf Robert Hitchins Ltd v International Computers Ltd* [1997] CLY 467 in which *Ventouris* was distinguished on its facts.

15 *Sumitomo Corporation v Credit Lyonnais Rouse Ltd* [2001] CP Rep 72, upheld by the Court of Appeal in [2001] 1 WLR 479, although no specific consideration is given to this statement by that Court.

16 Citing *The Palermo* (n 9) and *Watson v Cammell Laird & Co* (n 13).

17 Citing *Dubai Bank Ltd v Galadari* [1990] Ch 98, in which it was held that photocopies were generally discoverable, although there would usually be no point in ordering their separate disclosure.

18 Citing *Land Corporation of Canada v Puleston* [1884] WN 1 and *Chadwick* (n 12).

136. In summary, *Sumitomo* at first instance holds that a copy of an original document, which is not itself privileged, is privileged only if (a) the copy came into existence for the purpose of litigation, and (b) the original document is not and has not at any time been in the control of the party claiming privilege. This statement, so formulated, was held to be uncontroversial on appeal in *Sumitomo*.

Translations

137. In *Sumitomo*, the next issue for the Court to consider was whether the translations of which Credit Lyonnais sought production were to be treated as copies? Sumitomo argued that the decision in *Ventouris*[19] as regards copies applied only to photocopies, because photocopies of a document are virtually indistinguishable from the original document. It should not, Sumitomo argued, be applied to translations. Andrew Smith J disagreed. He considered that the principles drawn together in *Ventouris* dealt with manuscript copies of documents and he could not believe that in the nineteenth century a short-hand copy of a document would be treated any differently to a long-hand original. Equally, he thought, a copy of a computer disk in a different computer language from the original would today surely be treated as a copy

The 'real question', as the judge put it, was whether the translation imports any 'relevant extrinsic element' into the document. By this he meant:

> something which, as a matter of principle and policy, should import privilege because it is of a confidential nature.

He went on to explain that this is because the justification for legal professional privilege is the requirement that the client:

> should be able to place unrestricted and unbounded confidence in the professional agent, and that the communications he so makes to him should be kept secret, unless with his consent, . . . that he should be enabled properly to conduct his litigation. . .[20]

In addition:

> It is the protection of confidential communications between client and legal adviser which lies at the heart of legal professional privilege.[21]

In *Sumitomo*, there was no relevant extrinsic element imported into the translations and they were held to be copies that, being in the control of Sumitomo, could not be privileged.

[19] See also *Dubai Bank* (n 17).
[20] *Anderson v Bank of British Columbia* (n 10).
[21] *Ventouris* (n 3) 475 (Bingham LJ).

Selections—the Rule in Lyell v Kennedy

138. The 'important qualification' to the general copies rule referred to by Andrew Smith J in *Sumitomo* is found in *Lyell v Kennedy (No 3)*.[22] This case concerned an entitlement claim to land through a purchase from the heir-at-law to an intestate. The case raised issues of the intestate's pedigree and the heirship to her estate. In the course of preparing the case, the defendant's solicitors obtained copies of and extracts from entries in public registers, together with photographs of tombstones and houses. The defendant objected to the production of these documents on the ground that they had come into existence for the purpose of litigation and also seemingly because his solicitor, counsel and clerks had gone to considerable efforts to obtain the documents for the purpose of his defence. The Court of Appeal was unanimous in finding that the documents should be protected, as summarised in *Ventouris* by Bingham LJ:

> The ratio of the decision [in *Lyell v Kennedy*] is, I think, that where the selection of documents which a solicitor has copied or assembled betrays the trend of the advice which he is giving the client the documents are privileged.

However, whilst approving the above statement, the Court of Appeal in *Sumitomo*, considering whether the 700 translations betrayed a trend of advice, explained that *Lyell* was not authority for the proposition that a selection made from own client documents may attract privilege.[23] The Court considered it a gloss on *Lyell* that the principle that a lawyer's advice is privileged from discovery should not result in the right of a party to refuse discovery of documentary evidence that was in the possession of that party before the selection was made, or copies or translations of such evidence. Also, the underlining or highlighting of documents does not, in itself, give rise to privilege protection.[24]

A Note on Production

139. If documents are not privileged, must they necessarily be produced for inspection? The answer seems to be that production may be resisted at the court's discretion, as Bingham LJ noted in *Ventouris*:[25]

[22] *Lyell v Kennedy (No 3)* (1884) 27 Ch D 1.
[23] Holding *Dubai Bank* (n 17) to be wrong on this point.
[24] *Vivian Imerman v Robert Tchenguiz* [2009] EWHC 2902 (QB).
[25] *Ventouris* (n 3) 622.

> [Counsel for the Defendant's] argument appeared to assume that there was no choice between a finding of legal professional privilege and an order for immediate disclosure and inspection. In my judgment, that is not so. The process of discovery is not an uncontrollable juggernaut . . . the House of Lords[26] . . . and the Court of Appeal[27] made plain that production and inspection are not automatic once relevance and the absence of entitlement to privilege are established. While the court's ultimate concern must always be to ensure the fair disposal of the cause or matter, it need not be unmindful of other legitimate concerns nor is it powerless to control the terms upon which production and inspection may be ordered. I would not wish it thought that because, as I conclude, production and inspection may be ordered therefore they must at once be ordered unconditionally.

Chapter Summary

140. *Ventouris*, as later considered by *Sumitomo,* holds that privilege does not attach to a document obtained by a party or the party's adviser for the purpose of litigation if the document did not come into existence for that purpose.

141. The situation in respect of copies is less straightforward. There is a distinction in status between copies of documents in the control of a party, or at one time in their control, and copies of documents that have never been in their control. A copy of any original which would have to be produced, because it is in the control of a party and not privileged, must itself be produced. This is an intuitive and sensible result. Furthermore, it is trite that a document which is not privileged and not in a party's control cannot be produced.[28] Yet, this is a matter of production for inspection. It is more difficult to understand why such a document, which is not privileged, can take on the nature of a privileged document just because it is copied and the copy is provided to a party, where the original remains outside the control of that party. It is easy to understand how such a document may attract confidentiality, but this does not imply privilege. In practice, there may be limited applications for this rule. An example where this privilege may attach is where a third party academic is asked to supply a copy of an unpublished article for the purpose of an action and duly does so. However, would it make a difference if the academic posted his draft article to the solicitors for them to copy? The answer to this seems to hinge on whether it has come under their control. In any case, it seems a somewhat artificial basis on which to determine whether a document is privileged or not. Translations are more straightforward.

26 *Science Research Council v Nassé* [1980] AC 1028.
27 *Dolling-Baker v Merrett* [1990] 1 WLR 1205.
28 There is a category reserved for such documents on the disclosure list.

These are to be treated the same as copies, provided there is no relevant extrinsic element imported into the translation.

142. Where a selection of original documents which a solicitor has copied or assembled betrays the trend of the advice which he is giving the client, the documents are privileged. This is unless that documentary evidence was in the possession of that party before the selection was made.

7

Joint Experts, Statements and Discussions

Introduction

143. Chapters 4 to 6 discuss situations in which each party to litigation instructs its own, unilateral, expert. However, unilateral experts will not always be appropriate. The court has the power in appropriate cases to direct that evidence is to be given by a single joint expert. Alternatively, both parties may agree to instruct a single joint expert. Furthermore, the instruction by each party of its own, unilateral expert on every, or any, issue is not to be assumed as the normal approach. The courts' attitude to this issue was summarised by Lord Woolf, the Lord Chief Justice (as he then was):[1]

> The starting point is: unless there is reason for not having a single expert, there should be only a single expert. If there is no reason which justifies more evidence than that from a single expert on any particular topic, then again in the normal way the report prepared by the single expert should be the evidence in the case on the issues covered by that expert's report.

Ten years on from the Woolf Report, Jackson LJ notes in his Review of Civil Litigation Costs: Final Report[2] that in the small claims track or the fast track there is a presumption that there will only be one expert witness (who may, or may not, be a single joint expert) on any particular issue. In relation to multi-track cases, however, section 7 of Civil Procedure Rules (CPR) Practice Direction (PD) 35 now gives guidance on the factors which the court should take into account when deciding whether to order that a single joint expert should be used.[3]

What is the privilege status of the dealings of the parties with the joint expert?

144. The court can also require that discussions take place between experts and that the conclusions of these meetings be recorded in a joint written statement, explaining with reasons the points of difference and agreed opinion between the experts. What is the privilege status of these discussions

[1] *MP v Mid-Kent Healthcare NHS Trust* [2002] 1 WLR 210.
[2] Jackson LJ, 'Review of Civil Litigation Costs: Final Report' (The Stationery Office, 2010).
[3] CPR PD 35, 383.

and the joint statement? This chapter looks at these and related issues arising from the use of joint experts and expert discussions.

Instructions to Single Joint Experts

The Applicable Rules and their Effect

Appointment of a Single Joint Expert—CPR 35.7

145. The court's power to direct that a single joint expert be appointed is provided in CPR 35.7. This states:

> (1) Where two or more parties wish to submit expert evidence on a particular issue, the court may direct that the evidence on that issue is to be given by a single joint expert.
> (2) Where the parties who wish to submit the evidence ('the relevant parties') cannot agree who should be the single joint expert, the court may –
>
> > (a) select the expert from a list prepared or identified by the relevant parties; or
> >
> > (b) direct that the expert be selected in such other manner as the court may direct.

Right of Parties to Instruct—CPR 35.8

146. Chapter 4 discusses the privilege status of instructions to a unilateral expert. However, CPR 35.7 concerns the appointment of an expert to give evidence on issues that more than one party would otherwise instruct experts of their own. How then do the rules explored in chapter 4 apply to joint expert reports appointed under CPR 35.7? How is the joint expert to be instructed at all? The starting point is to look at CPR 35.8(1) and (2):

> (1) Where the court gives a direction under rule 35.7 for a single joint expert to be used, any relevant party may give instructions to the expert.
> (2) When a party gives instructions to the expert that party must, at the same time, send a copy to the other relevant parties.
> ...

147. CPR 35.8(1) provides that even though the parties may be directed to use a single joint expert, each of the parties is entitled to send instructions to that expert. This apparently obvious observation nonetheless required stating by the Court of Appeal in *Neil Edward Yorke v Antoine Katra*.[4] This case

[4] *Neil Edward Yorke v Antoine Katra* [2003] EWCA Civ 867.

concerns a claim in respect of building work, in which it was stated that one party is not bound by the instructions formulated by the other side, but may put forward its own instructions to the expert.

Difference from Unilateral Instructions

148. The difference between the instructions supplied to a single joint expert and those given to a unilaterally appointed expert is apparent in CPR 35.8(2). This rule makes it clear that any instructions provided to the joint expert are, at the same time, to be provided to the other parties. It must follow as an obvious consequence of disclosing these instructions between the parties that there cannot be the same privilege protection afforded to these instructions as are discussed in chapter 4 for unilaterally instructed experts. Privilege must be waived between the parties upon service of those instructions to the other parties.[5]

Exchange of Information—CPR 35.9

149. CPR 35.9 is a potentially very significant rule and it is therefore surprising how little guidance there is on its application. It is not expressed to be restricted in application to single joint experts. However, it is included at this point in the discussion because it has much in common, in terms of effect on privilege, with CPR 35.8, which immediately precedes it. CPR 35.9 states:

> Where a party has access to information which is not reasonably available to another party, the court may direct the party who has access to the information to –
>
> (a) prepare and file a document recording the information; and
> (b) serve a copy of that document on the other party.

CPR 35.9 does not clarify the nature of information not reasonably available to the other party that it has in mind. However, it may be important that the rule stops short of mentioning 'expert reports' in favour of 'information'. At one extreme, an order under this rule could amount to an exercise in the disclosure of any document (see chapter summary and discussion). However, a less onerous possibility is that the rule is intended merely to apply to exchanges of information with the single expert. Support for this view comes from the Protocol for the Instruction of Experts to give Evidence

[5] Technically, it may be said that the instructions are in their nature privileged and remain so and hence it is perhaps more accurate to talk in terms of losing the right to withhold production of the instructions on the basis of privilege, rather than the privilege itself. The practical result is the same—the documents must be produced. As regards the rest of the world, it is submitted that such instructions would form part of the expert evidence to which the rules of collateral use discussed in chapter 12 apply. It seems doubtful that such instructions fall within the compulsion rule. Documents supplied to the expert as part of the instructions may be treated differently, for which again see chapter 12.

in Civil Claims. To some extent, this mirrors the obligation in CPR 35.9 by requiring the expert to keep the parties informed of the steps they are taking, including disclosing all their correspondence to the instructing parties, per para 17.10:

> Single joint experts should keep all instructing parties informed of any material steps that they may be taking by, for example, copying all correspondence to those instructing them.

150. Although it does not say so expressly in the rules, Lord Woolf comments in *MP v Mid-Kent Healthcare NHS Trust*[6] that it was anticipated in framing the CPR that written instructions would be given to the single expert. In doing so, he refers to CPR 35.9 but it is not clear whether he actually may also have had CPR 35.8 in mind when saying this. In any case, such information must be served on the other party and again this would appear to be inconsistent with any possibility that the information can benefit from the protection of privilege.

The Role of CPR 35.10(3)

151. There is nothing in the CPR to suggest that the provisions of CPR 35.10 (discussed in chapter 4) should be restricted in their application to experts instructed unilaterally. However, the role of CPR 35.10 is nonetheless somewhat unclear in the context of single joint experts. For example, whilst it appears to remain an obligation that a statement of instructions should be set out in a joint expert's report pursuant to CPR 35.10(3), it is not actually necessary to do so, in practical terms, in order to guarantee transparency of instructions given to the expert as it is for unilaterally instructed experts. This effect should already have been achieved by CPR 35.8 and/or 35.9. However, the obligation in the rule no doubt remains that of assisting the court.

The Role of CPR 35.10(4)

152. The application of CPR 35.10(4) to joint experts is more opaque. So far as CPR 35.10(4) states that the instructions referred to in CPR 35.10(3) are not privileged, it would appear to do no more than achieve the effect of CPR 35.8 and/or 35.9. In this respect it may again be otiose. Furthermore, subparagraph (a) of 35.10(4) is considerably narrower in scope than 35.8 and 35.9. It merely requires disclosure of a specific document in circumstances where the statement of instructions is inaccurate or incomplete. The rules for single joint experts, as we have seen, provide for the blanket exchange of information in 35.8(2) and if necessary, 35.9(b). Nonetheless, the power

[6] *MP v Mid-Kent Healthcare NHS Trust* (n 1).

of the court to order the disclosure of a specific document may remain a useful second string to the bow of an applicant who suspects another party of withholding information, such that the copy of the instructions given to the single joint expert that is provided by that other party is inaccurate or incomplete.

Similarly, the application of CPR 35.10(4)(b) can still be envisaged in circumstances where the court is satisfied that there are reasonable grounds to consider the statement of instructions inaccurate or incomplete. Although, again, it might be expected that the need for questioning of the expert on his or her instructions from the other party would be limited in the context of a joint expert, because of 35.8(2), and 35.9(b) where ordered. Nonetheless, this may be a particularly useful resort, given a general judicial reluctance for unnecessary cross-examination of single joint experts:

> . . . there should be no need for that report to be amplified or tested by cross-examination. If it needs amplification, or if it should be subject to cross-examination, the court has discretion to allow that to happen. The court may permit that to happen either prior to the hearing or at the hearing. But the assumption should be that the single joint expert's report is the evidence. Any amplification or any cross-examination should be restricted as far as possible.[7]

Access to Joint Experts

Expert Conferences

153. *Mid-Kent Healthcare* concerned a claim for medical negligence following the birth of twins, one of whom was born suffering from four limb cerebral palsy of a type that limited the child's mobility. After settlement of liability, Master Turner ordered that there should be jointly instructed non-medical expert evidence dealing with quantum, limited to seven witnesses: an educational psychologist, an employment consultant, a nursing specialist, an occupational therapist, a physiotherapist, an architect and a speech therapist. This was ordered by consent.

The issue that arose was that the claimant's father, acting as a litigation friend, wanted a conference with the experts to take place without any representative of the defendant being present so that he, with his wife, could discuss the joint experts' evidence. In his words, their wish was to:

> express ourselves freely, without fear that any of our comments might be used or taken up by the other side. . . it is vital that [the experts] are allowed to give advice to us and our representatives without the presence of the defendant's legal representatives.

[7] *Mid-Kent Healthcare NHS Trust* (Lord Woolf) (n 1); see also *Popek v National Westminster Bank Plc* [2002] EWCA Civ 42.

In other words, the claimant was effectively seeking privileged discussions with and advice from the joint experts.

154. The Court of Appeal would not allow a one-sided conference to take place. As Lord Woolf commented:

> . . . the idea of having an experts' conference including lawyers without there being a representative of the defendant present, as was suggested by the claimant's solicitors, in my judgment is inconsistent with the whole concept of the single expert. The framework to which I have made reference is designed to ensure an open process so that both sides know exactly what information is placed before the single expert. It would be totally inconsistent with the whole of that structure to allow one party to conduct a conference where the evidence of the experts is in effect tested in the course of discussions which take place with that expert.[8]

155. Simon Brown LJ took a similarly strong line on the issue, emphasising the bar on hiding instructions, or the advice received:

> When, if at all, should one party, without the consent of the other party, be permitted to have sole access to a single joint expert, ie an expert instructed and retained by both parties? In common with my Lord, I believe that the answer to this question must be an unequivocal 'Never'
>
> . . .
>
> The good sense of this is surely plain. There can be no point in a unilateral meeting or conference unless what transpires between the party enjoying sole access and the expert is, at least in part, intended to be hidden from the expert's other client. What is to be hidden will necessarily be either the information which the party enjoying access is giving the expert, ie part of expert's instructions, or the expert's view expressed in the light of that information, or more likely both.
>
> The hiding of such material seems to me necessarily inconsistent with the very concept of a jointly instructed expert, owing, as much as an expert does, an equal duty of openness and confidence to both parties, besides his overriding duty to the court. That, in short, is the fundamental objection in principle to what the appellant seeks to achieve by this appeal. I too would dismiss it.

156. The Court of Appeal also pointed to paragraph 17.12[9] of the Protocol for the Instruction of Experts to give Evidence in Civil Claims for directing that both parties must attend a joint expert conference:

> 'Single joint experts should not attend any meeting or conference which is not a joint one, unless all the parties have agreed in writing . . .' It seems to me that this admirably summarises the position whether it is the claimants or the defendants who wish to have a conference of that nature.

[8] An earlier example of the same approach being taken in the inferior courts can be seen in *John Sutton Smith v Reginald David Stephens* [2001] QBD Birmingham 26 1 2001 CILL 1802 where the judge held that it was clear that CPR 35.9 went behind legal professional privilege in relation to expert witnesses. It was inconsistent with the appointment of a joint expert for one side to secretly try to test the strength of the evidence.

[9] Formerly, and at the date of judgment, para 19.9.

Single Expert Interviewing One Party

157. On the other hand, Lord Woolf in *Mid-Kent Healthcare* was anxious to make it clear that there is no nothing improper about a single expert interviewing a party for the purpose of obtaining information necessary to write his or her report:

> One of the experts whose expertise is nursing has interviewed the parents of the claimant for the purposes of the preparation of her report. There can be no objection to that. A single expert is perfectly entitled to interview the parents for the purposes of preparing a satisfactory report. There was no suggestion, as I understand it, for the defendant to be represented when instructions of that sort were being taken by the expert, and I would not expect the defendant to raise any objection to what happened in this case . ... I emphasise . . . does not prevent one expert from communicating with another expert in order to obtain any information which that expert requires to include in his or her report.

Although it should be assumed that any information moving between the expert and one party is subject to CPR 35.8 and 35.9, the Court in *Mid-Kent Healthcare* was clearly concerned that these rules should not be subverted by inappropriate discussions between the expert and one party. However, making a distinction, as Lord Woolf does, between a party having sole access to an expert (not permissible) and allowing an expert to interview one party alone (permissible) is not easy to do. The difference may be that, in the latter case, the process is not only one in which the information flows from the party to the expert, it is one in which the expert controls what that information relates to.

Use of a Unilateral Expert by another Party

158. Risks to privileged expert evidence will arise in situations where experts who are initially instructed to give evidence by one party, later find they are in the position of giving evidence for another party, or they become jointly instructed.

Unilateral Experts Used by another Party

159. *Harmony Shipping Co v Saudi Europe Line Ltd*[10] was a shipping case that featured a dispute as to the authenticity of a letter put forward as evidence of a genuine charterparty. The defendants maintained that the letter was not authentic. To answer this issue the plaintiffs instructed an expert in

[10] *Harmony Shipping Co v Saudi Europe Line Ltd* [1979] 1 WLR 1380.

handwriting, Mr Davis. Mr Davis met with the plaintiff's solicitor and viewed copies of the letter in issue. He also expressed his view as to the authenticity of one or other of the copies. Although Mr Davis commonly worked on about 200 cases at any given time, his conflict checks revealed that he was not instructed by the defendants and he gave his undertaking that he would not accept instructions from them. However, Mr Davis's assessment of the letter copies was such that the plaintiff's solicitors said they would not want his assistance any further.

Some weeks later, Mr Davis was instructed by another firm of solicitors who wanted him to look at some letters. He gave his view on them, which it can be inferred was that they were not genuine. Shortly afterwards, Mr Davis realised that these were the same letters as those he had viewed for the plaintiff. He declined to act and was consequently subpoenaed by the defendants.

The question for the Court of Appeal was whether the well-established rule that there is no property in a witness could be applied to an expert, given that the expert may have been told the substance of a party's case, been given confidential information on it and given advice to that party. The Court's answer was that an expert witness falls into the same position as a witness of fact. The Court is entitled to have the actual facts which the expert has observed adduced before it and to have the expert's individual opinion on those facts, in order to ascertain the truth.

However, this situation immediately raises a concern about what happens to privileged communications between the party who initially instructed the expert and the expert. Are these to be disclosed to the party which has subpoenaed the expert? Mindful of these concerns, the Court in *Harmony Shipping* stipulated that there is an important qualification to the above, based on the court's concern to protect privilege, as Lord Denning MR commented:

> Many of the communications between the solicitor and the expert witness will be privileged. They are protected by legal professional privilege. They cannot be communicated to the court except with the consent of the party concerned. That means that a great deal of the communications between the expert witness and the lawyer cannot be given in evidence to the court. If questions were asked about it, then it would be the duty of the judge to protect the witness (and he would) by disallowing any questions which infringed the rule about legal professional privilege or the rule protecting information given in confidence—unless, of course, it was one of those rare cases which come before the courts from time to time where in spite of privilege or confidence the court does order a witness to give further evidence.

160. Thus, the expert could be subpoenaed to answer questions, but a judge should be quick to prevent the expert from being led into privileged matters. This is quite a considerable qualification to the finding that there is no property in an expert witness. In effect, it seems to imply, another party may

subpoena an unwanted expert, but they will have to start their discussions with that expert afresh. They may not rely on material that the expert has produced for their former instructing party.

Unilateral Expert Becoming a Joint Expert

161. Whilst of limited authority, a case in the County Court, *Sage v Feiven*,[11] indicates the cautious approach that may be taken to the protection of privileged expert material in circumstances where an expert who was originally instructed on a unilateral basis is later sought as a joint expert.

Sage had initially agreed to the appointment of an expert orthopaedic surgeon from a list provided by a third party insurer. The expert was instructed, but Sage did not agree with the content of the report, advised the insurer that it would not be disclosed and sought the instruction of another expert. However, accepting Feiven's argument, a district judge considered that it would be cheaper for Feiven to instruct the same expert who had already been seen (and disavowed) by Sage as a joint expert between the parties. Sage appealed on the basis that this would be tantamount to disclosing the report the expert had prepared for Sage and thus undermine privilege in it.

On appeal, Judge Thompson ordered that the parties should instruct a new joint expert. He held that Sage could claim privilege in a report that had not been obtained as a joint expert report. Hence, to allow the author of that report to be subject to questioning put him in an invidious position, as the answer to those questions might require the disclosure of privileged information.

162. This is a decision of the County Court, but it illustrates how decisions made every day at that level may not always appear consistent with higher authorities. In particular, *Sage v Feiven* is difficult to reconcile with *Harmony Shipping*—why should one party be able to subpoena a disavowed expert in one case, but not use them as a joint expert, when privileged information of the first instructing party would seem equally at risk? Actually, *Sage v Feiven* may be correct for another reason. If the disavowed expert were imposed as the joint single expert then it would appear to follow that privileged material would have to be shared between the parties in satisfaction of CPR 35.8 and possibly CPR35.9.

[11] *Sage v Feiven* [2002] CLY 430.

Discussions and Statements between Experts

Joint Statements—CPR 35.12

Scope of the Rule

163. Section 7.2 describes the requirement for information flowing between the instructing parties and the joint expert to be disclosed to the other parties instructing that expert, pursuant to CPR 35.8. It seems that this rule must therefore abrogate the general rule that litigation privilege attaches to communications between a solicitor and a unilateral expert. It follows that the report prepared by such an expert must also be available to both parties, and there is therefore no question of the statement being privileged as between one party and another.

164. However, CPR 35 provides for another situation where a statement may be produced on behalf of both the parties. This occurs where unilateral experts are appointed, but a statement is produced between them jointly, further to CPR 35.12. What is the privilege status of joint material and discussions of experts that go into the production of such a statement?

CPR 35.12 states that the court can direct a discussion between different parties' experts, with a view to the experts agreeing as many issues that are common ground as possible:

> (1) The court may, at any stage, direct a discussion between experts for the purpose of requiring the experts to –
>
> (a) identify and discuss the expert issues in the proceedings; and
> (b) where possible, reach agreed opinion on those issues.
>
> (2) The court may specify the issues which the experts must discuss.
> (3) The court may direct that following a discussion between experts they must prepare a statement for the court setting out those issues on which –
>
> (a) they agree; and
> (b) they disagree, with a summary of their reasons for disagreeing.
>
> (4) The content of the discussion between the experts shall not be referred to at the trial unless the parties agree.
> (5) Where experts reach agreement on an issue during their discussions, the agreement shall not bind the parties unless the parties expressly agree to be bound by the agreement.

Status of Joint Statement and Discussions

165. Further to CPR 35.12(3), the court can also direct that a joint statement be produced on the basis of the expert discussions, such statement to give the

issues on which the experts agree and those on which they disagree, together with reasons for any disagreement. Unlike the discussions that foreshadow it, the very purpose of the statement is to assist the court. It is, therefore, perhaps unsurprising that the CPR does not offer the statement the same protection as the discussions that underlie it. The application of privilege to joint statements is discussed in *Robin Ellis Ltd v Malwright Ltd.*[12]

Robin Ellis Ltd v Malwright Ltd

Background

166. A Technology and Construction case, *Robin Ellis v Malwright* concerns certain building works carried out by the plaintiff builder for the defendant, his employer. The defendant alleged the works were not completed and refused to pay the plaintiff. Proceedings ensued for, inter alia, money alleged to be due for work done. The defendant counterclaimed for damages arising from the alleged failure to complete the work.

In the first order for directions the parties were given leave to call expert witnesses in the following terms:

> Leave to the parties to call expert witnesses limited to two experts per party on condition that their reports shall have been offered for exchange by [date]...
>
> Experts of like disciplines are to meet on a 'without prejudice' basis to try to narrow issues and agree facts by [date]...
>
> The experts are to agree a joint statement indicating those parts of their evidence on which they are, and those on which they are not, in agreement by [date]...

Subsequently, expert quantity surveyors met on numerous occasions, telephoned and wrote to each other, without prejudice. Though all of these discussions had not been completed, so as to comply with the ordered timetable, a statement was eventually signed off and titled an 'Interim Joint Statement of the Valuation Experts'. Later, the parties shifted their ground and the defendant wanted to use the joint statement to cross-examine the plaintiff's witnesses. The plaintiff objected.

Joint Statement not Privileged

167. Despite being titled an 'Interim' report, Judge Bowsher QC held that the joint statement was not privileged and that it would be available to the parties and the Court at trial. However, the discussions and correspondence between the experts would remain privileged.

[12] *Robin Ellis Ltd v Malwright Ltd* [1999] EWHC Technology 256. Although decided pre-CPR, the judge was mindful throughout his decision of the upcoming CPR and did not believe that any statement he made regarding the current law would be altered by the new Rules. The relevant rule pre-CPR was Ord 38 r 38.

Reasoning in Robin Ellis

168. The judge in *Robin Ellis* applied *Rush & Tompkins Ltd v Greater London Council*,[13] which, although on very different facts—whether documents containing admissions made without prejudice with a view to settlement of one piece of litigation should be disclosed in related litigation—he considered to contain a statement of public policy of prime importance that formed the basis of 'without prejudice' privilege:

> The 'without prejudice rule' is a rule governing the admissibility of evidence and is founded on the public policy of encouraging litigants to settle their differences rather than litigate them to a finish. It is nowhere more clearly expressed than in the judgment of Oliver LJ in *Cutts v Head*[14]:
>
> 'That the rule rests, at least in part, on public policy is clear from many authorities, and the convenient starting point of the inquiry is the nature of the underlying policy. It is that parties should be encouraged so far as possible to settle their disputes without resort to litigation and should not be discouraged by the knowledge that anything that is said in the course of such negotiations (and that includes, of course, as much the failure to reply to an offer as an actual reply) may be used to their prejudice in the course of the proceedings. They should, as it was expressed [by] (Clauson J in *Scott Paper Co v Drayton Paper Works Ltd*[15], be encouraged freely and frankly to put their cards on the table . . . The public policy justification, in truth, essentially rests on the desirability of preventing statements or offers made in the course of negotiations for settlement being brought before the court of trial as admissions on the question of liability.'
>
> The rule applies to exclude all negotiations genuinely aimed at settlement whether oral or in writing from being given in evidence. A competent solicitor will always head any negotiating correspondence 'without prejudice' to make clear beyond doubt that in the event of the negotiations being unsuccessful they are not to be referred to at the subsequent trial. However, the application of the rule is not dependent on the use of the phrase 'without prejudice' and if it is clear from the surrounding circumstances that the parties were seeking to compromise the action, evidence of the content of those negotiations will, as a general rule, not be admissible at the trial and cannot be used to establish an admission or partial admission. I cannot therefore agree with the Court of Appeal that the problem in the present case should be resolved by a linguistic approach to the meaning of the phrase 'without prejudice'. I believe that the question has to be looked at more broadly and resolved by balancing two different public interests, namely the public interest in promoting settlements and the public interest in full discovery between parties to litigation.

Furthermore:

> In ordering without prejudice meetings of experts, the Court has in addition a more limited immediate public interest, namely that the litigation (if it cannot

[13] *Rush & Tompkins Ltd v Greater London Council* [1989] AC 1280.

[14] *Cutts v Head* [1984] 1 All ER 597, 605–606, [1984] Ch 290, 306.

[15] *Scott Paper Co v Drayton Paper Works Ltd* [1927] 44 RPC 151, 157.

> be settled) should be prepared for trial and fought at trial upon issues which have been carefully limited and refined by appropriate agreements. If that objective is followed, then the action, if fought, will be fought with less cost to the parties and the public. Pursuit of this more limited objective will in fact also go far to aid the broader interest that the litigation should be settled if possible. Closer definition of the issues helps the parties to reach a settlement.

Judge Bowsher then went on to state that experts' meetings and the communications associated with them are without prejudice and protected by privilege for public policy reasons. What is agreed as a result of those without prejudice meetings is not privileged. It is only as an open document that the joint statement can serve its purpose in limiting the issues in the action.[16]

As regards discussions, the rule is now implicitly found in CPR 35.12(4): the content of the discussions between the experts shall not be referred to at the trial unless the parties agree. In other words, whilst the content of those discussions cannot be protected by litigation privilege as such between the parties, it is effectively deemed to be without prejudice. Either party may therefore veto any reference to the discussions at the trial.

Losing Without Prejudice Protection in a Joint Statement

169. Difficulty may arise in determining when agreement is reached for the purpose of the loss of without prejudice privilege. Referring to *Tomlin v Standard Telephone & Cables*,[17] Judge Bowsher in *Robin Ellis* drew a parallel between agreed expert statements and any other without prejudice negotiation. If without prejudice negotiations result in an agreement, the privilege does not apply to the agreement. To determine whether an agreement has been reached, it may be necessary to look at privileged material, but once it has been decided that there is an agreement, the material containing the agreement is held not to be privileged.

Further to CPR 35.12(5): 'Where experts reach agreement on an issue during their discussions, the agreement shall not bind the parties unless the parties expressly agree to be bound by the agreement.'

Does it follow from this and *Standard Telephone & Cables* that the test of whether material in a joint statement should lose its privilege is whether the parties have agreed that the statement will bind them, not merely that it has been agreed between the experts?

The Court of Appeal in *Stanton v Callaghan*[18] suggests that an agreed joint statement signed by both experts may be put in cross-examination to an expert who later seeks to depart from the views recorded in it. To do otherwise

[16] See also Chadwick LJ in *Stanton v Brian Callaghan* [1999] 15 Cons LJ 50.

[17] *Tomlin v Standard Telephone & Cables* [1969] 3 All ER 301.

[18] *Stanton v Callaghan* [1999] 2 WLR 745.

would deprive a joint statement agreed between experts of the purpose for which it was intended to serve. In other words, the Court implicitly viewed a joint statement agreed by the *experts* as an open document not protected by privilege.[19]

170. *Stanton v Callaghan* was decided pre-CPR, but the reason for the availability of joint statements agreed between the experts remains the same—to fulfil the purpose of the experts to assist the court. The parties instructing them should be prevented from subverting this duty, as expressed by Lord Woolf in Chapter 13 of Access to Justice:

> Among the criticisms I made in my interim report was that the present system does not encourage narrowing of issues between opposing experts, or the elimination of peripheral issues. There has been widespread support for my suggestion that experts' meetings were a useful approach to narrowing the issues. In areas of litigation (such as Official Referees' business) where experts' meetings are already the usual practice, there is general agreement that they are helpful. In areas where they are not at present widely used, including medical negligence, the majority of respondents accept that they could be helpful . . ..
>
> Two principal reservations have been expressed, even by those who support experts' meetings in principle. The first (mentioned in my interim report) is that meetings can be futile because the experts are instructed not to agree anything; or, alternatively, are told that any points of agreement must be referred back to their instructing lawyers for ratification. This subverts the judge's intention in directing the experts to meet, because the decision as to what to agree becomes a matter for the lawyers rather than the experts. I recommend in the interim report that it should be unprofessional conduct for an expert to be given or to accept instructions not to agree, and this has been widely supported.

Consequently, the correct status of statements agreed between experts, and the correct application of CPR 35.12(5), remains that the joint statement of the experts is open when it is agreed by the experts, though it may not be agreed by the parties themselves.

Can the Experts Bind the Parties?

171. In *Aird and Aird v Prime Meridian Ltd*,[20] the Court of Appeal addressed this question. It held that although possibly influential, the agreed statement of the experts will not be regarded as an admission by either party unless it is agreed by the parties, as May LJ noted:

> In my view, the structure of this rule is clear. It provides a balance between the need for the parties' experts to be able to have a free discussion about the issues amenable to their expert opinion which are relevant in the case without the details

[19] See also *Murray Pipework Ltd v UIE Scotland Ltd* (1990) 6 Const LJ 56 and Richard *Roberts Holdings Ltd v Douglas Smith Stimson Partnership* (1990) 6 Const LJ 70.

[20] *Aird and Aird v Prime Meridian Ltd* [2006] EWCA Civ 1866.

> of those discussions becoming material which can be used in the proceedings, with the court's need to have some proportionate and useful product of those discussions. The statement for the court for which rule 35.12(3) provides is a statement which, if it is directed, the experts must produce. It is a statement which, from the very wording of the rule, is available for use in the proceedings. It is not protected by privilege. One of its purposes is to define and narrow the contentious issues. An agreement of this kind is likely to influence any decision the court may reach and the court is likely to make findings consonant with what the experts have stated to be their agreement. But the court is not bound to do so and rule 35.12(5) expressly says that the experts' agreement shall not bind the parties unless they expressly so agree to be bound.
>
> A stated agreement by the experts is not therefore, strictly speaking, an admission. It is certainly not an admission by the parties, because it is not their statement and they are not bound by it. It is not perhaps apt to characterise it as an admission by one or both experts, but rather as an expression of agreement or, as the case may be, disagreement by them in response to an order of the court and in performance of their overriding duty to the court. As I have said, by instructing experts in civil proceedings the parties authorise their experts to do this. It would no doubt be possible for a party instructing an expert in civil proceedings to instruct that expert not to proceed in accordance with an order under rule 35.12(3). But I think that, if this happened, the expert would have to decline to act as an expert in the proceedings, or at least to seek the court's direction in that respect. For, in truth, the instruction would be an instruction not to perform the expert's duty to the court. It would be so because the postulated instruction would be an instruction to disobey an order of the court for which the Rules provide, and an instruction to the expert not to perform his overriding duty to the court, for which again the Rules provide.

The Court of Appeal is thus echoing the concerns of Lord Woolf in Chapter 13 of Access to Justice, described in chapter 3 of this book.

Joint Statements Ordered for Mediation

172. The Court of Appeal decision in *Aird v Prime Meridian* is of further interest because the joint statement in that case had been directed at the case management stage of proceedings for the purpose of facilitating mediation between the parties. Does the fact that the joint statement is ostensibly prepared for a mediation change its privileged status?

Aird v Prime Meridian

Background

173. *Aird v Prime Meridian* concerned a claim for negligence and breach of professional duty brought against the defendant for alleged failures in providing architectural services for the construction of a house. At a hearing in the Technology and Construction Court, HHJ Thornton QC ordered a stay of the proceedings for alternative dispute resolution to take place, the implementation of which was delayed whilst schedules of damages were prepared by both sides. Further to a request, which made explicit reference to CPR35.12(3), and against the background of the stay, a joint statement was ordered by Judge Thornton at a further case management conference six months later for the purpose of facilitating a mediation between the parties. The judge made the order in the following terms:

> . . . the parties' architectural experts (Peter Blockley for the Claimants and Frank Cleveland for the defendants) do meet without prejudice and prepare a statement of the issues upon which they are agreed and those upon which they are not agreed with a brief statement of the reasons for the disagreement.

The experts met and a draft joint statement was prepared, which was stated to be made without prejudice. Then the experts prepared a final joint statement on which the without prejudice notice was removed. The statement was used in a mediation, but this mediation proved unsuccessful and the proceedings resumed. The defendants subsequently sought to use the joint statement of the experts in the proceedings on the basis that the statement was ordered by the Court under CPR 35.12 and so could be used as such. The claimants, on the other hand, argued that the joint statement was prepared for the purpose of, and used in, mediation and was therefore protected by without prejudice privilege, preventing its use in the proceedings.[21]

Status of Statement in Aird v Prime Meridien

174. At first instance the Court held that since the joint statement was ordered for the purpose of mediation its subsequent status in litigation was privileged,[22] and this was unaffected by its origins in CPR 35.12(3). The Court of Appeal overturned this finding. It held that the joint statement was an order made under CPR 35.12(3), despite the fact that there was evidence that Judge Thornton and the parties had intended the statement to be used primarily for the purposes of the mediation. The Court of Appeal said that this was

[21] See *Rush & Tompkins* (n 13).

[22] The Court of First Instance and Court of Appeal refer to privilege, apparently meaning without prejudice.

immaterial—it was not appropriate to look into the motivation that lies behind the case management order. Instead the order must be viewed objectively. The factual question is therefore whether the joint statement which the experts produced should be regarded as that which the Court had ordered.

It was held that the statement could not, in the context, have been anything else but a CPR 35.12(3) statement. This is because, whilst the court can encourage mediation, it has no power to order the parties how to conduct that mediation. Accordingly, as a CPR35.12(3) joint statement, the statement was not privileged and did not become privileged because it was used in mediation, as May LJ commented:

> The experts met and discussed, as they were obliged to do. They produced a joint statement originally marked 'without prejudice'. A final version of that statement was produced with the 'without prejudice' marking removed. The impetus for this was Mr Cleveland's understanding, correct in my view, that it was normal—I would say necessary—for a final version of the statement to have the 'without prejudice' marking removed because it had by then become the considered and agreed statement of both parties for the purpose, I would add, of doing that which the court had ordered. Accordingly, in my judgment, what both experts had prepared was a joint part 35.12(3) statement which was not privileged. It did not acquire a privileged statement [sic] by being used in the mediation, any more than would the pleadings in the action, if they were so used. Judge Coulson's idea, that an originally privileged document did not lose the status of privilege, put the matter the wrong way round.

175. In coming to this decision, the Court of Appeal in *Aird v Prime Meridian* was careful to reiterate that mediations are conducted 'without prejudice' and that material prepared for mediation should only lose this status in clear and unequivocal circumstances. However, the joint statement was not mediation material in this context even though it was referred to in the mediation. Nor would marking it 'without prejudice' make a difference:

> I have dealt with the question, adverted to by the judge, whether it would be fair and just to allow a party to rely on mediation material and that the court should only hold that that material loses its 'without prejudice' statement in clear and unequivocal circumstances. The joint statement was not, in my judgement, mediation material in this context, although it was subsequently referred to in the mediation. It was an antecedent document, ordered by the court for the court. . . .. If it were necessary to do so, I would say that it was perfectly clear and unequivocal that the statement which had been marked 'without prejudice' lost its 'without prejudice' statement because both the experts took a considered decision to remove the words 'without prejudice'. It is not necessary to do so because [counsel for the claimants] would derive a without prejudice status from the fact that the document was used in mediation and because we are concerned with the eventual open document, not with an earlier without prejudice document.

Chapter Summary

176. CPR 35.7 and 35.8 provide that in circumstances where parties provide their own instructions to a single joint expert, the parties must keep the other parties served with any instructions they provide to the expert. The Protocol for the Instruction of Experts to give Evidence in Civil Claims places a responsibility on the single joint expert to keep all the parties informed of the steps they are taking, including copying correspondence from one party to another. The distribution of information between parties provided for by these rules is inconsistent with the right to refuse production based on privilege in that information and to this extent that right is abrogated by these rules.

CPR 35.9 is apparently much broader in scope. It is not expressly restricted to single joint experts, but instead provides for information to be exchanged, subject to an order of the court, between the parties. Little light is thrown upon what 'information' is in this context. However, given that the objective of the rule is apparently to level the playing field between the parties (see chapter 3), it is possible that in appropriate circumstances it could be used to order the exchange of not only instructions, but expert material itself, where it is available to one party, but not another. There is very little comment in the case law on the rule, which is perhaps surprising given its potential power. It remains open whether the rule could be applied, for example, to obtain reports from in-house experts or 'behind the scenes' experts, even where they have been prepared for the dominant purpose of the litigation in question. Were there to be such a result it would obviously have profound implications for litigation privilege and it must be doubtful that a court would be quick to apply it to this effect.

177. The relationship between CPR 35.7 to 35.9 and CPR 35.10 is also unclear. The blanket loss of privilege that the former rules would seem to affect goes further than the CPR 35.10 regime. However, the latter may remain useful in circumstances where a party suspects that the instructions provided to it under the rules concerning joint experts are inaccurate or incomplete and wishes to ask the expert questions in court. This may be a useful tool given that the courts are generally reluctant to order the cross-examination of joint experts.

178. Where a joint expert has been instructed, the expert may interview a party in order to assist them with the preparation of their report. However, the courts will not allow a one-sided conference to take place. Both parties and their lawyers must be present to ensure an open process and allow the parties to know exactly what information is being placed before the single expert. In *Mid-Kent Healthcare*, the Court draws a distinction between the above situation and a case in which an expert interviews one party, alone, in order

to gather information. The latter is permissible, the former is not. In practice, it may prove difficult to distinguish the two and so care needs to be taken.

179. Where a unilateral expert engaged by one party has been subpoenaed by another party, there is no rule preventing that expert from giving evidence before the court for the new party, but the court will be quick to prevent questions on privileged matters being asked to the expert. However, it is difficult to see, in such a situation, how the courts can adequately protect privileged material from accidental disclosure by an expert. The burden is, in reality, on the expert and it is an onerous one. Indeed, *Sage v Feiven* provides an example of where the county court has been reluctant to appoint a joint expert who was originally instructed by one party and thus likely to have privileged information which risks being disclosed in the course of its duties.

180. The content of discussions between experts pursuant to CPR 35.12 is protected by without prejudice privilege and may not be adduced at court without agreement by both parties. A joint statement prepared by experts further to these discussions and pursuant to CPR 35.12(3) is treated differently. A statement of agreed issues, and stipulated issues that are not agreed, even if titled 'interim', is an open statement to the court and is not protected by privilege (even though the discussions and correspondence underlying it will remain so). However, the agreement of the experts on certain issues in the statement will not constitute an admission by the parties.

181. A joint statement of experts ordered by the court will be treated as a statement under CPR 35.12(3), even if the purpose of the statement was to assist in mediation. Therefore, such a report will not attract without prejudice privilege even if it is marked 'without prejudice'.

8

The Status of Draft Reports

Introduction

182. In very complex cases expert reports may be drafted over a long period of time, through many iterations. Each draft may be marked up with further questions, alterations, removals of material and general editing that can give away the thinking and strategy of the legal team and also embarrass the expert if it is seen by the opposing party and appears to show inconsistencies or a change of mind. Are earlier drafts privileged?

Unserved Expert's Reports

183. The case of *Carlson v Townsend*[1] was discussed earlier in chapter 3. It is a second tier appeal case, discussing the privilege status of expert reports in the context of paragraph 3.14 of the Pre-Action Protocol for Personal Injury Claims,[2] as follows:

> 3.14 Before any party instructs an expert he should give the other party a list of the name(s) of one or more experts in the relevant speciality whom he considers are suitable to instruct.
>
> . . .
>
> 3.16 Within 14 days the other party may indicate an objection to one or more of the named experts. The first party should then instruct a mutually acceptable expert.
>
> 3.17 If the second party objects to all the listed experts, the parties may then instruct experts of their own choice. It would be for the court to decide subsequently if proceedings are issued, whether either party had acted unreasonably.
>
> 3.18 If the second party does not object to an expert nominated, he shall not be entitled to rely on his own expert evidence within that particular speciality unless: (a) the first party agrees, (b) the court so directs, or (c) the first party's expert report has been amended and the first party is not prepared to disclose the original report.

[1] *Carlson v Townsend* [2001] 1 WLR 2415.

[2] 3.14 *Pre-Action Protocol for Personal Injury Claims, Civil Procedure 2000* vol 1 1607.

The claimant duly gave the defendant a list of three names of consultant orthopaedic surgeons. The defendant objected to one of these experts and the claimant subsequently instructed one of the remaining names on the list, Mr Trevett. However, after obtaining Mr Trevett's report, the claimant declined to disclose it to the defendant and instead instructed another expert whose name had not been on the list, Dr Smith.

At first instance in the County Court it was held that Mr Trevett's report must be disclosed. This was appealed successfully to a Circuit Judge. The issue that then came before the Court of Appeal was, in addition to whether the protocol had been breached, does the Court have the power to order the disclosure of Mr Trevett's report?

Simon Brown LJ gave precise reasons why the report of Mr Trevett should not be disclosed:

> (1) Although the protocol plainly encourages and promotes the voluntary disclosure of medical reports, it does not specifically require this.
> (2) Withholding Mr Trevett's report did not constitute non-compliance with the protocol although the instruction of Dr Smith without first giving the defendant an opportunity to object plainly did.
> (3) Paragraphs 2.1 and 2.3 of the Practice Direction on Protocols (*Civil Procedure 2000*, vol 1, p 1600) provide the court with ample and various sanctions – in particular with regard to directions, costs and interest – for non-compliance with a protocol. In the present case, of course, the claimant has still to obtain the necessary permission from the court to call Dr Smith. The defendant for her part would almost certainly, if she wished, be permitted to call an expert of her choice. The court would, after all, know that one expert at least, Mr Trevett, had reported less favourably to the claimant's cause than Dr Smith.
> (4) One sanction not available to the court, however, would be to override the claimant's privilege in Mr Trevett's report.
> (5) This appeal in truth could only succeed if Mr O'Brien established his central contention that, on a true understanding of the protocol, the defendant's non-objection to a nominated expert of itself transforms that expert, once instructed, into a single joint expert whose report is accordingly available to both parties. This is not an argument I can accept either in principle or upon the scheme or language of the protocol.

Despite instances of non-compliance with the protocol, the Court could not order disclosure of Mr Trevett's draft report. To do so would override the claimant's privilege in that report. Similarly, Brooke LJ quoting the earlier authority of *Causton v Mann Egerton*[3] reiterated that the common law has always recognised a privilege in communications, such as medical reports in personal injury cases, which come into existence when litigation is contemplated, if they have been made with a view to such litigation:

> I am clearly of the view that this court has no power to order production of privileged documents. Medical reports are in no different category

[3] *Causton v Mann Egerton* [1974] 1 WLR 162.

> from other expert's reports and it would be quite wrong to engraft a qualification upon the doctrine of privilege according to the nature of the report or the class of professional qualification attaching to its maker . . . so long as we have an adversary system, a party is entitled not to produce documents which are properly protected by privilege if it is not to his advantage to produce them, and even though their production might assist his adversary if his adversary or his solicitor were aware of their contents or might lead the court to a different conclusion from that to which the court might come in ignorance of their existence.

Earlier Drafts by the Same Expert

Jackson v Marley Davenport

Background

184. The question of whether an earlier report of an expert could be disclosed was considered in *Jackson v Marley Davenport Ltd.*[4] This was an accident at work case in which Alan Jackson claimed damages for personal injuries sustained in a construction site accident in the Leuna chemical site, Mersburg near Leipzig, Germany, in the course of the claimant's employment with the defendant, Marley Davenport Ltd.

Mr Jackson's supervisor had instructed him to work in a concrete pond or sump, known as the steam turbo set and cooling tower. Access down into the pond or sump was gained by a lightweight ladder provided by the defendant. Mr Jackson alleged that the ladder was not tied or secured in any way and also that the means of access to the top of the ladder was obstructed by pallets on which various materials were strapped. While attempting to gain access to the ladder, or while he was on the ladder, he claimed to have lost his balance, falling backwards into the sump, sustaining severe injury to his head and spinal cord. As Mr Jackson could remember nothing of the accident, he sought leave to obtain expert assistance about the cause of the accident and the method in which he was likely to have sustained his injuries.

The parties were given leave to instruct one engineering expert each and one pathologist each. Mr Jackson instructed Professor Rutty as his pathologist. Professor Rutty prepared a report for the purpose of a conference with Mr Jackson's lawyers. He then prepared a further report, which was served on the defendant.

On 20 July 2004, after disclosure of expert pathologists' reports, District Judge Mort on an application by the defendant, ordered disclosure of the

[4] *Jackson v Marley Davenport Ltd* [2004] 1 WLR 2926.

first report of the claimant's pathology expert, Professor Rutty. In the served report Professor Rutty answered a number of questions put to him, which he answered in turn. Then in conclusion he said in his report:

> Thus in summary, *having now gained additional information in relation to this case*, I am of the opinion that it is entirely possible that the claimant fell from the top of the sump in a backwards and slightly to the left direction probably whilst trying to get onto the ladder. During this process the ladder appears to have pivoted around one of its legs moving into the position shown within the reconstruction photographs. The claimant has gone backwards and to the left, possibly striking his head on the cross-beam sustaining his neck injury and losing his hard hat in the process or sustaining the neck injury as he hit the floor. (Emphasis added.)

His later report thus contained an inference that his opinion had changed since the earlier, unserved, report.

Application under CPR 35.10(3) and 35.13

185. The defendant sought disclosure of the earlier report under Civil Procedure Rule (CPR) 35.10(3) and (4):

> (3) The expert's report must state the substance of all material instructions, whether written or oral, on the basis of which the report was written.
> (4) The instructions referred to in paragraph (3) shall not be privileged against disclosure but the court will not, in relation to those instructions (a) order disclosure of any specific document; or (b) permit any questioning in court, other than by the party who instructed the expert, unless it is satisfied that there are reasonable grounds to consider the statement of instructions given under paragraph (3) to be inaccurate or incomplete.

The defendant also argued that Professor Rutty's earlier report should be disclosed pursuant to CPR 35.13:

> A party who fails to disclose an expert's report may not use the report at the trial or call the expert to give evidence orally unless the court gives permission.

Failing that, it was argued, the Court's general case management powers should apply, so that if an expert's view of a case 'develops' after fresh information is given, an earlier report containing different views becomes disclosable, even if it is privileged. It was said by the defendant that this was especially so given the CPR had adopted a 'cards on the table' approach.

The Court of Appeal on CPR 35.13

186. As regards CPR 35.13, the Court of Appeal held that this rule was meant to refer to the final report that the expert intended to give in evidence, not earlier drafts of that report. The expert could not give evidence at trial unless

such a report had been prepared and served on the other side. However, it was argued by the defendant that there would be a failure to comply with CPR 35.13 if the earlier report were not disclosed, because the earlier draft formed part of the totality of Professor Rutty's evidence. The Court of Appeal considered that earlier drafts could not be considered in this way and that to require the disclosure of every draft of an expert's report on this basis would be a 'retrogression and not an advance in our law'.

The Court of Appeal on CPR 35.10

187. The Court was also clear about the status of draft expert's reports:

> There can be no doubt that, if an expert makes a report for the purpose of a party's legal advisers being able to give legal advice to their client, or for discussion in a conference of a party's legal advisers, such a report is the subject matter of litigation privilege at the time it is made. It has come into existence for the purposes of litigation. It is common for drafts of expert reports to be circulated among a party's advisers before a final report is prepared for exchange with the other side. Such initial reports are privileged.
>
> I cannot believe that the CPR were intended to override that privilege. CPR, r.35.5 provides that expert evidence is to be given in a report unless the court directs otherwise. CPR, r.35.10 then changed the previous law by providing in paragraph (3) that the expert's report must state the substance of all material (whether written or oral instructions) on the basis on which the report was written. By paragraph (4) it is, moreover, expressly provided that these instructions shall not be privileged. But the reference in rule 35.10 to 'the expert's report' is, and must be, a reference to the expert's intended evidence, not to earlier and privileged drafts of what may or may not in due course become the expert's evidence.
>
> The specific and limited exemption from privilege of the instructions given to the expert as the basis on which the report is to be written, shows, to my mind, that there cannot have been any intention in the minds of the draftsmen of the CPR to abrogate the privilege attaching in other respects, e g to earlier drafts of a final report or to earlier reports whether said, in terms, to be draft reports or not.

Complications from County Court Decisions

188. The principle enunciated in *Jackson v Marley Davenport* and *Carlson v Townsend* seems clear. Earlier drafts of experts' reports are protected by litigation privilege and will remain so unless served. However, complications creep into the application of this principle in the County Courts. The following cases illustrate the application of the principle: *Nyiry v*

Intercontinental Hotels;[5] and, how it has apparently been avoided: *Carruthers MP v Fireworks*.[6]

Reports Prepared after Disclosure of Earlier Report

Nyiry v Intercontinental Hotels

189. *Nyiry v Intercontinental Hotels* is a personal injury case. It concerns injuries sustained by Mr and Mrs Nyiry when falling down an automatic escalator, having climbed it in the wrong direction. The claimant and the defendant jointly instructed an orthopaedic expert, Mr Hubble, pursuant to the personal injury pre-action protocol. Mr Hubble prepared a report and provided it to both parties. Subsequently, the claimant instructed a further orthopaedic surgeon to prepare a report, Professor Rushton. This report was also disclosed to the defendant. Later, but before proceedings were issued, the claimant obtained a second expert report from Professor Rushton, but this was not disclosed to the defendant. When proceedings were commenced only Mr Hubble's report was relied upon. Professor Rushton's evidence was neither relied upon nor referred to. Furthermore, permission was granted at the case management conference for both parties to rely on Mr Hubble's report.

Knowing that a second report was being prepared for the claimant by Professor Rushton, the defendant sought an order that the second report should be disclosed to them. The District Judge at first instance ordered disclosure of the second report and this decision was appealed to a circuit judge, HHJ Griggs.

190. Claimant's counsel argued that legal professional privilege was a matter of substantive law and not merely procedural. It could not therefore be overridden by the rules of the CPR.[7] Counsel also referred the judge to the decision in *Carlson* to support the argument that privilege attached to the work of an expert that one party alone had instructed. Reference was also made to *Jackson* for the general principle that the court had no power to order the disclosure of an earlier report. Defendant's counsel sought to distinguish these two cases on the basis that they were concerned with first drafts not later, concluded views, as here.[8]

191. It was held that having instructed a second expert, as they were entitled to do, they were not obliged to rely on the second report and not obliged to make it available to the defendant. This did not mislead the Court as the Court

[5] *Nyiry v Intercontinental Hotels* (Unreported Torquay & Ntn Abbott CC, 22 February 2006) HHJ Jeremy Griggs.

[6] *Carruthers MP v Fireworks* (Bristol CC 26 January 2007) Recorder Moxon-Browne QC.

[7] See *General Mediterranean Holdings SA v Patel* [1999] 3 AER 673.

[8] It was also argued that *Beck v Ministry of Defence* [2005] 1 WLR 2206 and *Vasiliou Michael Vasiliou v Nicos Varnavas Hajigeorgiou* [2005] EWCA Civ 236 applied, to prevent expert shopping (see chapter 9).

was aware of the first report and could properly be told that a second report had been prepared. Although the courts will do what they can to prevent the mischief of expert shopping, they cannot prevent parties instructing whoever they wish. Waiving privilege in the contents of the first report by disclosing it did not waive privilege in the contents of subsequent reports.

Fairness and Justice Overriding Privilege?

Carruthers v MP Fireworks

192. It is in this context that the decision of *Carruthers v MP Fireworks Ltd.*[9] This personal injury case arose from an accident with a firework. Before proceedings commenced, the claimant instructed a fireworks expert, Mr Harriman, to examine the remains of the firework. The defendants knew about this. For unexplained reasons, the claimant then decided he did not wish to rely on Mr Harriman's report and did not disclose it. Instead he instructed a second pyrotechnics expert, Mr Miller, and applied to the Court to rely on him.

Mr Recorder Moxon Browne QC thought that absent an explanation for the change, the claimant was vulnerable to the inference that the reason for non-disclosure is that the report was, to a greater or lesser extent, adverse to the claimant's case. There was, therefore, an inference of 'expert shopping'.

The judge was referred to the Court of Appeal in *Carlson* as authority that there was nothing in the personal injury pre-action protocol to enable the Court to override the substantive law of legal professional privilege. However, the judge appeared to distinguish *Carlson* as being concerned entirely with a simple issue, under the pre-action protocol, of whether a report obtained by one party with the approval of the other was disclosable. On the other hand, the judge thought this case was different, because the claimant was seeking permission to rely on an expert after proceedings had started. It followed, in his view, that the Court had the power to make sanctions.

Furthermore, the judge acknowledged the principle set out in *Jackson* that the privilege in subsequent expert reports is not lost as a result of the disclosure of the first report by the same expert. However, the judge said, it is equally clear that if fairness and justice require the disclosure of an earlier report by the same expert (or another expert), the court has the power to make that order:

> If for example the omission of material from an earlier report had the effect (or might be perceived to give rise to the risk) that a subsequent report was partial or incomplete, and hence potentially misleading, there is no doubt that the court

[9] *Carruthers* (n 6). See also chapter 9 for further facts and discussion of this interesting and perplexing case.

could order the first report to be disclosed so that the full picture was before both parties and the court.

The Decision

193. Influenced by Court of Appeal cases on changing experts (discussed in chapter 9),[10] the judge stated that the disclosure of an earlier report could always be made a condition of permission to rely on a later report; but if no such permission is sought (as in *Carlson*), the court simply has no power to override the privilege in the earlier report.

It seems that an important consideration in the judge's mind was the fact that the expert in this case had been instructed to perform tests on an exploded firework and there was a perception that those tests may have caused some physical alteration of the firework. In these circumstances, it would be unfair for the examinations and their results to remain a secret to the defendants.

Chapter Summary

194. An unserved expert report is effectively outside the reach of the rules of Part 35 of the CPR. Such a report is subject to the general rule that the protection of litigation privilege applies. Similarly, earlier drafts of a report that is later served in proceedings should normally be protected by privilege. Similarly, subsequent drafts by an expert who has served a report in proceedings should be protected.

195. However, the case of *Carruthers* suggests that the protection of privilege may be lost in circumstances where it would do an injustice to the other party to keep from them a report that may record details of an experiment which has altered the evidence available to subsequent experts. This case is not of high authority and it remains unclear whether it can be relied upon for any broader principle that the protection of privilege can be abrogated where there is a risk of injustice. The decision is a reminder that seriously unusual results can occur. It is discussed again in the context of changing experts, in the next chapter.

[10] *Beck v Ministry of Defence* and *Vasiliou v Hajigeorgion* (n 8).

9

Changing Experts

Introduction—When will this Problem Arise?

196. Chapter 8 discusses circumstances in which there are earlier draft reports (or, as the case may be, later drafts) of an expert whose evidence is served and relied upon in proceedings. Also, in chapter 3, the use of 'behind the scenes' experts was discussed in the preparation of a case and/or during proceedings. As those chapters explain, in the normal course of preparing expert evidence such drafts and behind the scenes advice should be protected from production by privilege. However, as this chapter will demonstrate, problems may arise in a situation where a party decides to change one or more of its experts. This is not an unusual occurrence and could prove necessary at any point between instructing the expert and trial.

197. In fact, there are numerous circumstances in which an expert may have to be changed. For illustration, take for example the following, broad scenarios:

- Illustration 1: A claimant is preparing a negligence claim and instructs an expert as a part of the preparations before proceedings have been started. The expert is instructed to assess the circumstances of an incident that has caused damage to the claimant's property. There is not a complete picture of these circumstances at the time of instruction, because these were under the control of the prospective defendants. On the information that is available, the expert comes to a preliminary view which is very favourable to the claimant on the key points and less favourable on points that are thought to have less importance. Encouraged, the claimant instructs the expert to start preparing a formal report. The expert is later named in an order for directions pursuant to a case management hearing. Notices to admit and requests for further information are served and responses to them follow. After service of the responses it becomes apparent that the principal matters at issue between the parties are not those that the claimant had originally thought. The issues on which the expert was very strong have diminished in significance and instead the defendants are building their case largely on the issues on which the expert was less supportive.
- Illustration 2: Alternatively, picture a similar scenario where instead of a different case emerging from the pleadings, unhelpful disclosure

is obtained. Upon inspection of the disclosure it can be seen that the disclosed documents put a significantly different complexion on the circumstances of the incident than had previously been supposed by the claimant. On these facts the claimant's expert's view is unfavourable.

These are just two generalised situations where the claimant has instructed an expert at an early stage, before the precise issues in the dispute become clear, only to find that what appeared to be favourable opinions at the beginning later become unfavourable. Furthermore, there are cases where the expert simply has a change of mind, gets cold feet about giving evidence and/or even turns out to be less than competent. Any of these problems can happen at a late stage, after a number of drafts have been prepared and after it is known by the other party that an expert has been instructed. Perhaps the expert's name has also been disclosed or even included in an order giving permission to rely on that expert's evidence.

198. In the above circumstances, it may be possible to take pragmatic steps to sideline the expert by restricting the issues dealt with to those on which the expert is most favourable, and supplementing the evidence with that of a more favourable and/or capable expert. Alternatively, there may be no option but to change the expert completely. In the latter situation, what is the status of the draft expert reports prepared by the disavowed expert? Are they privileged, or must they be disclosed?

The cases that are discussed in this chapter form an apparently discrete group that can be traced back to a Court of Appeal decision from the early 1970s called *Lane v Willis*:[1]

Personal Injury Cases

Lane v Willis

Background

199. *Lane v Willis* concerned an action against Willis for injuries suffered in a road accident in May 1968 that was alleged to have caused the plaintiff, Lane, physical injuries and 'nervous shock, depressive anxiety state'. Lane was examined by a neurologist, Dr Carroll, on behalf of the defendant, following which the defendant denied liability. The plaintiff later amended the particulars of his injuries by adding that he had received electro convulsive therapy treatment at Holloway Sanatorium for severe depression, bouts of which he was still suffering. He also claimed to be suffering other symptoms

[1] *Lane v Willis* [1972] 1 WLR 326 (CA).

which affected his ability to do his job properly. The plaintiff was examined on two further occasions by Dr Carroll, but the defendant also asked that he should be examined by a well-known psychiatrist, Dr Leigh. That request was refused and the defendant accordingly applied for a stay of the proceedings in default of the plaintiff submitting to such examination. The application was refused by a master and Talbot J.

Evidencing Need for Further Expert

200. It was held in the Court of Appeal that although no expert or medical evidence had been put forward to show that a psychiatric examination was desirable and necessary for the defendant properly to conduct his defence to the claim, given the substantial difference in the injuries originally pleaded and those pleaded by the amendment, the request for such an examination was reasonable. The important statement from the Court of Appeal for present discussion came from Sachs LJ. He said that, when the refusal of a medical examination is alleged to be unreasonable, the onus lies on the party which applies for the order to stay to show that the party is unable properly to prepare his or her case without that examination:

> . . . the fact that some medical evidence should have been put before the master or the judge—and preferably, to my mind, the reports of Dr. Carroll—has been ventilated, and it has become plain that in future cases of this particular type (if these should ever recur) such medical evidence should be produced: no room should be left for a plaintiff to wonder whether the application is really due to the reports of a defendant's medical expert being favourable to the plaintiff.

In Sachs LJ's view, as well as evidencing the need for further examination, the requirement that such evidence be produced has a wider function. In circumstances of this seriousness, it shows that the defendant is not trying to merely replace an unwanted expert. In other words, it is intended to avoid expert shopping. In this case, the defendant was permitted to adduce evidence from Dr Leigh and an undertaking was given by counsel that all of Dr Carroll's reports would be disclosed as well—the disclosure of Dr Carroll's reports was not actually ordered. How would similar concerns to those in *Lane v Willis* be addressed in subsequent cases?

The Beck v Ministry of Defence 'Principle'

Background

201. *Beck v Ministry of Defence*[2] was an appeal from a circuit judge, Judge Langan QC, sitting as a judge of the Queen's Bench Division. It concerned an action

[2] *Beck v Ministry of Defence* [2005] 1 WLR 2206.

in clinical negligence brought by a flight lieutenant in the Royal Air Force (RAF), Mr Beck, against the Ministry of Defence. Whilst serving in the RAF, Beck developed a psychiatric illness. He was later treated for this condition by an RAF general practitioner at the Duchess of Kent Hospital, Catterick, under the charge of a consultant psychiatrist. Beck alleged that the treatment he received during this time was negligent, and that instead of curing him it made his condition worse. As a result he developed a major depressive illness which caused his medical discharge from the RAF and the end of his long-term employment prospects. The case was thus both high value and involved serious allegations against practising doctors.

In addition to other directions, an order was made in the form:

> Each party shall exchange expert evidence limited to one psychiatrist per party concerning the issues of liability, causation, condition and prognosis in the form of experts' reports by way of simultaneous exchange, . . .

By the date of this order, the defendant had selected its expert psychiatrist, who proceeded to examine the claimant. However, the defendant later lost confidence in this expert, because in their solicitor's words:

> the expert did not have sufficient knowledge of the Ministry of Defence psychiatric referral system which is relevant to this case. In addition, the presentation and flow of the report was poor.

A day before his evidence was due to be served the defendant asked the claimant's permission that another expert be allowed to examine the claimant. This request was refused and the defendants applied to the Court for permission to change experts.

202. The district judge who heard the application granted leave because it was considered the only way in which an informed and fair trial could be conducted. So, Beck appealed to the circuit judge on the basis, amongst other matters, that following *Lane v Willis* the defendant could not establish that it was unable to prepare a defence without requiring the further expert; in particular, without disclosing the medical evidence already prepared. The appeal was dismissed and a second appeal was made to the Court of Appeal.

Disclosure—a Condition of Permission

203. The issue that the Court of Appeal had to decide was whether, and if so on what terms, the defendant should be allowed to instruct a new psychiatric expert. The Court of Appeal held that once a change of expert had been permitted, they could see no reason for continuing to withhold disclosure of the unwanted expert's report and every possible reason why such disclosure should be made. The Court of Appeal gave particular note to the passage from Sachs LJ's judgment in the earlier authority of *Lane v Willis* (which was referred to throughout the Court of Appeal's decision):

> no room should be left for a plaintiff to wonder whether the application is really due to the reports of a defendant's medical expert being favourable to the plaintiff.

Consequently, the defendant was permitted to change expert, but only upon the condition that they should disclose the report of the unwanted expert, the disclosure of this report to take place only after the permission had been granted, and not before, so not to expose the unwanted expert to later cross-examination on earlier drafts of their report, if permission should then not be granted.

Is Beck a Narrow Authority?

204. A characteristic of the *Beck* case was that much of the debate was concerned with the detriment that might be caused to the claimant—a fragile and continuing psychiatric patient—by being re-examined without good reason. Much of this debate went to the issue of how the court's discretion should be applied to permit a further expert in such a case. However, on the issue of whether the unwanted expert's report should be disclosed as a condition of such permission, the decision of the Court of Appeal appears more wide-ranging. In particular, this is indicated by the statement by Brown LJ:

> I do not say that there could never be a case where it would be appropriate to allow a defendant to instruct a fresh expert without being required at any stage to disclose an earlier expert's report. For my part, however, I find it difficult to imagine any circumstances in which that would be properly permissible and certainly, to my mind, no such circumstances exist here.

The suggestion here is that the Court is making a general statement about the need to disclose unwanted reports once permission has been obtained to change expert. In fact, the statement appears to establish a general presumption that this should be the correct approach.

How would the courts treat the issue in non-personal injury cases?

Broader Application of the 'Beck Principle'

A Valuation Case—Vasiliou v Hajigeorgiou

205. The Court of Appeal returned to the subject of changing experts in *Vasiliou Michael Vasiliou v Nicos Varnavas Hajigeorgiou.*[3] This case gives further scope for reflection on whether there is a general principle, beyond application

[3] *Vasiliou Michael Vasiliou v Nicos Varnavas Hajigeorgiou* [2005] EWCA Civ 236.

to personal injury cases alone, that the disclosure of an unwanted expert's report should be a condition of changing the expert.

This decision ensued from a successful action brought by the claimant for breach of covenant for quiet enjoyment of its lease of restaurant premises in Green Lanes, London. Liability having been determined, damages were ordered to be assessed. In order to assist this process, the trial judge, Judge Levy QC, ordered a Case Management Conference (CMC). In preparation for this CMC the defendant's solicitor identified the expert it wished to rely on, Mr Watson, in a witness statement. However, Mr Watson was not named in the subsequent order, made pursuant to Civil Procedure Rule (CPR) 35.4. Instead, the order gave permission to the parties to 'instruct one expert each in the specialism of restaurant valuation and profitability'.

Some time afterwards, Mr Watson inspected the claimant's restaurant premises by appointment. Watson prepared what was described as a 'draft interim report', but subsequently the defendant decided that he did not wish to rely on Watson and his report. As a result, the defendant's solicitors wrote to the claimant's solicitors asking if a second appointment could be arranged. This time the inspection would be conducted by an expert called Mr Negus. However, the claimant opposed permission to adduce the evidence of Mr Negus and the defendant argued that it didn't need permission. Judge Cowell held that permission was required and that as a condition of that permission, the evidence of Mr Watson should be disclosed to the claimant.

Permission not required if Expert Unnamed

206. The Court of Appeal held that the wording of the specific case management order directed only that one expert could be called to give evidence in the area of restaurant valuation and profitability. No specific individuals had been named in the order and CPR 35.4 provides:

> (1) No party may call an expert or put in evidence an expert's report without the court's permission.
> (2) When parties apply for permission they must identify–
>> (a) the field in which expert evidence is required; and
>> (b) where practicable, the name of the proposed expert.
>
> (3) If permission is granted it shall be in relation only to the expert named or the field identified under paragraph (2).

It was therefore open to the defendant to change its expert without permission because the proposed expert would be in the same field of expertise, satisfying CPR 35.4(3). In these circumstances, there was no need to require the disclosure of the earlier report as a condition of a second inspection of the claimant's premises.

Effect of Naming the Expert in an Order

207. In fact, the defendants in *Beck* had also not needed the permission of the Court to change experts, because the Court in that case had also not given permission to adduce expert evidence by reference to a specific, named expert. As the Court of Appeal in *Vasiliou* noted, this point appears never to have been taken in *Beck*. Instead, they observed, the argument in that case seems to have proceeded on the basis that the question was much wider:

> whether it can ever be appropriate to allow a party to substitute one expert for another without, at some stage at least, being required to disclose the first expert's report.

The Court of Appeal in *Vasiliou* clearly thought that this point had been missed and that whether the expert was named or not made a difference. The expert was not named here and so the Court did not need to make a decision about the issue of disclosure. However, the Court of Appeal did comment, obiter, on circumstances in which a first expert had been named by order of the Court and permission to call the second expert therefore was *necessary*. In these circumstances, the Court confirmed that *Beck* made an important statement of principle—the court has the power to permit a party to rely on a second expert which it should usually exercise only on condition that the report of the first expert is disclosed.

Expert Shopping

208. Explaining the rationale for this principle, the Court repeated the policy that expert shopping is undesirable and that, wherever possible, the court would use its powers to prevent it. The principle established in *Beck* was an example of the way in which the court will control the conduct of litigation in general, and the giving of expert evidence in particular. Indeed, in his supporting judgment in *Beck*, Ward LJ makes a similar general statement about preventing expert shopping:

> . . . expert shopping is to be discouraged, and a check against possible abuse is to require disclosure of the abandoned report as a condition to try again.

Privilege not 'Abrogated' but 'Waived'

209. To summarise, where an order had been made by the court to allow expert evidence, a condition of changing the expert to be relied upon would be the disclosure of the unwanted expert's report. It is interesting that at no point in the deliberations is privilege referred to by the Court in *Beck*. This is surprising given that a requirement to disclose unwanted experts' reports

is clearly an incursion into the general rule of privilege seen in cases such as *Carlson v Townsend*,[4] discussed in chapters 3 and 8. Did the Court of Appeal really intend it to be an abrogation of the general rule of privilege in these circumstances, and could it be even more wide-ranging?

Unlike the Court in *Beck*, the Court in *Vasiliou* did discuss the issue of changing experts in the context of privilege, although the Court would not accept that the Lords Justice in *Beck* had overlooked the issue. The Court reasoned that there was indeed privilege attaching to a draft report of an unwanted expert.[5] However, it was not an 'abrogation or emasculation' of this privilege to order that such an unwanted draft be disclosed. Instead, it was simply a condition of changing expert that the privilege existing in such reports should be waived.

Which Draft Report should be Disclosed?

210. The Court in *Vasiliou* also addressed a further question. This is whether the condition of disclosure should relate only to the first expert's 'final' report, being the report signed for disclosure, or whether it should also relate to his or her earlier draft reports. The Court thought that such disclosure should not be limited to the final report, but could extend to an earlier draft if that contained the substance of the first expert's opinion.

Application in the County Court—Carruthers

211. The *Carruthers MP v Fireworks* case,[6] first discussed in chapter 8, must be revisited in the context of this chapter, because it provides another example in which permission was sought to replace an expert. It is also of interest as an example of how the rule established by the Court of Appeal above can be applied by the inferior courts, with apparently far reaching effect.

Background

212. In *Carruthers*, the claimant was injured by a firework manufactured and sold by the first and second defendants, respectively. Details of what happened are limited, but it would appear the claimant suffered serious injuries, including to his left eye, as a result of the firework exploding at the wrong

[4] *Carlson v Townsend* [2001] 1 WLR 2415.

[5] It also referred to *Jackson v Marley Davenport Ltd* [2004] 1 WLR 2926 as authority for the same principle.

[6] *Carruthers MP v Fireworks* (Bristol CC 26 January 2007).

time or the wrong way. Before the action started, and without any direction by the Court, the claimant instructed an expert, Mr Harriman, to examine the firework. This examination was conducted on an undertaking to the defendants that any testing of the remains of the offending firework would not be destructive.

Having examined the firework, Mr Harriman proceeded to prepare a report which the claimant then decided it did not wish to rely on. The claimant instead wanted to rely on the report of another pyrotechnics expert, Mr Miller. The claimant's reasons for this disavowal of Mr Harriman were not explained and neither was the work that he had carried out on the firework.

213. In the Bristol County Court, Deputy District Judge Howell gave permission to rely on the evidence of Mr Miller, subject to the disclosure of the report prepared by Mr Harriman. The judge based his reasoning for this on the *Vasiliou* decision. However, the claimant had argued that he was not seeking to rely on Mr Miller *in place of* Mr Harriman, because Mr Harriman had never been named pursuant to an order of the Court. However, Deputy District Judge Howell said that it did not matter because in this context there was no relevant distinction between unidentified experts' reports obtained before an action is started, and identified reports obtained with the Court's permission after the action has started.

Disclosure of any Report

214. On appeal, Recorder R Moxon Browne QC, sitting in the Bristol County Court, agreed. In doing so the Recorder relied on statements of the Court of Appeal in *Vasiliou* and *Beck* to the effect that 'the disclosure of an earlier report can always be made a condition of permission to rely on a later report'.

In doing so, the judge was apparently unconcerned whether the expert had been named in a court order or not. The fact that the claimant needed permission to rely on Mr Miller under CPR 34, gave the Court the opportunity to exercise its power to order disclosure of *any* earlier report (that is known about), in order to prevent expert shopping and abuse of the process of the Court.

Problems with Carruthers

215. The *Carruthers* decision seems particularly unsatisfactory for two reasons. First, the difference in outcome between *Carruthers* and *Vasiliou* (disclosure rather than non-disclosure) results purely from the technical matter of whether permission is required. In both cases, the courts knew that there were earlier reports in existence, but the defendant in *Vasiliou* was able to hide behind the fact that they already had permission to bring the evidence in the

field of valuation and profitability, generally, and so no further permission was required. Conversely, in *Carruthers,* the claimant was penalised for not having such an order. This has the result that it would have been better for the claimant in *Carruthers* to have denied the Court and the other party any knowledge of its intentions with experts. It disadvantages the claimant in circumstances where they did not 'use' the Court to their advantage—the claimant could have obtained a general order from the Court, like that in *Vasiliou,* and used it as a 'licence to expert shop', thus defeating the point of the Court's power to order disclosure in these circumstances.

216. There is a, more serious, second concern raised by *Carruthers. Carruthers* would seem to suggest, at its broadest interpretation, that the court has the power to override privilege in any 'behind the scenes' expert advice of the kind discussed in chapter 3, whether the expert is identified or not. This approach seems to extend to circumstances in which permission is required either for a change of expert or, alternatively, just to seek permission to rely on an expert at all.

If correct, such an approach would cut across the whole concept of protecting documents by privilege; any discussions with experts on the merits of a claim, whether for the purposes of eventually giving evidence or not would be susceptible to disclosure. Even given the court's concerns about preventing expert shopping, it is submitted that this cannot be right. It 'would deprive a Claimant of confidential pre-action advice about the viability of his claim, which he would be at liberty to discard if he did not agree with it', to use the words of Brooke LJ in the context of the *Carlson* decision.

Could there be a different way to read *Carruthers*?

A Narrower View of Carruthers

217. A closer reading of *Carruthers* shows that the judge seemed particularly concerned that the tests on the firework by Mr Harriman may have caused some physical alteration to it. This meant that if he did not order disclosure of Harriman's draft expert, there was a risk of injustice:

> . . . if fairness and justice required the disclosure of an earlier, privileged, report as a condition of permission to rely on a subsequent report by the same expert, (or indeed another expert) the Court would have power to make that order. If for example the omission of material from an earlier report had the effect (or might be perceived to give rise to the risk) that a subsequent report was partial or incomplete, and hence potentially misleading, there is no doubt that the Court could order the first report to be disclosed so that the full picture was before both parties and the Court.

If a risk of injustice was the concern, it raises the question whether it might have been preferable for the judge to resolve the problem by directing the replacement expert to address this issue and then weighing up his evidence with that of the defendants.

Chapter Summary

218. It should be remembered that *Carruthers* is a County Court decision and of lesser authority than the *Beck* and *Vasiliou* decisions. Fortunately, it is submitted, the more sensible approach is that of the Court of Appeal in *Vasiliou*, albeit obiter. Under the CPR, if a party wishes to call an expert, it must seek permission. The cost of that permission, if the expert is named in an order of the court, is that the court should not then countenance abuse of its process by allowing the order to be changed without the cost of disclosing the unwanted expert's report.

This approach does leave open the unsatisfactory avoidance of this condition by the simple expedient of naming a field of expertise rather than a particular person. However, it is a far cry from penalising a party for discussing its case with a number of behind the scenes experts, where the courts have not been involved and formal proceedings cannot be said to have been exploited. This sanction, which is suggested by the *Carruthers* case, seems particularly inappropriate given that the advice of behind the scenes experts might enable litigation to be avoided.

219. Clearly, care should be taken in these circumstances to ensure that experts are chosen wisely and that they have developed their opinion as far as possible before committing them to proceedings by naming them. Practitioners should also be sure that that expert is fully competent to give the evidence at issue. It is also wise to remember that anything put into a draft report by one party may end up in the hands of the other party. A vigorous observance by an expert of his or her duties to the court should be encouraged by this possibility.

10

Experiments and Surveys

Introduction

220. At first sight, the privilege issues arising from experiments may seem only a matter reserved for a narrow breed of intellectual property practitioners. In particular, it is frequently the case that patent proceedings, inherently technical as they are, will require experiments in order to support anticipation, insufficiency, or even infringement and obviousness arguments about a particular patent. Experiments may also be used to try to demonstrate the infringement or even obviousness of a particular patent. The fact that experiments are common in the jurisdiction of the Patents Court is reflected in Practice Direction (PD) 63 paragraphs 7.1 to 7.3, to the specialist Civil Procedure Rule (CPR) for patents and other intellectual property claims, CPR 63. PD 63 states:

> 7.1 A party seeking to establish any fact by experimental proof conducted for the purpose of litigation must, at least 21 days before service of the application notice for directions under paragraph 7.3, or within such other time as the court may direct, serve on all parties a notice –
>
> (1) stating the facts which the party seeks to establish; and
> (2) giving full particulars of the experiments proposed to establish them
>
> 7.2 A party served with a notice under paragraph 7.1 –
>
> (1) must within 21 days after such service, serve on the other party a notice stating whether or not each fact is admitted; and
> (2) may request the opportunity to inspect a repetition of all or a number of the experiments identified in the notice served under paragraph 7.1.
>
> 7.3 Where any fact which a party seeks to establish by experimental proof is not admitted, that party must apply to the court for permission and directions by application notice.

However, despite their confined position in the intellectual property practice direction, there is no reason why these directions should not apply generally to any proceedings in which experiments need to be conducted to prove facts.[1] This chapter addresses the privilege issues of which practitioners

[1] This is envisaged in the editorial introduction to Civil Procedure Rule (CPR) 63 which states 'The application of the other Civil Procedure Rules and their practice directions is subject to the provisions of this practice direction [PD63].'

need to be aware when conducting experiments, whether there is a wider application of these rules and their relationship to expert evidence.

Experiments in Patent Cases

Experiments without Notice

221. Before turning to the role of privilege in experiments as such, attention should first be given to the effect of a failure to fulfil the formalities of the notice required by CPR PD 63[2] by looking at a case decided under its predecessor Rules of the Supreme Court (RSC) Ord 104 r 12, *Electrolux Northern Ltd v Black & Decker*.[3] *Electrolux* was a patent infringement action relating to lawn mowers. The lawn mowers at issue could hover above the ground on a cushion of air. In the claimant's patent this cushion was created by a fan mounted above the cutting blade on the drive shaft. It was designed so that air flowing towards the fan would in turn suck up cut grass. The claimants argued that this patent was infringed by the defendant's lawn mower. The defendant's lawn mower employed two fans; the lower fan creating most of the uplift, while the upper fan sucks air through a collecting nozzle lifting up cut grass.

The size of the air-flow in this lawn mower, and its contribution to grass pick-up, was hotly contested and resulted in the parties carrying out a number of experiments. Notices of experiments were served for these experiments. During the repeat of one air-flow experiment conducted by the defendant, an experimenter acting for the plaintiffs made measurements of the apparent height of the cut grass. To do so, they used an improvised device with a scale up the vertical edges. Its points were pushed into the ground where the mower had passed and certain measurements were taken of grass height at those points. The defendant's experimenter was asked to confirm the measurements but no explanation of this additional experiment was given at the time.

It was not until later, based on these measurements of cut grass height, that the plaintiffs advanced an argument in their skeleton sent to the defendant just before trial. It appeared with hindsight that this argument had earlier been foreshadowed in the plaintiffs' expert report but not made clear. No notice of experiments was advanced and the defendant objected to these results being relied on or admitted at the trial.

[2] A number of the cases discussed are based on the predecessor provision to Practice Direction (PD) 63 from Ord 104 r 12 of the Rules of the Supreme Court (RSC). The discussion and conclusions in this chapter are common to both.

[3] *Electrolux Northern Ltd v Black & Decker* [1996] FSR 595.

222. In Laddie J's view, the plaintiffs had failed to comply with the mandatory requirements of RSC Ord 104 r 12 and it would be unfair to the defendant to allow the experiments to be admitted in the action. The plaintiffs were not given leave to rely on the results of their grass height measurements. Consequently, if a party does not comply with the requirement to give a notice of experiments they should not be surprised if they are not then permitted to adduce those experiments in evidence. However, what is the situation if a party wishes to rely on the experiments of another party, given under notice, or not?

Abandoned Experiments

Inconsistent Cases

223. In addition to the effect of failure to serve a notice of experiments, *Electrolux* also dealt with the status of abandoned experiments. Both the defendant and the plaintiffs in *Electrolux* suggested that the other parties had conducted additional experiments which they had not disclosed. It was argued that Laddie J should infer that these experiments had proved helpful to the opposing party and that they had been abandoned for that reason. Reliance for this argument was placed on the judgment of Jacob J in *Honeywell Ltd v Appliance Components Ltd and Mayne Pty Lt*,[4] in which it was said: 'It can hardly be right that a party can put forward an argument (whether supported by experiments or not) and suppress experiments he has conducted which do not support that argument or indeed undermine or destroy it.'

And furthermore:

> I do not say that experiments not relied upon should be placed before the court. But the opposite party should know about them, as in the trade mark cases. It may well be that, at least in some cases, leave to adduce evidence of experiments conducted for the purpose of the action should only be given on condition that all such experiments are disclosed to the opposite party.

For reasons which are explored in greater depth in the section entitled 'Laddie J's Critique of Honeywell in Electrolux', in *Electrolux* Laddie J was reluctantly, but vehemently, opposed to this finding:

> with much regret I am unable to accept that those considerations justify the imposition of a general requirement on parties to disclose abandoned experiments, or abandoned endeavours to find any other form of evidence. Nor do I accept that the admission or disclosure by a party that it conducted other experiments which it has chosen not to rely on should lead the court, in a normal

[4] *Honeywell Ltd v Appliance Components Ltd and Mayne Pty Lt* Unreported, Patents Court, February 1996.

case, to draw any adverse inferences as to what those experiments might have proved.

Practice Direction (Patents Court: Practice Explanation)

224. *Electrolux* thus provides a clash of first instance authority in the Patents Court with the more sweeping statement of the law in the earlier authority of *Honeywell.* As a result of this clash Laddie J and Jacob J released Practice Direction (Patents Court: Practice Explanation),[5] which states:

> The Intellectual Property Court Users' Committee has discussed the question of experiments conducted by a party for the purposes of litigation but not disclosed or adduced by it following the Judgments in [*Honeywell* and *Electrolux*]. As a result it is proposed that in future it should be a requirement that an expert's report should include the statement 'I know of no experiment which is inconsistent with my evidence.' Further, practitioners are reminded that it would be contrary to their duty to the court to allow any expert evidence to be given inconsistent with an experiment of which they, but not the expert, have knowledge.

Consequently, it remains unclear whether abandoned experiments will be disclosable or not. The Practice Direction, which makes the call on a practice level of requiring an expert to disclose inconsistent or adverse experiments, does not explicitly, or by implication, address the issue. Nonetheless, given the propriety required from experts and practitioners on this issue, the problem may be merely an academic one.

Electrolux is concerned only with the status of *abandoned* experiments which have not been introduced into the action by means of a notice of experiments. The next section deals with experiments where a notice of experiments has been served, but for which the work-up experiments have not been disclosed.

'Work-Up' Experiments

225. When producing any experimental method it may be necessary to undertake a number of 'work-up' experiments. These are the ground work, trial and error experiments that are conducted to hone the experimental method, such as finding the correct settings on equipment, temperatures, solvents, etc. The notice of experiments that is served on the other party may be the result of many such work-up experiments. What is the status of the work-up experiments? Is another party entitled to look behind the notice at everything that tried and failed in arriving at the method set out in the notice?

[5] [1996] 1 WLR 1567 (replaced by (1998) 1 WLR 1414).

Mayne Pharma

226. The issue of work-up experiments was dealt with in *Mayne Pharma Plc v Debiopharm SA and Sanofi-Synthelabo.*[6] The case was about two patents relating to oxaliplatin, an anti-neoplastic platinum complex used for treating cancer. One of the patents claimed pharmaceutical formulations of oxaliplatin, and the other claimed a process for its preparation. The validity of both patents was challenged and infringement was also alleged of the process patent. In connection with their revocation case, the claimants served a notice of experiments which attempted to establish certain facts about the pH of the reaction mixture in a prior disclosed method which, if followed, would anticipate certain claims of the patents in suit.

When following the method set out in the notice of experiments, the defendants' expert could not get it to work. The expert also pointed to ways in which the notice of experiments did not follow the disclosure in the prior art. Consequently, the defendants applied for disclosure of documents relating to any work-up or preliminary investigation leading to the experiment described in the notice of experiments.

227. Pumfrey J allowed the application. He did so, even though he was well aware of the *Honeywell* and *Electrolux* decisions. However, as the judges in those cases had not done,[7] Pumfrey J directed himself according to the decision in *Nea Karteria Maritime Company Ltd v Atlantic & Great Lake Steamship Corporation and Cape Breton Development Corporation (No 2)*,[8] in particular the following parts (reported in quotation):

> I believe that in summary and perhaps not in very concise terms one can see a rule of positive law being stated in the interest of justice, that where a party chooses to deploy evidence which would otherwise be privileged the court and the opposition must, in relation to the issue in question, be given the opportunity to satisfy themselves that they have the whole of the material and not merely a fragment. Thus I must start by asking myself what are the issues in relation to which the material has been deployed? Of course, the prime issue is whether and, if so, in what circumstances, the seaman accepted the truth of an account of events different from one which on two other occasions he has put forward. This involves the question whether he did give the answers recorded in document P35, whether that document represents a complete record of the meeting, having regard to the seaman's evidence that he signed the statement to get rid of the lawyers.

And further (in report form):

> It was essential, therefore, for the court to see the meeting as a whole, and for that purpose the Judge's view was that the whole of the substance of the meeting was 'a legitimate subject for disclosure and for cross-examination.'

[6] *Mayne Pharma Plc v Debiopharm SA and Sanofi-Synthelabo* [2006] FSR 37.

[7] Apparently because counsel had not raised the case in argument.

[8] *Nea Karteria Maritime Company Ltd v Atlantic & Great Lake Steamship Corporation and Cape Breton Development Corporation (No 2)* [1981] Com LR 138 (see also chapter 5).

228. Pumfrey J had no difficulty in saying that the waiver in *Mayne v Debiopharm*, effected by the giving of the notice of experiments in relation to an experiment conducted on the instruction of the lawyers for the purposes of litigation, extended to the work-up of the particular experiment forming the subject matter of the notice: 'I will be willing to declare that any legal professional privilege otherwise attaching to documents relating to workup experiments for the experiment in the notice of experiments has been waived by service of the notice of experiments.'

Pumfrey J thus seemed to be drawing an analogy with *Nea Karteria* to the effect that (adapting the quotation above):

> where a party chooses to deploy [a notice of experiments] which would otherwise be privileged the court and the opposition must, in relation to the [experiments] in question, be given the opportunity to satisfy themselves that they have the whole of the [work-up experiments conducted] and not merely a fragment.

Survey Evidence

Disclosing the Context of Surveys

229. Both in *Honeywell* and *Electrolux*, Jacob J and Laddie J, respectively, refer back to the *Imperial Tobacco v Philip Morris* case.[9] Jacob J did so to adapt its principles and Laddie J did so to ask whether it needs reconsideration. The case concerns the use of surveys in a passing off matter.

Imperial Tobacco

230. The plaintiffs in *Imperial Tobacco* had introduced a new brand of cigarette which was marketed under the brand name 'Raffles'. It was alleged by the claimants that the similarities of the 'Raffles' packet to their own John Player Special ('JPS') brand amounted to passing off. This is because, they said, there would be confusion between the packs—purchasers would think that Raffles was a JPS cigarette because of the black and gold pack, the use of a crest resembling a Royal crest and the word Raffles appearing in calligraphic form.

At the trial the plaintiffs relied on certain surveys. The surveys were intended to evidence an association in the minds of the consumer of the colours black and gold with the JPS brand. Other surveys suggested that because of the black and gold colouring people thought that Raffles cigarettes

[9] *Imperial Tobacco v Philip Morris* [1984] RPC 293.

came from the same source as JPS cigarettes. A number of other surveys were also conducted by the plaintiffs which were not put in evidence. Smokers and retailers were also called to give evidence on actual confusion.

231. Although not directly influential on his decision in this case, there were a number of faults which Whitford J found with the survey evidence put before him. In particular, he was concerned about those surveys that may not have been brought to the Court's attention:

> Apart from those surveys as to which direct evidence was led, there were quite plainly a number of other surveys on which the court is in this difficulty. The court knows very little about them other than that they took place. How exactly they were conducted and what number of people were in fact interviewed.
>
> If survey evidence is to be of any weight at all it can only be of weight if in any case where, as here, a number of surveys have been carried out the plaintiffs give—and they must give this to the defendants before ever the action comes on—the fullest possible disclosure of exactly how many surveys they have carried out, exactly how those surveys were conducted and the totality of the number of persons involved, because otherwise it is impossible to draw any reliable inference that answers given by one or two or three people in one survey might conceivably be said to indicate that similar answers would be given if a survey covering the entire smoking population or the entirety of retail tobacconists were carried out.
>
> It is also important that the totality of all answers given to all surveys should be disclosed and made available to the defendants. Unfortunately in some of the surveys which were here conducted provision was made for objection to be entered by any person interviewed to the use of the answers to the questions for some purposes without his consent, as a result of which only a limited disclosure on one survey was or could be offered.
>
> Great importance inevitably attaches to the way in which the questions are cast. It is very difficult in connection with an exercise such as this to think of questions which, even if they are free from the objection of being leading, are not in fact going to direct the person answering the question into a field of speculation upon which that person would never have embarked had the question not been put. It must necessarily be the case that the exact answers given and not some sort of abbreviation or digest of the exact answer should be recorded. For the purpose of an analysis coding is in general carried out, as is well known, and it is of vital importance that any such coding should be accurately carried out. Of course one has to know exactly what instructions were given to persons carrying out the interviews upon which answers to questionnaires are secured, and indeed, in the instance of those surveys upon which reliance was placed, we have got information as to the instructions given, the way in which the interviews were carried out and the coding. What emerges at the end of the evidence is that there may be doubt as to whether in fact in all cases the answers which were given were correctly recorded. There may be doubt as to whether the instructions in all cases were sufficiently carefully followed by those carrying out the interviews. There is no doubt whatsoever that, so far as the coding is concerned, in some cases it must be considered to have been incorrect and in other cases it might be considered to be misleading.
>
> I make these comments about these surveys, not because I think it is of vital importance to the final decision in this case, but there is an increasing reliance

> upon material of this character which results in a vast amount of paper being brought before the court, which in fact if it is to be of any value should be even larger than was the amount brought in this case, I have found the results of the plaintiffs, save and in so far as what is in fact established is that one would reasonably expect to find established, of very little value.

232. *Imperial Tobacco* therefore says, analogously to the result in *Honeywell*, that for a survey to have evidential value all other surveys which may have been conducted in the proceedings must be disclosed.

O2 v Hutchison

233. In *O2 Ltd and O2 (UK) Ltd v Hutchison 3G (UK) Limited (Admissibility)*,[10] Pumfrey J went a step further than *Imperial Tobacco* by attempting to actively manage survey evidence, *ab initio*. The case concerned alleged trade mark infringement in an advertising campaign of the defendant. When the question of survey evidence was raised at an interim stage, the judge made this remark:

> If you want to do first shot surveys, you can and come back with the results. You know what I mean. . .But you are not to embark on a fully blown survey without having the questions and what you are seeking to demonstrate considered by the court first.

As a result, an order was drawn up in the following terms:

> Neither party has permission to adduce survey evidence without first having obtained the leave of the court. Any application for such leave is to include details of any questions proposed to be used in any such survey.

Despite this order, the claimants went ahead and conducted a 'first shot survey' at two locations with 20 respondents, two supervisors and 12 interviewers. It produced about 280 completed questionnaires. The material collected was not disclosed to the other side as part of the parties' disclosure exercise but did appear at the time of exchange of evidence later on.

234. Lewison J held that the evidence of eight members of the public whom the claimants wished to call was not probative. But even if it had been, he would exclude it under his case management powers under the CPR, on the basis that it had not been foreshadowed by disclosure of the various questionnaires used. The judge was also aggrieved by the claimants' failure to abide by the spirit or the letter of the order of Pumfrey J.[11]

[10] *O2 Ltd and O2 (UK) Ltd v Hutchison 3G (UK) Limited (Admissibility)* [2006] RPC 30.

[11] *cf D Jacobson & Sons v Globe Ltd* [2008] EWHC 88 (Ch) in which there were agreed directions for permission to adduce survey evidence.

Surveys in Relation to Experiments

235. A further issue tied up with the admissibility of survey evidence in *O2 v Hutchinson 3G* was the nature of survey evidence generally. The claimants sought to call an employee of the market research company conducting the surveys, Mr Mumford. He was to give evidence on how the survey had been carried out. The defendant objected to the admission of the evidence of Mr Mumford on the basis that it was to be properly characterised as expert evidence. If this were correct, Mr Mumford's evidence would fall within Part 35, in particular the requirement that permission be sought for leave to call him. No such leave had been sought.

In determining this question, Lewison J accepted that surveys are a form of experiment:

> In the present case Mr Hobbs submits, and Mr Arnold did not dispute, that what has been carried out in the exercise I have described is an experiment. It is an experiment in the sense that stimuli have been applied to subjects under controlled conditions and their reactions have been observed. In my judgment, Mr Hobbs is right about that. This is, in effect, an experiment. This is not a question of members of the public who have spontaneously reacted either to seeing the claimants' advertising material in actual use or the defendant's allegedly offending advertisement in actual use. They have been given particular questions and shown particular things and their responses have been recorded.

Consequently, if the surveys were a form of experiment, for the judge it followed that the evidence of Mr Mumford must properly be considered as expert evidence.[12] If he did not give evidence then the results of the 'experiments' could not be explained.

Reconciling the Experiment Cases—a Discussion

Honeywell

236. When discussing the correct approach to the disclosure of experiments, in both *Mayne v Debiopharm* and *Electrolux* the judges refer to the earlier decision of Jacob J in *Honeywell* (discussed earlier). All are first instance decisions of the Patents Court and yet between them they appear irreconcilable. If the authority of *02 v Hutchison* is included on the basis that surveys are another form of experiment, then the picture becomes even more complex. Is there an underlying principle to be found, that applies to

[12] Etherton J implicitly assents to this characterisation in *D Jacobson & Sons v Globe Ltd* (n 11) when holding that the directions had included permission to adduce expert evidence in relation to the methodology of any footwear marketing survey.

intellectual property cases and also to experiments conducted in proceedings generally?

237. *Honeywell* concerned a claim for infringement by Honeywell of their patent entitled 'Motor Control Apparatus' and related to a control valve for central heating systems. The claim was met with a counterclaim for invalidity of the patent on the grounds that it was anticipated and obvious in the light of certain pieces of prior art.

It emerged from the correspondence of Appliance Components Ltd's ('ACL') patent agents, that an experiment had been tried relating to whether a so-called 'November' circuit fell within one of the patent claims. Furthermore, another experiment was performed by ACL on the heat generation of a DC current. Despite the fact that there was a direct way of proving invalidity of the patent by anticipation through experiment, neither of the experiments conducted was put in. Instead ACL adopted what Jacob J called a 'convoluted' way to prove anticipation. Jacob J concluded, by inference, that the experiments did not support the defendant's case.

Jacob J then went on to make the following general statement about experiments for which notice had not been served:

> It may be noted that I have referred to two lots of experiments conducted by ACL for the purpose of this action which were not put in. One only emerged in the course of cross-examination. I think it highly desirable in future, if experiments are conducted which are not relied upon that the opposite party is told of this. This seems to me to be an exact parallel to what is done in relation to experiments by way of opinion polls in trade mark and passing off cases, see *Imperial Tobacco v Philip Morris*[13]. Indeed the principle would seem to apply to all cases (not just intellectual property cases) where a party seeks to rely upon experiments. It can hardly be right that a party can put forward an argument (whether supported by experiments or not) and suppress experiments he has conducted which do not support that argument or indeed undermine or destroy it. I do not say that experiments not relied upon should be placed before the court. But the opposite party should know about them, as in the trade mark cases. It may well be that, at least in some cases, leave to adduce evidence of experiments conducted for the purpose of the action should only be given on condition that all such experiments are disclosed to the opposite party.

238. This statement appears to be intended to have broad application in two respects. First, it appears to apply to all experiments conducted in patent proceedings; and, secondly, Jacob J expressly states that he thinks the same principle applies to experiments of any kind, that is those conducted outside the context of intellectual property proceedings. Given that this decision pre-dates those in *Electrolux* and *Mayne v Debiopharm*, how is it reconciled with those decisions and, if it is not, what is left of the general principle that Jacob J seems to espouse?

[13] Discussed earlier in the section entitled 'Disclosing the Context of Surveys'.

Laddie J's Critique of Honeywell in Electrolux

239. In *Electrolux*, Laddie J held that it was not required that abandoned experiments be disclosed. Perhaps because of his reluctance to disagree with his fellow Patents Court judge, he goes to great lengths to explain in detail why he thinks Jacob J is incorrect in *Honeywell*:

> I have given this matter long and careful thought. I would not lightly disagree with a judge of Jacob J's eminence in this field, not only out of respect for his views but because it is hardly helpful to practitioners to have conflicting views from two current patent judges. However, with much regret, I have come to the conclusion that I must differ from Jacob J. In view of the potential importance of this issue to other cases. I think that I must explain why I feel constrained to do so.
>
> Our system proceeds on the basis that, save in relation to discovery, each party puts before the court the material which it believes supports its case or undermines the case of its opponent. The evidence is subject to testing by cross-examination at the trial. That is frequently, but not inevitably, assisted by discovery which each party is compelled to give. Even if advised by its lawyers that its case is weak, no party is obliged to call witnesses who are hostile to its case, whether that be a witness of fact or an expert witness. Indeed, a party is not obliged to proffer evidence on any point. He may hope that he can achieve enough by cross-examination of his opponent's witnesses or by relying on the burden of proof where that rests on his opponent. Patent actions in this respect do not differ from any other type of action.
>
> It is against this background that experiments in patent actions should be considered. In many patent cases one or both parties decide to rely on experiments. The rules about notices of experiments and repetition before the opponent's experts, referred to already in this judgement, are designed to ensure that a full and fair analysis of what was done and what, if anything, it proves can be carried out by the parties. However, the fact is that in many cases, of which this is a typical example, by the end of the trial and as a result of the technical criticism in the evidence of the expert witness, many of the experiments fail to support the propositions for which they were advanced. Indeed frequently the experiments are shown to have no probative value one way or the other to the issues in the case. A number of the experiments in this case exemplify that. By the end of the trial it was agreed by both parties that a number of the experiments were, on proper analysis, valueless. I would be surprised if relevance was proved for more than 20 per cent of the experiments deployed in an average patent action. There have been many cases where eventually it was found that all the experiments were valueless. But whether my pessimistic assessment of the average success rate of experiments is accurate or not, I am sure that experiments frequently prove to be a waste of time and effort. It is because of this that efforts and suggestions have been made over the years to curtail the freedom of parties to put in experiments. It is also the reason why the courts will penalise in costs any party who puts in and seeks to rely on unnecessary experiments . . .
>
> . . . it may be useful to start by considering the simplest and best case...Assume that the defendant in an action carries out an experiment which appears to show,

contrary to his expectation, that his product infringes the plaintiff's patent. He has no desire to rely on it. However, as a result either of an inquiry or some expanded obligation of discovery or disclosure, he is forced to disclose the existence of the experiment to the plaintiff. The plaintiff will call for full discovery relating to it (a topic I will return to later). Notwithstanding what was said in *Honeywell*, the plaintiff *will* seek to place the experiments before the court. The defendant will then have to produce evidence to undermine his own experiments. The possibility of calling no evidence and arguing that the plaintiff has failed to prove his case would not arise. But it can be argued that this is not unjust because, by this method, the court will be made aware of the evidence of infringement and therefore be assisted to come to the right result. However, this benefit, in most cases, is more theoretical than real. If the defendant can run experiments which prove infringement so, save in exceptional cases, can the plaintiff. No substantial injustice is likely to result from following the normal course of requiring the plaintiff to prove infringement. However even if, in this case, some benefit might accrue to the plaintiff by reason of forcing the defendant to disclose, for the reasons set out below, I think the price paid is far too high.

I deliberately started with this simple example. I suspect that it is not only simple but unreal. As those who have been involved in the conduct of patent actions will know, frequently experiments are discarded for a variety of reasons: they are either not clear enough, or the experimental technique is too open to attack to make it worthwhile relying on them, or the expert who would give evidence in relation to them would make a dreadful witness, or counsel and solicitors come to the conclusion that there is a better and simpler way of proving the point or they appear to support the other side's case and it would take a lot of complicated evidence to prove that the initial impression is not the right one and that they really support the experimenting party's case. In relation to any such experiments the norm is for solicitors and counsel to discuss the pros and cons of relying on them with experts and clients. That may well include experts who, because of the limitations on the number of expert witnesses, are not to be called to give evidence. Bearing in mind the costs of penalties emphasised in the *Pall* case[14], it is the lawyers' obligation to advise their clients to jettison any experiment that is not clearly necessary to the case. The withholding of experiments will frequently, and perhaps normally, not be because they proved the other side's case. For the court to draw a contrary inference would be wrong. Somewhat similar considerations apply when clients rely on a claim to privilege to withhold documents from discovery. The court does not assume that they have been withheld because they are damaging.

In these circumstances, we should consider what would be the result of forcing the withholding party to disclose the abandoned experiments. In the passion of litigation, the other side would assume that there is a good prospect that the experiments were aborted because they were unhelpful. They would ask for full discovery. There would be little to be lost by so doing. I do not see how the court could refuse the application. But whether it did or not, the withholding party would be put in a quite impossible position. He would be aware, because of *Honeywell*, that the court is likely to infer that they prove the other side's case.

[14] *Pall Corp v Commercial Hydraulics (Bedford) Ltd* [1990] FSR 329.

He will therefore have to disclose not only the details of the experiments but the reasons why they were jettisoned. Since the major reason may well be the advice of counsel and solicitors, is he going to be forced to waive privilege? Furthermore if the decision was based in part upon the advice of an expert who was going to be called and could not be called because of the number limit on such witnesses, is he now going to have to apply to the court for leave to put in evidence from him to explain why he thought the experiments were unnecessary and unhelpful? If the experiments were equivocal, is the withholding party now going to be forced to carry out further experiments to prove that he was right to believe that there were good non-incriminating grounds for jettisoning them? And is the court now going to add to the burden of trying the case the time and expense of considering, with expert evidence, whether in fact there was, as there will be in most cases, a perfectly sensible and non-incriminating reason for doing so? In my view the prospect of adding all this to a patent or any other action is most unappealing. It will simply result in the parties being driven to spend time and money on what is likely to turn out to be an irrelevant exercise. The courts in general and the patents court in particular are trying to slimline proceedings and cut down on costs. This seems to be a step in the wrong direction.

My concerns do not end there. The central reason for suggesting this course is to be found in the following sentence in *Honeywell*: 'It can hardly be right that a party can put forward an argument (whether supported by experiments or not) and suppress experiments he has conducted which do not support that argument or indeed undermine or destroy it.'

As I have pointed out above, the inference that this is the reason for withholding experiments, in my view, will be unjustified in most cases. But ignoring that, if this reason holds in respect of experiments, why should it not hold in respect of witnesses, including expert witnesses? If, as is normal in a patent action, a party interviews five or six experts with a view to finding one who will best support the case on obviousness, can it be right to put forward arguments based on his evidence and to suppress the draft witness statements of other interviewed experts? It is possible that some of those others do not support that argument or indeed undermine or destroy it. I have difficulty in seeing why different principles should apply in this area. For much the same reasons as are set out in relation to the disclosure of abandoned experiments. I cannot believe it is in the interests of the administration of justice to force parties to disclose all the other unfruitful avenues they have pursued on the off chance that some of them might be arguably supportive of their opponent's case.

For these reasons I am afraid I cannot agree with the broad thrust of the *Honeywell* decision. I should mention that I have not thought it appropriate to consider, in the absence of argument, whether the same reservations apply to the decision in *Imperial Group PLC v Philip Morris Ltd* [15].

This does not mean that the existence of abandoned experiments can never be relevant. The *Honeywell* case is a good example of where it was useful for there to have been cross-examination on this issue. It appears that there was a direct experimental way of proving anticipation. The infringer did not put in such experiments. Instead he tried to use a 'convoluted' route to try to prove

15 *Imperial Group PLC v Philip Morris Ltd* [1984] RPC 293.

> it. It was legitimate to ask the relevant witnesses why the direct route was not taken. If the witness said that the experiment was tried and seemed to show non-anticipation, so much the better. In deciding on the question of validity, the court was entitled to take into account and give weight to the fact that a direct method of proving anticipation appeared to exist but was not taken or relied on by the defendant. From my reading of the judgement in the *Honeywell* case, Jacob J was fully entitled in all the circumstances of that case, including the failure by the defendant to produce direct experiment proof of anticipation, to conclude that that issue had not been proved. But for the reasons set out above and with much regret I am unable to accept that those considerations justify the imposition of a general requirement on parties to disclose abandoned experiments, or abandoned endeavours to find any other form of evidence. Nor do I accept that the admission or disclosure by a party that it conducted other experiments which it has chosen not to rely on should lead the court, in a normal case, to draw any adverse inferences as to what those experiments might have proved.

240. In summary, Laddie J's reasoning why there should be no general requirement that abandoned experiments should be disclosed seems to boil down to seven points:

1. The system of notice and repeat already enables scrutiny of the way experiments are conducted.
2. More experiments by the disclosing party to show why its earlier experiment is not unhelpful to its case would be necessary.
3. The other party can equally demonstrate the facts it wants to prove with its own experiments without relying on unhelpful experiments from the opposing party.
4. Experiments may be abandoned for a number of reasons other than because they undermine the experimenting party's case.
5. Disclosure of abandoned experiments may require additional experts to be called to interpret those abandoned experiments.
6. It may be necessary to use court time to try the issue of whether there was a sensible and non-incriminating reason for abandoning an experiment.
7. Parity of reasoning suggests that disclosure of discussions with experts that have not been called would follow as a requirement.

Pumfrey J's Critique of Electrolux in Mayne v Debiopharm

241. In *Mayne v Debiopharm*, Pumfrey J takes a different view to Laddie J, beginning with point 7 above, the view that experiments are comparable with expert evidence:

> I think, with respect, that the suggested parallel with experts is wide of the mark. Experimental evidence is intended to provide a degree of objective confirmation or corroboration of the subjective views of the experts. It is evidence of a kind

> different from that advanced as experts' opinions. It may provide, and from time to time does provide, a fixed point against which the experts may themselves be assessed. It is one place in litigation of this class where an appeal to scientific technique is directly made. It is employed because it trumps the experts, however cogent their views may be.
>
> I take the view that the opinion generally expressed by Jacob J in the passage, to which I have referred, reflects a need to reveal the full story rather than just its culmination in the context with which I am presently concerned; which is to say the workup of an experiment. I do not wish to be taken to be expressing a view in any other context at all.

242. For Pumfrey, the issue he was being asked to address was limited to whether work-up experiments should be disclosed. He thought this should be approached on the same basis as any other issue of the waiver of privilege:

> On the hypothesis that workup experiments at least are in principle subject to legal professional privilege, the question for me is whether disclosure should be ordered. It is unfortunate that neither Jacob J nor Laddie J, no doubt the former by reason of the deficiencies of counsel, were shown the relevant authorities or addressed on the correct question of waiver of privilege, although it is clear that Jacob J was concerned with a really wider question than mere workup experiments and Laddie J was concerned with experiments which had been abandoned.

In summary, Pumfrey J thought the reason that confusion and inconsistency had crept into his fellow judges' decisions on experiments was that they had overlooked the central role of privilege in these issues.

A General Principle?

243. As discussed in the section entitled 'Work-Up Experiments', the correct approach according to Pumfrey J was to apply the authority of *Nea Karteria.* However, as Pumfrey makes clear in the passage from his judgment above, he was dealing with the issue of work-up experiments. He was not making a general statement about experiments and he was not dealing with experiments which had been abandoned and on which the experimenting party was not seeking to rely. Hence, it makes sense for him to use the general principle that reliance should warrant disclosure of all the material relied upon, derived from *Nea Karteria.* In that sense, there is a general principle governing notices of experiments that is similar to the 'cherry-picking' principle discussed in chapter 5. Pumfrey J was not sure whether his finding in *Mayne v Debiopharm* extended to a wider application.

244. In *Mayne v Debiopharm,* Laddie J is concerned with circumstances of a different kind, those experiments which have been abandoned and on which the party has never sought to rely. In his impassioned objection to the general principle expounded in *Honeywell,* Laddie J focuses in particular on parallels between abandoned experiments and uncalled experts (referred

to as 'behind the scenes' experts in chapter 3). If this comparison is correct, there is consistency between Laddie J's approach in *Electrolux* and the behind the scenes expert cases. Indeed, Laddie J appears to recognise this from his concerns in point 7 above. As Laddie J suggests, it is accepted that the work undertaken with behind the scenes experts who never become Part 35 experts is privileged. Pumfrey J objects to this analysis and thinks experiments are akin to objective points against which the subjective opinion of an expert may be tested. However, even if this is correct, the experiments are investigations of fact, recorded in documentary evidence, that have come into being for the purpose of litigation. They should, it seems, therefore benefit from the protection of litigation privilege under general principles. Providing the experiments are not relied upon, the analysis for abandoned experiments should, therefore, be different to that for work-up experiments.

245. Should there be a general principle, as suggested by Jacob J in *Honeywell*? Jacob J says the rules governing experiments in intellectual property proceedings should be the same as those for experiments in any other proceedings, and this seems sensible. However, for the rules governing experiments to be consistent with other fields in which privilege applies (discussed in the earlier chapters of this book), the rules governing experiments themselves are divided between those cases where there is reliance and those where there is not. However, it is submitted that in the context of abandoned experiments the scope of a general rule such as that suggested by Jacob J would have a similar far reaching effect on experiments to the decision that *Carruthers MP v Fireworks*[16] has for expert reports (see chapter 9). That is, a party can never try out its case by any form of investigation resembling an experiment, without the risk that it must be disclosed later. Given the fact that behind the scenes advice is really only a kind of 'thought experiment', Jacob J's general rule is inconsistent with the treatment of such behind the scenes experts.

246. The survey cases present a further difficulty. In *02 v Hutchison 3G*, Lewison J held that surveys are merely a species of experiment. However, the decision in *02 v Hutchison 3G*, following *Imperial Tobacco*, is to the effect that when survey evidence is brought forward, all undisclosed materials related to that survey evidence and *all other surveys* conducted must be disclosed. This approach is akin to the decision in *Honeywell*.[17] If Laddie J and Pumfrey J are correct in their approaches and the dividing line between disclosure and non-disclosure is reliance then clarification with regard to surveys is needed. In particular, it is submitted that the consistent course would be for a party to notify the opposing party of any survey evidence that will be relied upon. The opposing party then ought to be able to seek all the documents that formed the work up to the survey evidence adduced, including questions, responses, numbers surveyed, and so on. However, consistency of approach would also

[16] *Carruthers MP v Fireworks* (Bristol CC 26 January 2007).

[17] And indeed Jacob J cites the *Imperial Tobacco* (n 9) authority.

require that those surveys that have been conducted but abandoned should remain privileged.

The key difficulty in this area is that all the leading decisions are first instance. Court of Appeal authority is needed to provide a comprehensive approach.

11

Use of Reports in proceedings by Third Parties

Introduction

247. It is an established principle that when a party serves an expert report, without restrictions, the protection afforded by privilege in that report is waived. The practical extent of this loss of privilege is much less clear—what use can the expert report be put to? This chapter looks at the use an expert report can be put to by the other parties in the proceedings. What happens when one or more of the parties have served their own expert evidence, but then drops out, by settlement or otherwise? What do the Civil Procedure Rules (CPR) say about the issue and is there any rule by which a quasi-privilege may be retained over the evidence of the ex-party?

The Basic Rule—CPR 35.11

Gurney Consulting Engineers—Background

248. In *Gurney Consulting Engineers (a Firm) v Gleeds Health & Safety Ltd and Gleeds Management Services Ltd*,[1] a Part 20 claimant sought to prevent the Part 20 defendant from relying on reports of the parties no longer in the proceedings. The Part 20 claimant, Gurney, was originally sued by a pension property fund called Pearson as a result of the collapse of part of a row of terraced properties in London that they owned. At the time of the collapse the properties in question were being refurbished by a number of parties, for which Gurney were the appointed structural engineers. In turn, Gurney issued Part 20 proceedings against the other parties employed in the refurbishment—the architect, the contractors, and the two Gleeds companies which acted as the planning supervisors and the project managers—seeking a contribution under the Civil Liability (Contribution) Act 1978.

[1] *Gurney Consulting Engineers (a Firm) v Gleeds Health & Safety Ltd and Gleeds Management Services Ltd* [2006] EWHC 43 (TCC).

Shortly before trial, Gurney settled with Pearson and settled all its Part 20 claims except those against the two Gleeds companies, but not before the parties had prepared and served expert evidence from a number of engineering experts. There was a broad measure of agreement between those experts and indeed they had prepared a CPR 35.12 statement on those issues where agreement had been reached. The exception was the Part 20 claimant's engineering expert, Mr Jackson. Mr Jackson disagreed with the other experts on a number of important issues, particularly causation. Amongst those experts with whom he was at odds was the expert for Gleeds, Mr Price. Finding their expert's opinion outnumbered by the other experts, Gurney sought to prevent the Gleeds companies from relying on the expert engineering reports of the parties no longer in the proceedings. Equally, Pearson wanted to rely on the opinions expressed in those reports and also on the agreement signed pursuant to CPR 35.12.

Gurney—the Argument

249. In order to try to prevent the Gleeds companies from using the favourable reports of the other parties, Gurney asserted that the Gleeds companies required permission to serve the additional reports under CPR 35.4. The Gleeds companies argued that they could rely on those other reports without seeking the Court's permission, pursuant to CPR 35.11, which states simply 'Where a party has disclosed an expert's report, any party may use that expert's report as evidence at the trial.'

However, the Gleeds companies did accept during the course of argument that it would be appropriate for them to notify Gurney of the reports that they sought to rely on in accordance with CPR 35.11. They also accepted, apparently without argument, that they could not cherry-pick those parts of the reports on which they wished to rely and exclude those parts that may be unfavourable to them—if the Gleeds companies were entitled to rely on CPR 35.11 to use another party's reports then they must be content to have regard to all of the report and not just a part of it.

In response, Gurney argued that 'a party [that] has disclosed an expert's report' refers to a party which is still participating in the proceedings and not, as in this case, a party or parties who have settled the action. Secondly, they added that even if CPR 35.11 applied, this did not mean permission should still not be required.

Relationship between CPR 35.11 and CPR 35.4

250. In *Gurney*, Judge Peter Coulson QC held that for the reports of the parties to be served in the proceedings in the first place they must already have

been permitted under CPR35.4 and so it was not necessary for the Gleeds companies to seek permission again to rely on them:

> In my judgement the answer to [Gurney's] two points can be found in CPR 35.11 itself. It only applies where party A has already disclosed an expert's report and party B wants to rely on it as evidence at the trial. The disclosure of party A's report could have occurred in accordance with CPR 35.4. In other words, it is a fundamental assumption within CPR 35.11 that there has already been compliance with CPR 35.4, and the report which party B now wishes to use is one for which the court has already given permission. In such circumstances, it is not necessary for party B to seek permission all over again; party B merely wishes to use a report for which permission has already been given.
>
> Similarly, because CPR 35.11 assumes that party A's report has been disclosed in accordance with CPR 35.4, it does not matter whether, sometime after disclosure of that report, party A ceased to be a party to the proceedings. The reference to 'a party [that] has disclosed an expert's report' in CPR 35.11 cannot be limited to those who happen to be parties to the proceedings at the time that that report is sought to be used by another: there is nothing in the rule which could limit its scope in that way. The reference in r.35.11 is to any party who has disclosed a report in accordance with r.35.4, whether they subsequently remain a party to the proceedings or not.

251. The Judge in *Gurney* also added that this result was, in his judgment, consistent with the overriding objective in CPR 1.1. In particular, he thought it artificial, and possibly misleading, for the Court to disregard entirely the reports of the other experts, or the part they played in reaching the detailed contents of the CPR 35.12 joint statement.

Notification of Use and Reliance

252. In *Gurney*, the Judge added that use of a third party report came with certain obligations:

> . . . I am mindful of the need to ensure that any orders/directions in respect of expert evidence are proportionate. I also consider that it is important that Gurney fully understand which of the other engineering expert's reports Gleeds wish to rely on, and for what purpose. That would necessarily involve a consideration by Gleeds of the component parts of each report, even if it is right, as I think it must be, for the court to have regard to the report as a whole when arriving at its conclusions. In particular, I consider that [Gurney's counsel] needs to know, in advance of his cross-examination of Mr Price, Gleeds' expert engineer, what, if any, points arising from the other engineers' reports he may need to raise during his questioning. In addition, I believe he is also entitled to raise with the court any aspect of Gleeds' attempt to use particular parts of the other experts' reports if he considers that such use would, for specific reasons, be disproportionate or unfair. Of course, he cannot do that until he knows what reports and/or parts of the reports Gleeds wish to use, and why they wish to use them.

In other words, the party wishing to rely on the report should notify its opponent of the reports it seeks to use, which parts it seeks to rely on and why they are important.

Other Applicable Rules?—CPR 35.1 and 35.7

253. The approach in *Gurney* was applied by Akenhead J in another Technology and Construction Court case called *Shepherd Neame v EDF Energy Networks (SPN) Plc.*[2]

Shepherd Neame—Background

254. *Shepherd Neame* concerns an application made during a trial of an action that arose from a fire at the City Arms in Canterbury which left the premises badly damaged. It was owned by the fourth claimants and managed and occupied by the fifth claimants. The remaining sets of claimants were owners or occupiers of neighbouring properties that had also been affected by the fire. The first defendant, EDF Energy Networks ('EDF'), was the electricity distributor at the time of the fire and the second and third defendants were the previous owner of the City arms (until eight weeks before the fire), Whitbread Plc, and electrical contractors retained by Whitbread from time to time, respectively.

As a result of various orders, the two sets of claimants and the three defendants retained experts, the experts met to discuss issues without prejudice, exchanged reports and produced joint statements on those matters about which they agreed and disagreed. All experts, except EDF's expert, Mr Fletcher, agreed that the source of the seat of the fire was on the electricity supply side of the electrical meter, which left an issue as to whether EDF was liable. Mr Fletcher's opinion was that the fire started on the consumer's side of the meter, which would mean EDF was not liable. Shortly after trial began, a number of settlements took place which left both the sets of claimants in dispute with EDF only.

Shepherd Neame—the Argument

255. The neighbouring claimants, supported by the fourth and fifth claimants, made an application during opening to use the reports of the two experts retained by the second and third defendants, who were by then longer

[2] *Shepherd Neame v EDF Energy Networks (SPN) Plc* [2008] EWHC 123 (TCC).

involved in the proceedings. The application was made on the basis of CPR 35.11.

The first defendant argued that the claimant should not be permitted to rely on these reports as the expert evidence should be restricted to that which was reasonably required to resolve the proceedings. This, they argued, was in accordance with CPR 35.1, which states that 'Expert evidence shall be restricted to that which is reasonably required to resolve the proceedings.'

256. The first defendant also relied on CPR 35.7, which allows the court to appoint a single joint expert, as supporting the position that the court should be sparing about allowing in expert evidence:

> (1) Where two or more parties wish to submit expert evidence on a particular issue, the court may direct that the evidence on that issue is to be given by a single joint expert.
> (2) Where the parties who wish to submit the expert evidence ('the relevant parties') are called 'the instructing parties' cannot agree who should be the single joint expert, the court may –
>
> > (a) select the expert from a list prepared or identified by the relevant parties; or
> >
> > (b) direct that the expert be selected in such other manner as the court may direct.

Relationship with CPR 35.11

General Position

257. In *Shepherd Neame*, Akenhead J echoed the decision in *Gurney* in ruling that the wording of CPR 35.11 entitled the claimants to rely on the experts' reports of the second and third defendants, because it gave them an unequivocal and unqualified right to do so. He said it applies where any party has put in an expert's report so that any party may rely upon it as evidence. The party wishing to rely on the report as evidence is not limited to the party who disclosed it in the first place. Furthermore, there is no qualification that it only applies to a party whose expert's report has been disclosed, so long as they remain a party to the proceedings.

Even if CPR 35.11 had only given the Court discretion as to whether to allow a party to use a report, the Court would have allowed the claimants to rely on the reports pursuant to its case management powers. This was because the five experts had undoubtedly spent a considerable time talking together and producing four joint statements. The joint statements were before the Court in any event and contained the views of the settled parties' experts whose reports were sought to be relied upon. So to understand the joint reports in context, it is likely to be necessary to understand what the free-standing reports say.

CPR 35.1

258. The judge held that CPR 35.1 should be read together with CPR 35.11:

> Whilst the indiscriminate use of experts and in particular the reliance by one party on more than one expert in each relevant discipline is discouraged, often parties will be allowed each to call one expert in each material discipline, if necessary or otherwise desirable.

Hence, it is inferred, that it is reasonable under CPR 35.1 for those reports already in existence to be used to resolve the proceedings.

CPR 35.7

259. Similarly, whilst CPR 35.7 provided the Court with the power to restrict evidence in appropriate circumstances, if reports already existed the Court must already have deemed them reasonable:

> CPR 35.7 is an example where the Court can, to save cost, resources and time, order that a single joint expert is appointed; that applies, for example, in cases where the amount in issue is relatively small and the single joint expert can relatively easily address the issues from the joint perspective of the parties. Thus, in this Court, quantity surveyors are sometimes appointed (often by agreement) as a single joint expert to address quantum matters in cases on final accounts and defects cases. Where, however, the Court has gone down the route, as here, of permitting all five parties to rely upon their own technical experts, with the concurrence of the parties, the Court has accepted that it was reasonable in the first place to permit the introduction of such expert evidence as is presaged in their reports.

Proportionality and Prejudice

260. Furthermore, Akenhead J did not consider it disproportionate to permit the claimant to rely on the reports. If the case against the settled defendants had proceeded, then EDF would have been prepared for trial on the basis that all the experts would have given evidence. There was no prejudice to the defendant, who had time to either call the two experts for cross-examination or rely on the proposition that no great weight was likely to be attached to the views of an expert who does not give oral evidence at trial. For this latter point, Akenhead J referred back to HHJ Coulson in *Gurney*:

> Although I consider that, in general terms, it would be artificial for me to ignore entirely the views of the other engineering experts, it should not be thought that any great weight can be attached to the views of any expert who will not give oral evidence at the trial. Moreover, the fact that the majority of the engineering reports reach broadly similar conclusions on causation is also, of itself, of little

account: cases of this kind are decided by reference to the quality of the expert evidence adduced at trial, and in particular the oral evidence. They are not determined by weight of numbers.

Costs

261. The question of costs had to be weighed up between the time saved by the removal of parties by settlement, the preparation that had already been undertaken to allow for the experts in question and the limited extra time that might be needed to deal with them in cross-examination. If the additional reports proved unnecessary to the reasonable resolution of the case, a special order for costs could be made in the defendant's favour.

Chapter Summary

262. By virtue of *Gurney* and *Shepherd Neame*, the central issue in this area is relatively clear. Once a report has already been disclosed in an action, the other parties in the action are entitled to use it to attempt to resolve those proceedings. They can do so pursuant to CPR35.11 and they are not fettered by CPR 35.1, 35.4 or 35.7. It is not necessary for the party relying on the report to be the party who disclosed it in the first place, and nor is it necessary for that party to remain involved in the proceedings.

263. What does this mean for privilege? It should be noted that the reports at issue in the decisions of *Gurney* and *Shepherd Neame* had already been disclosed to the other parties to the litigation. There is therefore an assumption underlying both decisions that those reports had already lost the protection against production by virtue of their privilege and so the proper use of the reports could be decided entirely on the basis of the provisions of the CPR.[3] The CPR does not create in these circumstances any form of 'quasi-privilege' to restrict their use by the other parties to the proceedings.

264. However, these cases do not deal with the issue of whether undisclosed reports of a third party which drops out of proceedings would be accessible to the parties remaining. However, it is to be implied from the application of CPR 35.11 to 'disclosed' reports only, and the general principles discussed in chapters 2 and 3, that such reports would be privileged and could not be obtained.

[3] Note that Civil Procedure Rule (CPR) 35.11 refers explicitly to disclosed reports.

12

Collateral Use of Expert Materials

Introduction

Context

265. Chapter 11 discussed the circumstances in which reports disclosed by parties that are no longer involved in proceedings may be used by other parties to those proceedings. The discussion was limited to the use of reports in the *same* proceedings. However, commonly, an action in the United Kingdom may be followed by a similar or related action. The proceedings in which the evidence is disclosed may also run concurrently with proceedings in another jurisdiction, between the same parties and in which the same facts and issues are in dispute. For convenience, all such proceedings are referred to as 'collateral proceedings' for the purpose of this chapter.[1]

In either case, there is frequently the scope for one or more of the expert reports disclosed in the original proceedings to be useful to one or other party in the collateral proceedings. Can the evidence from the original proceedings be deployed in the collateral proceedings?

Rules for Witness Statements and Disclosure Documents

266. Under the rules of the Civil Procedure Rules (CPR), witness statements, disclosure documents and expert evidence are dealt with according to separate rules. Accordingly, the rules governing the collateral use of these documents are also to be found in different places. The collateral use of witness statements is provided for under CPR 32.12:

> Use of witness statements for other purposes
>
> (1) except as provided by this rule, a witness statement may be used only for the purpose of the proceedings in which it is served.
>
> (2) paragraph (1) does not apply if and to the extent that –

[1] Although special considerations may apply in circumstances where highly sensitive documents are disclosed to a legal team only and that team also represents their client in concurrent proceedings concerning the same issues. See, *British Sky Broadcasting Group Plc v Virgin Media Communications Ltd* [2008] EWCA Civ 612.

(a) the witness gives consent in writing to some other use of it;
(b) the court gives permission for some other use; or
(c) the witness statement has been put in evidence at a hearing held in public.

Similarly, the collateral use of documents disclosed in proceedings is governed by CPR31.22:

Subsequent use of disclosed documents

(1) A party to whom a document has been disclosed may use the document only for the purpose of the proceedings in which it is disclosed, except where –

(a) the document has been read to or by the court, or referred to, at a hearing which has been held in public;
(b) the court gives permission; or
(c) the party who disclosed the document and the person to whom the document belongs agree.

(2) The court may make an order restricting or prohibiting the use of a document which has been disclosed, even where the document has been read to or by the court, or referred to, at a hearing which has been held in public.
(3) An application for such an order may be made –

(a) by a party; or
(b) by any person to whom the document belongs.

267. It will be noted that, whilst they are expressed differently, both CPR 31.22 and CPR32.12 appear to provide the same basic rule—subject to exceptions, witness statements and disclosure documents alike may only be used in the proceedings in which they were disclosed.[2]

A Rule for Expert Reports?

268. If the collateral use of witness statements and disclosure documents is subject to CPR32.12 and CPR 31.22, respectively, what is the rule applying to expert reports? It seems clear that the treatment of expert reports is intended to fall outside both of the above rules: rhetorically speaking, why should the rule for documents in CPR 31.22 apply to expert reports when witness statements have been provided with their own rule on collateral use? Similarly, why should CPR 32.12 on witness statements apply when disclosed documents have their own rule? Furthermore, expert reports are in all other respects subject to their own regime under CPR 35.[3]

[2] Civil Procedure Rules (CPR) 32.12(1) uses the word 'served', but it is not apparent that this is intended to do anything more than reflect the usage of the term 'served' in respect of witness statements rather than 'disclosed', used for documents.

[3] See *L'Oreal SA v Bellure NV* [2006] EWHC 1503 (ch) 'I am not persuaded. . . .that the experts' reports under CPR 35 are governed by the regime under CPR 32. In my view, they are different regimes with similarities, but significant differences.'

The problem is, however, that under CPR 35 there is no rule corresponding to CPR32.12 or CPR 31.22. As discussed in chapter 11, the only rule in CPR 35 dealing with the use of expert evidence by other parties is CPR 35.11. This provides only that any party that has served expert evidence in UK proceedings cannot prevent any other party from relying on it in the same proceedings.

269. In order to fill this gap and understand the extent to which expert evidence can, if at all, be used in collateral proceedings, it is necessary to go back and examine the rules governing the collateral use of witness statements, disclosure documents and expert reports under the pre-CPR regime—to what extent does this survive in current procedure? To answer this, it is necessary to address the so-called 'implied undertaking'. In particular, what was the effect of that undertaking? Did it ever apply to expert reports and, if so, does it still apply?

Collateral Use Pre-CPR

270. An introduction to the application of the implied undertaking to witness statements and expert reports is provided in *Prudential Assurance Co Ltd v Fountain Page Ltd.*[4]

Implied Undertaking

Prudential Assurance v Fountain Page

271. *Prudential* arose from an action in the English courts (the '1986 Action') for damages for deceit and breach of duty against three defendants, with a fourth defendant being added subsequently. During proceedings, the Court ordered that the parties should serve witness statements on each other pursuant to the old Rules of the Supreme Court (RSC) Ord 38 r 2A.In addition, the plaintiffs were ordered under old RSC Ord 38 rr 36 and 37 to serve on the defendants a copy of the proposed report of their expert, Mr Todd. Further to these directions, the plaintiffs served five witness statements, together with attached documents, and Mr Todd's report. Later, the plaintiffs and the fourth defendant agreed to settle the action, but their solicitors (and then their solicitor's successors) retained the witness statements, attachments and expert report. Due to the settlement of the action there was no trial and the documents were never put in evidence in open court.

[4] *Prudential Assurance Co Ltd v Fountain Page Ltd* [1991] 1 WLR 756.

A few months earlier than this, proceedings had been initiated in the District Court of Harris County, Texas (the 'Texas Action'), by two Texas insurance firms against, amongst others, the fourth defendant to the 1986 Action. In the Texas Action, the defendants, including the fourth defendant, put in evidence documents that had been disclosed in the 1986 Action, including documents attached to the witness statements served in those proceedings. Subsequently, the fourth defendant applied in the 1986 Action (which had been stayed as between them and the plaintiffs) to be released from the implied undertaking applying to the documents which they had obtained on discovery in that action. They also asked the English court to rule that the documents they had already disclosed in the Texas Action were not subject to restrictions on use or disclosure as a result of having been disclosed in the 1986 Action.

The plaintiffs responded by seeking a ruling that the following documents were subject to restrictions, breach of which was a contempt of court, inter alia:

> any witness statement or document attached or appended thereto disclosed by the plaintiffs in the 1986 Action pursuant to the order of the court made in that action; and
> any expert's report or document attached or appended thereto disclosed by the plaintiffs in the 1986 Action pursuant to the order of the court in that action.

Meaning of 'Implied Undertaking'

272. Hobhouse J began by looking at the established treatment of documents disclosed on discovery. The relevant principle is described as an 'implied undertaking'. It arises in circumstances where a party has been put under compulsion of a court order to disclose documentary or factual material, whether wishing to or not. The implied undertaking is explained by Lord Denning MR in *Riddick v Thames Board Mills Ltd*:[5]

> A party who has obtained access to his adversary's documents under an order for production has no right to make their contents public or communicate them to any stranger to the suit. . . nor to use them or copies of them for any collateral object. . . if necessary an undertaking to that effect will be made a condition of granting an order. . .

Further, in *Crest Homes Plc v Marks*,[6] Lord Aylmerton said:

> a solicitor who, in the course of discovery in an action, obtains possession of copies of documents belonging to his client's adversary gives an implied undertaking to the court not to use that material nor to allow it to be used for any purpose other

[5] *Riddick v Thames Board Mills Ltd* [1977] QB 881.
[6] *Crest Homes Plc v Marks [1987]* AC 829.

> than the proper conduct of that action on behalf of his client. . . It must not be used for any 'collateral or ulterior' purpose . . .

Consequences of Breach

273. Hobhouse J summarised the nature and consequences of breach of an implied undertaking:

> This undertaking is implied whether the court expressly requires it or not. The expression of the obligation as an implied undertaking given to the court derives from the historical origin of the principle. It is now in reality a legal obligation which arises by operation of law by virtue of the circumstances under which the relevant person obtained the documents or information. However, treating it as having the character of an implied undertaking continues to serve a useful purpose in that it confirms that the obligation is one which is owed to the court for the benefit of the parties, not one which is owed simply to the parties; likewise, it is an obligation which the court has the right to control and can modify or release a party from. It is an obligation which arises from legal process and therefore is within the control of the court, gives rise to direct sanctions which the court may impose (viz contempt of court) and can be relieved or modified by an order of the court. It is thus a formulation of the obligation which has merit and convenience and enables it to be treated flexibly having regard to the circumstances of any particular case. Treating the duty as one which is owed to the court and breach of which is contempt of court also involves the principle that such contempts of court can be restrained by injunction and that any person who knowingly aids a contempt or does acts which are inconsistent with the undertaking is himself in contempt and liable to sanctions.[7]
>
> The implied undertaking also applies to the parties' lawyers, and probably any third party that comes into contact with the protected documents.[8]

Hobhouse J distilled the following principle behind the implied undertaking—where a party is compelled to disclose documents or information, by enforcement of a rule of court or a specific court order, and whether it wishes to disclose that material or not, for the purpose of doing justice in litigation with the party to whom the documents are disclosed, it follows that such compulsion should be limited to that litigation between those parties and not for any other litigation or matter of any collateral purpose.[9]

The 'Compulsion' Principle

274. The 'compulsion' principle thus identified by Hobhouse J in *Prudential* does not, however, apply to documents obtained pursuant to orders or rules

[7] Referring to *Distillers Co (Biochemicals) Ltd v Times Newspapers Ltd* [1975] QB 613.
[8] See Laddie J, at first instance, in *Bourns Inc v Raychem Corporation* [1999] 1 All ER 908.
[9] For example, see *Home Office v Harman* [1983] 1 AC 280.

which if breached merely give rise to a default. It only applies to documents obtained under orders which if breached give rise to a contempt of court.[10] So pleadings, for example, are not covered by the compulsion principle and the implied undertaking will not be applicable to them. Furthermore, as Sir Nicholas Browne-Wilkinson VC commented in *Derby & Co Ltd v Weldon (No 2)*[11] concerning affidavits voluntarily put in evidence:

> The voluntary disclosure of documents in the course of interlocutory proceedings by a party does not come within the rationale which is the basis of the implied undertaking relating to documents disclosed on discovery. In relation to documents voluntarily disclosed, the court has not invaded the privacy of the party. The party has for his own purposes in defending a case, decided himself to use the documents rather than maintain his privacy. . . In my judgment the special protection given to documents disclosed under compulsion of discovery procedures does not apply to any wider class of documents.

The same would apply to documents which a party was required to produce because of the way they had been referred to in a voluntary affidavit.

Similarly, unlike disclosure documents, witness statements and expert reports served pursuant to directions under old Order 38 were not served under compulsion and were not protected by the duties or undertakings which the court implied in circumstances of compulsion.[12] Nonetheless, witness statements and expert reports were not treated alike, as the next section explains.

The Difference between Expert Reports and Witness Statements

275. As Hobhouse J discusses in *Prudential*, the issue of compulsion is not the only factor to apply when considering collateral use. The RSC themselves have to be considered to see if they impose their own restrictions. The judge found that on a consideration of the rules under which expert reports and witness statements were served, different conclusions were to be drawn about the confidentiality and privilege protection of expert reports and witness statements. As regards expert reports, there was to be no implied restriction or undertaking, because Part IV Order 38 had been made under section 2 (3) of the Civil Evidence Act 1972, which authorised rules overriding rights of privilege against disclosure. That the recipient of a report was entitled to use it in evidence is expressly provided in RSC Ord 38 r 42:

[10] See, for example, the Court of Appeal in *Bourns Inc v Raychem Corporation* [1999] FSR 641 where documents disclosed for the purpose of a taxation because they are relevant to an issue and therefore should in the interests of justice be disclosed, an implied undertaking arises so that the documents can only be used for the purpose of the taxation proceedings.

[11] *Derby & Co Ltd v Weldon, Chancery Division,* Sir Nicholas Browne-Wilkinson VC, The Times 20 October 1988.

[12] See *Comfort Hotels Ltd v Wembley Stadium Ltd* [1988] 1 WLR 872; *Derby & Co Ltd v Weldon. Chancery Division,* Sir Nicholas Browne-Wilkinson VC (Unreported, 18 October 1988).

A party to any cause or matter may put in evidence any expert report disclosed to him by any other party in accordance with this part of this order whereas in respect of witness statements there is to be a restriction, pursuant to rule 2A(8):

Not only did the implied undertakings relevant to documents disclosed under compulsion not apply to experts' reports, but the entitlement under RSC, Ord. 38, r.42 was unqualified and so a party's use of an expert report was not restricted to the proceedings in which he received the report[13].

On the other hand, a party on whom a witness statement had been served was bound by an implied obligation to the court, since Ord. 38, r.2A(8) expressly preserved rights of privilege.

Restrictions on Use of Expert Reports under the CPR

Limits on Interpretation of CPR 35.11

276. In *Prudential* it was held, under the old RSC, that expert reports could be used outside of the proceedings for which they were produced, because the implied undertaking does not apply to expert reports and RSC Ord 38 r 42 expressly provides for a party to any cause or matter to put in evidence any expert report disclosed to the party by any other party. However, as mentioned above, the CPR is silent on the issue of collateral use of expert reports and the commentary to CPR 35 provides no further guidance. Does it follow from this that CPR 35.11 allows use of such reports in parallel proceedings and that the finding of Hobhouse J in *Prudential* should prevail under the CPR?

The wording of CPR 35.11 only refers to use by any party 'at the trial' and so on first glance it seems possible that it is intended to infer a restriction on the use in other trials elsewhere when, by comparison, old RSC Ord 38 r 42 referred more broadly to use by 'a party to any cause or matter'. On the other hand, if CPR 35.11 is only concerned with the same proceedings, it does not necessarily follow that it is intended to do anything more than any prevailing rules on collateral use.

Guidance in L'Oreal v Bellure

277. The clearest statement on the position of expert reports comes in *L'Oreal SA v Bellure NV*.[14] In *L'Oreal* an application was made to use the evidence of a survey expert, Mr Barter, prepared for and used in an earlier action. It was put in argument to Peter Smith that the expert evidence can be used under

[13] An approach followed by the Court of Appeal in *Bourns Inc v Raychem Corporation* [1999] FSR 641.

[14] *L'Oreal SA v Bellure NV* [2006] EWHC 1503 (Ch).

CPR 35, the regime that applies to witnesses, under CPR 32, and in particular the restriction of 32.12, does not apply. The judge found as follows:

> That is a difficult question to answer. It seems to me that the position before the CPR was summarised in the case of *Bourns Inc v Raychem (No.2)* . . ., where service of a report waived the privilege. I see nothing in the CPR that takes that away. In the case of witness statements it is taken away by virtue of the provisions of CPR, r.32.12. I am not persuaded by Miss Reid's submissions that the experts' reports under CPR 35 are governed by the regime under CPR 32. In my view, they are different regimes with similarities but significant differences. First of all, the purpose of the evidence under the two regimes is entirely different. The witness statement regime is designed to allow a party to adduce their evidence in a particular way with a statement of truth attached to them. An expert report, whilst it is tendered on behalf of a party, is nevertheless tendered to the court to assist the court. The expert in his report gives a declaration which is far removed from the mere statement of truth that the witness gives. Further, his evidence is not called a witness statement. It is called a report. I do not believe that the regimes are merged together under CPR 32. They are separate. Therefore, in my view, Mr Moody-Stewart is quite right that there is no rule or privilege which the claimant can claim in respect of a report once it has been disclosed in an action.

Peter Smith J's view is therefore that the current law is the same as the pre-CPR regime applicable to expert reports. In other words, he appears to accept, without saying so expressly, that the implied undertaking does not apply to expert reports under the CPR and the CPR provides no restriction itself.

Restrictions on Using Documents Referred to in Report

278. In chapters 4 and 5 the rules relating to documents referred to in expert reports are discussed. Assuming that a document is produced further to the principles discussed in those chapters, how is the further use of that document in collateral proceedings governed? Does CPR 31.22 apply or are such documents to be dealt with in the same way as expert evidence itself?

Guidance in SmithKline Beecham

279. *SmithKline Beecham v Generics (UK) Ltd*[15] (the facts of which are discussed later in the section entitled 'Exercising Discretion to Protect Material') concerned an application by Generics (UK) Ltd to have restrictions placed on certain documents using CPR 31.22(2). It was submitted on behalf of SmithKline, and further to the decision in *Prudential*, that pre-CPR, the

[15] *SmithKline Beecham v Generics (UK) Ltd* [2004] 1 WLR 1479.

expert report of Professor Mullin,[16] and the documents referred to in it, were not subject to an implied undertaking. They therefore were in the public domain and could not now be restricted. It was also argued that another set of documents (called the Darmstadt documents) had been produced voluntarily, having been obtained from a third party by Generics. The consequence, SmithKline said, was that neither an implied undertaking nor CPR 31.22(2) would apply to these documents. Their argument is recorded by Aldous LJ:

> [SmithKline] accepted that CPR r.31.22 was a complete code. The first 25 words were a substitute for the implied undertaking that applied pre-CPR. CPR r.31.22(1)(a), (b) and (c) contained exceptions which also applied pre-CPR. CPR r.31.22(2) enabled the court to make a restriction or prohibition order in respect of a document 'which has been disclosed . . .' Such documents are those produced pursuant to the obligation of disclosure under such rules as CPR, r.31.5 and r.31.6. There was a difference between a document which had been disclosed and one which a party had a right to inspect. CPR, r.31.14 gave a right to inspect documents. At the date of the application the rule included a right to inspect documents referred to in expert's reports.[17] That difference between documents disclosed and those which could be inspected perpetuated the difference which existed under the RSC between documents produced on discovery which were subject to the implied undertaking and those which had to be produced or were produced voluntarily. It followed that documents which were produced voluntarily or in expert's reports were not documents 'which have been disclosed' and therefore the court did not have power to restrict their use under CPR, r. 31.22(2).

In other words, *SmithKline Beecham* is saying that although the Part 31 regime wiped away the old RSC rules, it actually preserved the distinction between documents produced on compulsion and those produced voluntarily. The former group fell under the compulsion rule discussed earlier in the section entitled 'The "compulsion" principle'and were therefore protected by the implied undertaking. The latter group, being voluntarily produced, was not covered by the implied undertaking and could be used in collateral proceedings. Documents produced further to reference in an expert report were in the latter group as, in this case, were the Darmstadt documents.

However, Aldous LJ agreed that Part 31 is a complete code, but rejected the submission that the CPR perpetuated in all respects the distinction between documents compulsorily produced further to disclosure in a list of documents and those that might be disclosed and produced in another way:

> The obligation to disclose and the ability to inspect are dealt with separately as is the ability to use a document after disclosure. CPR, r.31.3 is concerned with disclosed documents but reserves an ability to refuse inspection. CPR, r.31.14 adds to CPR,

16 The Court of Appeal did not need to decide the status of the expert report itself in this case.

17 See the discussion in chapter 4 regarding the change that has since occurred to the drafting of CPR 31.14.

> r.31.3. In any case the wide definition in CPR, r.31.2 must be determinative. That states that 'A party discloses a document by stating that the document exists or has existed'. No distinction is sought to be drawn between documents obtained from third parties and no limitation is placed on the way that the statement is made. In my view a reference by a party to a document in a witness statement is a statement that the document exists. I therefore reject Mr Turner's submission. It follows that the judge was right to consider the application by Generics as an application under CPR, r.31.22(2). He was also right to conclude that the *Lilly Icos* case gave guidance as to the considerations he should have in mind.

So, further to *SmithKline Beecham*, disclosure is disclosure. It is defined according to the simple definition in CPR 31.2. Any document obtained further to such disclosure may be subject to restriction under CPR 31.22, whether produced as part of expert materials, from a third party or in any other way.

The court's discretion under CPR 31.22(2) and the effect of reading a document in open court are discussed later in the section entitled 'Documents Read in Open Court'. First, how is expert deposition evidence treated?

Restrictions on Use of Deposition Evidence

280. How is expert evidence given by deposition treated under the CPR? Is it different to voluntarily produced expert evidence? Assistance on this question is given by the case of *Dendron GmbH v The Regents of the University of California.*[18]

Dendron—Facts

281. In *Dendron*, the claimants sought the revocation of a patent owned by the defendant. The patent related to a special apparatus for accurately getting a device called a Guglielmi Detachable Coil to a desired location in a patient's arteries, in order to treat aneurysms—the weakening and occasional rupturing of the artery walls. There were two other parallel sets of proceedings on foot in The Netherlands and Germany, and opposition proceedings in the European Patent Office (EPO).

The UK proceedings focussed on an issue of prior use of the invention, which, if made out, would render the patent invalid. The essence of the allegation was that the technique and apparatus of the invention covered by the patent had been used extensively and openly by a considerable number of people in a number of locations before the priority date of the patent. In support of this allegation the claimants applied for two letters of

[18] *Dendron GmbH v The Regents of the University of California* [2004] FSR 43.

request. The first was made under Council Regulation (EC) 1206/2001 of 28 May 2001 on cooperation between the courts of the Member States in the taking of evidence in civil or commercial matters, [19] by the English High Court to the Amtsgericht of Freiburg, Germany. It concerned an order for the examination of Professor Martin Schumacher, a neuroradiologist at the University of Freiburg. Professor Schumacher had been present, amongst others, during some of the pre-priority date surgical procedures which were alleged to constitute prior use.

The second letter of request was not made under Regulation 1206/2001, but instead directed to the courts in Alabama, USA. This request sought the deposition of a Professor Horton, who was also alleged to have seen procedures using the apparatus later claimed in the patent in suit.

The claimants wanted to use the documents and evidence gathered from the depositions of Schumacher and Horton in the EPO and in the German and Dutch courts.

Consequently, applications were made to Laddie J by the claimants to confirm that they could use the Schumacher and Horton testimony wherever they liked. Should permission be needed, they also applied for that permission.

Dendron—Application of the Compulsion Principle to Depositions

282. First, Laddie J found first that evidence collected under Regulation 1206/2001 had a limited purpose and hence there was a limitation on the power to use material produced under it to that sanctioned by the UK court. Having dealt with that issue, he then turned to the wider question of collateral use of deposition evidence.

283. It was argued by the claimants that there is no implied undertaking like that existing pre-CPR and applying to discovery that could be used to restrict the use of discovered documents. Furthermore, the claimants said, if there were an implied undertaking it only applied to documents produced on disclosure or on a compulsory inspection, not evidence obtained by deposition. In addition, the argument continued, the CPR is a complete code for dealing with the use of material obtained by compulsion during the proceedings and, insofar as evidence is concerned, the only limitation on the use of depositions is the narrow one relating to examinations about assets contained in CPR 34.12:

> (1) Where the court orders a party to be examined about his or any other assets for the purpose of any hearing except the trial, the deposition may be used only for the purpose of the proceedings in which the order was made.

[19] OJ C 314/2000 P 1

(2) However, it may be used for some other purpose:–
(a) by the party who was examined;
(b) if the party who was examined agrees; or
(c) if the court gives permission.

On the issue of whether depositions would be subject to the compulsion principle, and therefore an implied undertaking, Laddie J said:

> I do not accept that there is a difference in principle between obtaining disclosure or inspection by compulsion on the one hand and obtaining evidence by compulsion on the other. These are all different ways of achieving the same objective, namely the provision of information which can be used to prove relevant facts at the trial. I do not see why, as a matter of principle, it should make any difference whether the information is obtained in the form of a written document, examination of equipment or a process or by examination of a witness . . . I cannot see why the same information obtained by compulsion from an unwilling witness should be treated any differently. Of course, once the evidence is given in court, it will be free to be used subject to any special order made by the court.

That is, subject to the effect of the CPR, there effectively exists an implied obligation not to use, as there did with documents, without the permission of the court or the consent of the witness, evidence obtained by compulsion under letters of request in collateral proceedings.

Dendron—Effect of the CPR on Deposition Evidence

284. What was the effect of the CPR? In reliance on *SmithKline Beecham*, the claimants argued that since CPR 31 is a complete code, CPR 34 should be considered a complete code also. As such, it was said, there was no longer any place for the implied undertaking. However, Laddie J took the following view:

> In *SmithKline Beecham* the Court of Appeal said that CPR 31 is a complete code. That Part deals with the disclosure and inspection of documents only. In relation to that, there can be little doubt that the principles restricting the collateral use of material produced under compulsion has been lifted out of the case law and, with certain modifications, codified. That case and CPR 31 are not concerned with the taking of evidence under compulsion. That is dealt with by CPR 34. [The claimants] say if the principles in *Alterskye*[20] still apply, CPR 34.12 would be otiose.
>
> This is a powerful argument. However, with some hesitation, I reject it. If one were convinced that the provisions of CPR 34 were attempting to cover all possible situations and had clearly in mind all restrictions to be placed on the use of evidence obtained under compulsion [the claimants'] argument would

[20] *Alterskye v Scott* [1948] 1 All ER 469 is early authority for the implied undertaking that parties are not to make improper use of disclosed documents, later applied by *Home Office v Harman* [1983] 1 AC 280 and *Riddick v Thames Board Mills* [1977] QB 881.

be unanswerable. However, I do not think it is safe to assume that CPR 34 was intended to be a definitive code in relation to the issue of collateral use of evidence. It does not appear that such use has figured much in the jurisprudence before the CPR. The case law on collateral use of documents produced on disclosure was extensive and well known. For that reason it was an obvious candidate for codification and, where necessary, modification. The same does not apply where collateral use of evidence is concerned. I am not persuaded that the implied restriction on collateral use has been removed by the CPR.

285. The finding of the judge in *Dendron* therefore appears to be that evidence given under compulsion by deposition is covered by the implied undertaking. Unlike CPR 31, CPR 34 is not a complete code that replaces the rules pre-CPR. Consequently, because collateral use is not provided for in CPR 34, the implied undertaking survives to restrict the collateral use that may be made of deposition evidence. However, as with the use of documents referred to in expert reports (see earlier section entitled 'Restrictions on Using Documents Referred to in Report'), attention must be given to whether documents subject to an implied undertaking have later been 'referred to in open court' (see section entitled 'Documents Read in Open Court').

Restrictions on Use of Expert Material by Third Party

286. So far, this chapter has discussed the restrictions, or lack of restrictions, on the use of expert material in collateral proceedings by those parties on whom the material has originally been served. This section turns to look at how a third party may obtain such material.

Paul Sayers v SmithKline Beecham

287. Another important case on collateral use of expert reports is *Paul Sayers v SmithKline Beecham Plc.*[21] In *Paul Sayers*, the defendants started with the assumption that they were required to seek permission to use experts' reports in parallel proceedings. This is even though the documents sought were from UK defendants in whose interests it was that they should have them. Hence, the case does not throw light on the relationship between CPR Part 35 and the implied undertaking, but it illustrates that there is another avenue that may be used under the CPR in order to obtain expert evidence, if you are a third party which was not involved in the proceedings for which the evidence was served. That is, by using CPR 5.4C.

[21] *Paul Sayers v SmithKline Beecham Plc* [2007] EWHC 1346 (QB).

Background

288. *Paul Sayers* concerned an application by the Secretary of the Department of Health and Human Services of the United States of America for evidence prepared by the defendants in UK litigation. It was set against the MMR/MR vaccine litigation which comprised a large number of claims by children who had been vaccinated with the measles, mumps and rubella (MMR) combination vaccine or the measles and rubella (MR) combination vaccine. These vaccinations had been conducted as part of a mass immunisation programme introduced in 1988 by the NHS. Various adverse effects were alleged as a consequence of these vaccinations, including autism and inflammatory bowel disease. The evidence was sought from the records of the court that had been filed by the defendants in the UK litigation—a number of pharmaceutical companies which manufactured or licensed the vaccines.

The documents were needed by the Secretary of Health to assist in defence proceedings on similar litigation in the United States, called the Omnibus Autism Proceedings. The Omnibus Autism Proceedings were of considerable public interest and importance, because if it was decided that the MMR/MR vaccines caused or contributed towards autism, vaccination uptake could be reduced with the consequence that the diseases at issue would increase. Furthermore, the cost of compensating petitioners under the Omnibus Proceedings in the United States was estimated to run to several billion dollars.

The Documents Sought

289. A key allegation of the defendant in the first Omnibus Proceedings test case in the United States was that biopsy specimens of the defendant contained live measles virus. These tests were carried out by a Professor O'Leary. However, the specimens were no longer available for the Secretary of Health to attempt to replicate the tests. However, similar tests had been carried out by Professor O'Leary on biopsy specimens provided by claimants to the MMR/MR litigation in the United Kingdom. Reports of the results of these tests also revealed the presence of live measles virus. The UK defendants' experts had been sceptical about these results, as comparisons with reports of the small amount of data they had been given showed a number of inconsistencies.

These concerns were recorded in the reports of three experts instructed by the defendants in the United Kingdom, and filed pursuant to a court order. Subsequently, all the data from the biopsy tests became available to the UK defendants and one of the defendants' experts, Professor Bustin, visited Professor O'Leary and reviewed all the tests he had conducted and the methodology used. A second report was then produced by Professor Bustin which commented on this methodology in light of what he had seen. Because Professor O'Leary's evidence, and possibly his data, was not to be produced in the Omnibus Proceedings in the United States, the only way the Secretary of Health could examine the biopsy results of the US defendant was to apply to use the expert evidence of the defendants in the United Kingdom, including the two Bustin reports.

Application of CPR 5.4C(2)

Scope of the Rule

290. The application for the expert evidence in *Paul Sayers* was founded on CPR 5.4C(2). CPR 5.4C(2) deals with access by third parties to documents on the court file other than statements of case:

> A non-party may, if the court gives permission, obtain from the records of the court a copy of any other document [a document other than that which is referred to in rules 5.4C(1) and 5.4C(1A)] filed by a party, or communication between the court and a party or another person.

As the judge in *Paul Sayers*, Keith J pointed out that the rule applies only to documents which have been filed with the court. It does not apply to documents which have been referred to in documents filed with the court, but which were not themselves filed.

Even then, there is further consideration that must be given when seeking documents under CPR 5.4C(2). If documents are filed with the court, on the one hand '. . . the authorities draw a distinction between documents which have been read or been treated as having been read in open court, or which would have been read by the judge in preparation for a hearing in open court . . .' and on the other hand '. . . documents which, though filed, have never been read or been treated as having been read by the judge'.

The distinction between documents read, or treated as read, and documents unread, is an important one. As Keith J stated, anyone who has a legitimate interest in having access to a copy of a document which has been read or been treated as having been read by the judge should normally be allowed to have it. However, documents which have not been read or been treated as having been read by the judge, should not be made available as a matter of routine. Instead, they should only be made available if there are strong grounds for thinking that access to them is necessary in the interests of justice.[22] In *Paul Sayers*, the first expert report of Professor Bustin, and the reports of the other two experts, were not read or treated as ever having

[22] *Dian AO v Davis Frankel & Mead* [2005] 1 WLR 2951; in respect of the collateral use of disclosed documents see *Marlwood Commercial Inc v Kosemy* [2004] 3 All ER 648.

been read by the judge. Therefore, access could only be granted on strong grounds that it was in the interests of justice to do so. The meaning and consequences of this distinction are discussed further in the section entitled 'Lifting Restrictions on Collateral Use'.

Relationship between CPR 5.4C(2) and 31.22

291. The expert reports that were sought in *Paul Sayers* drew on materials that had been disclosed by the claimants in the UK proceedings, that is, the test results on the biopsy samples. Consequently, rather than dealing with these documents as simple expert reports, Keith J clearly characterised them as more akin to disclosure and held that the principles governing whether they should be disclosed should not be different to those on which questions under CPR 31.22 are determined. This also avoided a two-tier approach to obtaining documents—had the Secretary of Health tried to obtain the documents from the court file under CPR 5.4C(2), they would be in a better position than if they had made the application under CPR 31.22, and this could not be right.

292. The second report of Professor Bustin was in a different category to the other reports. This report had never actually been filed with the court and therefore CPR 5.4C(2) could not apply. However, the judge said this did not mean the report could never be obtained: Merck, which received the document in the original proceedings, was willing to provide it to the Secretary of Health, but to do so it would first need to make an application under CPR 31.22 for the court's permission. But, the judge could not see how such an application could be decided differently to the Secretary of Health's application under 5.4C(2).

The judge held that the interests of justice and the public interest in the outcome of the US proceedings were sufficient to require disclosure of the documents, since the US judge would otherwise have a one-sided view of the other evidence at issue and the outcome of the case was of '*immense public interest and importance*' (see section entitled 'Lifting Restrictions on Collateral Use' for a discussion of the circumstances under which the court will permit the disclosure of otherwise restricted documents).

There are therefore two apparent outcomes from this case: (i) the issues that must be determined by the court when deciding whether to permit the use of documents are the same under CPR 5.4C(2) and 31.22; and (ii) the hint that CPR 31.22 can be used indirectly by a third party to obtain documents through a party to the original proceedings in which the document was produced.

Identifying Documents with Precision

293. Anyone who does wish to obtain a document from the file should be aware that the court will not give permission for a party to trawl through the whole of the court file in the hope of finding something useful. Instead, in *Dian AO v Davis Frankel & Mead*,[23] Moore-Bick J stated that the court's permission is required before a search may be made for any document which, if found, may then be inspected and copied. Consequently, the documents which the applicant wants permission to look for must be identified with reasonable precision. In Moore-Bick's judgment, the rule[24] clearly did not contemplate permission to *inspect* the file as a whole.[25] Instead, it contemplates permission as a necessary first step to search the record for a particular document or documents. The judge considered it difficult to see on what basis the court could exercise its discretion to permit a search unless the applicant has first identified which documents it wishes to search for.

Documents Read in Open Court

294. As Keith J explains in Paul Sayers, there is a difference between documents which have been read in open court, or deemed to have been read in open court, and those that have not. The distinction is important, because if read, or deemed to have been read, in open court, a document should normally be made available to a third party which has a legitimate interest in having access to it. The basis for this rule is the principle of open justice.

Open Justice

295. There is a strong presumption in English law that cases should be both heard and decided upon in public. This is the principle of 'open justice' and it is held vital to the public scrutiny and awareness of the administration of justice. It is a principle that has come under increasing pressure with the increasing amount of written material that is now commonly placed before judges to read, but which is not necessarily read out aloud in court. This is particularly true of witness and expert evidence, where evidence in chief is

[23] *Dian AO v Davis Frankel & Mead* [2005] 1 WLR 2951.

[24] Decided under CPR 5.4(5) which has now been replaced with CPR 5.4C(2), however, the wording of the former 'Any other person may—(b) if the court gives permission, obtain from the records of the court a copy of any other document filed by a party, or communication between the court and a party or another person', closely resembles the latter.

[25] See also *The Queen on the Application of Mr Taranissi v Human Fertilisation and Embryology Authority* [2009] EWHC 130 (Admin).

given in written form rather than orally in court. There is therefore concern that access by members of the public to the content of such material will be diminished.[26] To counter this risk, the CPR provides rules to aid access to court documents.[27] For example, CPR 31.22 states:[28]

> (1) A party to whom a document has been disclosed may use the document only for the purpose of the proceedings in which it is disclosed, except where –
>
> (a) the document has been read to or by the court, or referred to, at a hearing which has been held in public;
>
> ...

The general tenor of the cases is in favour of disclosure to the public of materials that, in proceedings in open court, have been put into the public domain.[29] The example given by Keith J in *Paul Sayers*[30] has already been seen.

296. Before discussing the nature of the general presumption in favour of freedom of access to documents read in open court, the question arises, when is a document read in open court?

Meaning of 'Open Court'

297. In *Smithkline Beecham Biologicals SA v Connaught Laboratories Inc*[31] the basic principles applying to open documents were summarised:

> When, as in Home Office v Harman,[[32]] documents or the material parts of them are read aloud in open court it is plain that the implied obligation binding on the party to whom compulsory disclosure had been made comes to an end, in the absence of any contrary order by the court. The same result must follow if counsel in open court draws the attention of the judge to a document which the judge then reads to himself. These are the simplest cases. The present appeal obliges the court to consider the application of the rule in less obvious cases, and in doing so to take account of changing forensic practice. For reasons which are very familiar, it is no longer the practice for counsel to read documents aloud in open court or to lead the judge, document by document, through the evidence. The practice is, instead, to invite the judge to familiarise himself with material out of court to which, in open court, economical reference, falling far short of verbatim citation, is made. In this new context, the important private rights of the litigant must command

[26] See the line of authority beginning with the House of Lords in *Scott v Scott* [1913] AC 417 and continuing in *Clibbery v Allen* [2002] Fam 261 to *Hodgson v Imperial Tobacco Ltd* [1998] 1WLR 1056 and *Law Debenture Trust Corp (Channel Islands) Ltd v Lexington Insurance Company* [2003] EWHC 2297 (Comm).

[27] See *Chan U Seek v Alvis Vehicles Ltd, Guardian Newspapers* [2004] EWHC 3092 (Ch) for a discussion of this issue in the context of press access to documents.

[28] See also CPR 5.4C(2) and 32.13.

[29] Park J in *Chan U Seek* (n 26).

[30] See section entitled 'Application of CPR 5.4C(2)'.

[31] *SmithKline Beecham Biologicals SA v Connaught Laboratories Inc* [2000] FSR 1.

[32] *Home Office v Harman* (n 9).

> continuing respect. But so too must the no less important value that justice is administered in public and is the subject of proper public scrutiny.
>
> Derby v. Weldon (No. 2) establishes that Order 24, rule 14A applies even though a document is not read in open court if it is pre-read by the court and referred to by counsel in a skeleton argument which is incorporated in submissions in open court, or if the document is referred to (even though not read aloud) by counsel or by the court. We have no doubt this is a correct approach. If counsel did not summarise their submissions in a skeleton argument, and if the judge did not pre-read material before coming into court, it would be necessary for counsel in open court to make his full submissions orally and to read aloud to the judge or refer him to each page of the material relied on. In this way everything read or referred to would fall within Order 24, rule 14A and would be treated as having entered the public domain. To apply Order 24, rule 14A to such material does not derogate from the private rights of the litigant and preserves the rights of the public in a changed environment of practice.

In *Lilly Icos v Pfizer*[33] the Court of Appeal built on *Connaught Laboratories* with the following general observations:

> Although the principle of the orality of the English trial remains untouched, practice has moved greatly in the direction of the presentation of evidence and arguments in writing, the use of documents by reference to them in those writings rather than by their being read out in open court and the consideration by the judge of a large part of that material before the trial opens, so that it is not necessary to make specific reference to it during the trial itself.

The court in *Lilly Icos* then summarised the rules applicable to determining whether a document had been read in open court:

> In *Connaught Laboratories*[34] this court pointed out that the intent of (as it was then) RSC Ord 24, r.14A would be substantially frustrated if the rule were literally restricted to what had physically happened in open court. The rule was passed in the interests of the publicity properly attaching to the administration of justice, and of the interests of the recipient of the document under article 10 of the European Convention . . . To achieve those ends under modern practice it was necessary to take as falling under CPR, r.31.22(1)(a) any document pre-read by the judge, or referred to in for instance witness statements taken to stand as evidence, even if the document or the witness statement was not actually read out in court. Some further details of that regime may be mentioned, and then some comments offered.
>
> First, there are taken to fall under the rule certain categories of document, in particular those coming within the pre-reading of the judge. It does not have to be established that the judge has actually read the documents: once the category is established, it is for a party alleging that they have not in fact been read to establish that fact, something that has to be achieved without inquiry of the judge. [35] Second, it therefore follows that not everything that is disclosed or copied

[33] *Lilly Icos v Pfizer* [2002] 1 All ER 842.
[34] *Connaught Laboratories* (n 30).
[35] *Barings v Coopers & Lybrands* [2002] 1 WLR 2353.

in court bundles falls under this rule: the *Connaught* approach is restricted to documents to which the judge has been specifically alerted, whether by reference in a skeleton argument or by mention in the "reading guide" with which judges are now provided at least in patent cases. Third, since the *Connaught* approach is based upon the assumed orality of a trial, documents, however much pre-read by the judge, remain confidential if no trial takes place, but the application is, for instance, dismissed by consent, albeit by a decision announced in open court.[36]

The central theme of these rules is the importance of the principle that justice is to be done in public, and within that principle the importance of those attending a public court understanding the case. They cannot do that if the contents of documents used in that process are concealed from them: hence the release of confidence once the document has been read or used in court. As this court recognised in the *Connaught Laboratories Inc* case, there may be some artificiality about that approach. That is because full access to documents deemed to have been read or used in court may give third parties at least the possibility of much more fully studying and understanding the case and the issues in it than if they merely heard the documents read aloud. Nevertheless, that paradox helps to underline this court's concern that economical means of using and referring to the documents, understood amongst the lawyers, should not exclude the spectators from comprehension of the case.

Protecting Material Read in Open Court

Who Applies?

298. The last section quoted the following statement of the court in *Connaught Laboratories*:

> When, as in Home Office v Harman, documents or the material parts of them are read aloud in open court it is plain that the implied obligation binding on the party to whom compulsory disclosure had been made comes to an end, in the absence of any contrary order by the court.

If a document is read in open court so as to satisfy the rules in *Lilly Icos* and *Connaught*, the rule is that a person with a legitimate interest would normally be allowed to have it. However, this obviously implies that there are circumstances in which they would not. The basis for objection is that a document may still be protected pursuant to the judge's discretion under CPR 31.22(2):

> The court may make an order restricting or prohibiting the use of a document which has been disclosed, even where the document has been read to or by the court, or referred to, at a hearing which has been held in public.

However, further to *Connaught*, once read in open court the implied obligation is overridden and the onus on obtaining such an order in cases

[36] Connaught Laboratories (n 30).

under CPR 31.22(2) is with the party seeking to protect the document.[37] However, the position in respect of third parties is different. Whilst any party who has a legitimate interest in having access to a copy of a document, which has been read or been treated as having been read by the judge, should normally be allowed to have it, leave is still required by third parties to access such documents. As Potter LJ commented in *Gio Personal Investment Ltd*:[38]

> Thus, while the parties to an action have free access to affidavits and other documents filed in the action, a member of the public requires leave to obtain such access, which will normally be given if the affidavit or other document has been read in open court. It seems that this must also include third parties who wish to obtain expert reports. The position of parties to an original action who wish to use expert reports that have been read in open court for a collateral purpose is unclear. However, given that the better view is that such documents probably attract no implied obligation (see Section 12.3), it would be odd if a party were subject to greater constraint than under the rules applying to documents. Furthermore, there is no codified rule further to which a party can restrict expert evidence from collateral use, although it seems likely that, upon application, the court could use its inherent jurisdiction to do so.

Exercising Discretion to Protect Material

299. The way in which a judge should exercise his or her discretion under CPR 31.22(2) was at issue in *SmithKline Beecham v Generics (UK) Ltd*. Following *Paul Sayers* (see section entitled 'Application of CPR 5.4C(2)'), the same rules should apply to third parties seeking documents under CPR 5.4C(2).

SmithKline Beecham v Generics (UK) Ltd—Background

300. *SmithKline Beecham* concerned two appeals from decisions of Pumfrey J in the Patents Court. These related to the use of documents by SmithKline Beecham in collateral proceedings against Apotex. SmithKline Beecham was the proprietor of a patent relating to a process for producing a pharmaceutical called paroxetine hydrochloride anhydrate. In 2001, SmithKline Beecham started proceedings against Generics (UK) Ltd for infringement of this patent. Generics denied infringement and counterclaimed that the patent was invalid. Shortly afterwards, BASF AG began revocation proceedings against the same patent upon similar grounds to those raised by Generics.

[37] *Home Office v Harman* (n 9). Note that in this case the House of Lords held three to two that the implied obligation not to use documents disclosed in proceedings for a collateral purpose survived those documents being read or referred to in open court. In the aftermath of this decision, former RSC Ord 24 r 14A was introduced. The effect of this was to place the burden on the party disclosing the document as to why the implied undertaking should not be lifted (see *Civil Justice Quarterly 1999*, 18 Oct).

[38] *Gio Personal Investment Services Ltd v Liverpool and London Steamship Protection and Indemnity Association Ltd* [1999] 1 WLR 984.

These two sets of proceedings were not consolidated but came on for hearing at the same time.

During the proceedings between SmithKline and Generics, two sets of documents came into issue. These were the 'Darmstadt' and the 'Sumika' documents. The Darmstadt documents came to light because they had been referred to in emails disclosed in Generics's list of documents. These documents were eventually produced by Generics further to a 'confidentiality club' with SmithKline. The Darmstadt documents were also referred to in the expert evidence of Generics' expert, Professor Mullin. Professor Mullin also made a general comment in his expert report about the content of the documents and expressed an opinion on a particular point. He also gave an opinion in his expert report on the contents of the Sumika documents.

On the first day of trial, SmithKline and Generics settled, leaving the proceedings between BASF and SmithKline. On the second day of trial SmithKline applied to use the Darmstadt and Generics documents in the BASF proceedings.

On SmithKline's application to rely upon the documents in the BASF action Pumfrey J, applying his discretion, concluded that the interests of the owners of the documents could be preserved by ensuring the documents were kept confidential. The judge therefore admitted the documents on terms that they would be dealt with in private and made an order over trial under CPR 31.22(2). The documents were subsequently used in the BASF proceedings in cross-examination, which took place in private.

During the BASF proceedings, SmithKline started infringement proceedings against another party, Apotex, in respect of the same patent. It was SmithKline's belief that the Sumika and Darmstadt documents would be very important to the Apotex proceedings and SmithKline applied to be able to rely on them in those proceedings under restrictions of confidentiality. In the meantime, the BASF proceedings had come to an end and an application for a permanent prohibition on use of the documents was sought by Generics. Judgment on the Generics application, permanently preventing further use of the documents under CPR 31.22(2), said as follows:

> . . . I take the following into account. First, the subject matter of the documents is confidential. Second, they originate with third parties. Third, they are of peripheral relevance at best to explain the issues in the action. Fourthly, they are not part of the material which is needed to explain the judgment. Fifthly, they are not needed to explain the judgment of the Court of Appeal which does not refer to them. Sixthly, they cannot be explained without considerable context or speculation exposing their makers or the employers of their makers to further requests for further information.
>
> I keep at the forefront of my considerations the interests of public justice. Nevertheless, it seems to me that these documents do not require to be disclosed and in the circumstances I propose to continue the order made under CPR r 31.22 indefinitely accordingly.

This judgment was delivered three days before the application was heard to use the documents in the Apotex proceedings.[39] This latter application was dismissed

SmithKline Beecham v Generics—the Appeal

301. Appeals were made by SmithKline to (i) whether permanent restriction should have been put on the documents under CPR 31.22(2) further to the Generics' application (the 'First Appeal'); and (ii) whether use of the documents in the Apotex proceedings should be permitted under restrictions of confidentiality (the 'Second Appeal'). If the answer in the First Appeal was that it should not, this would have the effect of making the documents available in other proceedings and jurisdictions and thus provided the answer to the Second Appeal (see section entitled 'Identity between Implied Undertaking and CPR 31.22' for discussion on the Second Appeal).

Approach to CPR 31.22(2)

302. In the First Appeal in *SmithKline Beecham*, Aldous LJ referred to the *Lilly Icos v Pfizer*[40] case, in which the claimant patentee had disclosed to the defendants confidential designated material on the basis of a confidentiality agreement (a 'confidentiality club'). After the trial, all of which had been in public, the patentee made an unopposed application for an order under CPR 31.22(2) to maintain confidentiality in respect of the expenditure on advertising.

As Aldous LJ noted in the First Appeal, it was held in *Lilly Icos* that the Court would not be constrained by any confidentiality agreement when making a final order under CPR31.22(2) at the end of the proceedings.[41] The Court's approach to making a decision under CPR 31.22(2) was as follows:

> It may be convenient to set out a number of considerations that have guided us.
>
> (i) The court should start from the principle that very good reasons are required for departing from the normal rule of publicity. That is the normal rule because, as Lord Diplock put it in *Home Office v Harman*,[42] citing both Jeremy Bentham and Lord Shaw of Dunfermline in *Scott v Scott*:[43]
>
> 'Publicity is the very soul of justice. It is the keenest spur to exertion, and the surest of all guards against improbity. It keeps the judge himself, while trying, under trial.'[44]
>
> The already very strong English jurisprudence to this effect has only been

[39] Judgment on the application took some 11 months.

[40] *Lilly Icos v Pfizer* (n 32). See also section entitled 'Meaning of Open Court'.

[41] See *SmithKline Beecham v Connaught* (n 30).

[42] *Home Office v Harman* (n 9) 303.

[43] *Scott v Scott* [1913] AC 417, 477.

[44] *Benthamiana, or Select Extracts from the Works of Jeremy Bentham* (1843) 115.

reinforced by the addition to it of this country's obligations under articles 6 and 10 of the European Convention.

> (ii) When considering an application in respect of a particular document, the court should take into account the role that the document has played or will play in the trial, and thus its relevance to the process of scrutiny referred to by Lord Diplock. The court should start from the assumption that all documents in the case are necessary and relevant for that purpose, and should not accede to general arguments that it would be possible, or substantially possible, to understand the trial and judge the judge without access to a particular document. However, in particular cases the centrality of the document to the trial is a factor to be placed in the balance.
> (iii) In dealing with issues of confidentiality between the parties, the court must have in mind any 'chilling' effect of an order upon the interests of third parties:[45]
>
> (iv) Simple assertions of confidentiality and of the damage that will be done by publication, even if supported by both parties, should not prevail. The court will require specific reasons why a party would be damaged by the publication of a document. Those reasons will in appropriate cases be weighed in the light of the considerations referred to in sub-para (ii) above.
> (v) It is highly desirable, both in the general public interest and for simple convenience, to avoid the holding of trials in private, or partially in private. In the present case, the manner in which the documents were handled, together with the confidentiality agreement during trial, enabled the whole of the trial to be held in public, even though the judge regarded it as justified to retain confidentiality in respect of a significant number of those documents after the trial was over. The court should bear in mind that, if too demanding a standard is imposed under CPR r 31.22(2) in respect of documents that have been referred to inferentially or in short at the trial, it may be necessary, in order to protect genuine interests of the parties, for more trials or parts of trials to be held in private, or for instance for parts of witness statements or skeletons to be in closed form.

Patent cases are subject to particular considerations:

> (vi) Patent cases are subject to the same general rules as any other cases, but they do present some particular problems and are subject to some particular considerations. As this court pointed out in *SmithKline Beecham Biologicals SA v Connaught Laboratories Inc*,[46] patent litigation is of peculiar public importance, as the present case itself shows. That means that the public must be properly informed; but it means at the same time that the issues must be properly explored, in the sense that parties should not feel constrained to hold back from relevant or potentially relevant issues because of (legitimate) fears of the effect of publicity. We venture in that connection to repeat some words

[45] The Court of Appeal seems to have had two possibilities in mind: (i) if a party is at liberty to 'use' a disclosed document, the party may make it available to a non-party, in the absence of a special order preventing that; and (ii) if the court does make an order under CPR 31.22(2), but the document in question comes into the possession of a third party, for instance by accident or theft, then any use by the third party of the document with knowledge of the court's order will arguably be a contempt.

[46] *SmithKline Beecham v Connaught* (n 30).

> of one of our number in *Bonzel (T) v Intervention Ltd (No2)*: [47] "the duty placed upon the patentee to make full disclosure of all relevant documents (which is required in amendment proceedings) is one which should not be fettered by any action of the courts. Reluctance of this court to go into camera to hear evidence in relation to documents which are privileged which could be used in other jurisdictions, would tend to make patentees reluctant to disclose the full position. That of course would not be in the interest of the public."
>
> In our view, the same considerations can legitimately be in the court's mind when deciding whether to withdraw confidentiality from documents that are regarded by a party as damaging to his interests if used outside the confines of the litigation in which they were disclosed.

303. The first issue dealt with by the Court of Appeal in *SmithKline Beecham* was thus whether documents that had become available to the public should nonetheless be protected by a CPR 31.22(2) order. Applying the above guidance, their decision was that the first instance judge had been correct to use his discretion to place the documents under the protection of such an order.

Lifting Restrictions on Collateral Use

304. The last section discussed the consequences of reading a document in open court on an implied undertaking. It has the effect of opening that document up for use by a party in the absence of a restriction. However, what is the situation if the document is never read, such that the implied undertaking remains. Can it ever be used for a collateral purpose?

Identity between Implied Undertaking and CPR 31.22

305. Having come to this conclusion on the First Appeal, the issue that the Court of Appeal had to deal with in the Second Appeal in *SmithKline Beecham v Generics* was whether the documents protected by such an order should be released for collateral use in separate proceedings (the Apotex proceedings).

Aldous LJ began his analysis of this issue with the statement of the general principle set out by the House of Lords in *Crest Homes Plc v Marks*, per Lord Oliver:[48]

> Your Lordships have been referred to a number of reported cases in which application has been made for the use of documents obtained under Anton Piller orders or on general discovery for the purpose of proceedings other than those in

[47] *Bonzel (T) v Intervention Ltd (No2)* [1991] RPC 231, 234 [27].

[48] *Crest Homes Plc v Marks* (n 6).

> which the order was made[49] . . . I do not, for my part, think that it would be helpful to review these authorities for they are no more than examples and they illustrate no general principle beyond this, that the court will not release or modify the implied undertaking given on discovery save in special circumstances and where the release or modification will not occasion injustice to the person giving discovery. As Nourse LJ observed in the course of his judgment in the instant case . . . each case must turn on its own individual facts.

It will be noted that this statement of principle applies to documents protected by the implied undertaking. By referring to it, the Court of Appeal in *SmithKline Beecham* implies that documents made available to the public but then made subject to a CPR31.22(2) order should be treated in the same way as documents that, pre-CPR, would have been subject to the implied undertaking, or indeed are now automatically protected by CPR 31.22(1).[50] Consequently, the factors applying to expert documents restricted under CPR 31.22 and a deposition restricted by the implied undertaking should be the same. It remains unclear whether different considerations would apply to an expert report if it were subject to an order restricting its use.

The Cobra Golf Guidelines

306. Guidance on the matters that the court will take into consideration when deciding whether to permit collateral use of documents which are otherwise restricted is given by Laddie J in *Cobra Golf Inc v Rata.*[51] This was an application for leave to use discovery obtained by a party on the execution of their *Anton Piller* order for the purpose of possible contempt proceedings in an unrelated action. Having reviewed the leading cases, Laddie J set out the following matters and considerations as likely to be relevant to the exercise of the Court's discretion:

> 1. Documents may not be used for a collateral purpose without leave of the court or the party from whom they came.
> 2. That restriction on collateral use covers not only the documents themselves but also copies of them and the information they contain.
> 3. In this context collateral purpose means some purpose not reasonably necessary for the proper conduct of the action in which the discovery was given.
> 4. Strictly speaking, asking for release of the documents for use outside the

[49] *Sybron Corporation v Barclays Bank Plc* [1985] Ch 299 and *Halcon International Inc v Shell Transport and Trading Co* [1979] RPC 97; the Court of Appeal in *SmithKline Beecham* considered that the House of Lords in this passage of Lord Oliver's was not following the earlier statement of Whitford J in *Halcon* that '. . . the use of a document disclosed in a proceedings in some other context, or even in another proceeding between the same parties in the same jurisdiction, is an abuse of process unless there are very strong grounds for making an exception to the general rule. It does, I think, emerge that some overriding public interest might be a good example, but not the mere furtherance of some private interest even where that private interest arises directly out of or is brought to light as a result of the discovery made.'

[50] That is, they are documents disclosed that have not been read in open court.

[51] *Cobra Golf Inc v Rata* [1996] FSR 819.

proceedings in which they were disclosed is itself a collateral use, since it is a use of knowledge of the contents of the documents for a purpose collateral to those proceedings. However, this must be taken to be a necessary exception to the otherwise all-embracing effect of the undertaking.
5. The unsanctioned collateral use constitutes an abuse of process or contempt of court. Whether it gives rise to a civil cause of action is not clear.
6. The existence of the implied undertaking means that an application to release the party from restraint must be made before there is collateral use.
7. Normally the application will be made first to the other party and only after refusal will it be made to the court.
8. In exceptional cases, such as ones in which notice to the party of the intended use to which the documents may be put are likely to defeat the ends of justice, the application for release from the undertakings may be made ex parte.
9. When made ex parte, the court should normally impose an inter partes return date in the near future when the affected party will be able if he so wishes to argue that the documents should not be used. [[52]]
10. On any application to relax the undertaking, the court has a discretion which must be exercised to achieve justice on the basis of all the circumstances of the case.
11. The circumstances which may be taken into account include the following:

(a) The extent to which relaxation of the undertaking will cause injustice to the party which provided the discovery.
(b) Whether the proposed collateral use is in court proceedings or outside litigation (*e.g.* for disclosure to the press as in Harman[53]). Prima facie if it is for use outside litigation, it is not the court's function to release for that purpose.
(c) Whether, if the collateral use is in aid of criminal or civil proceedings, those proceedings are in this country or abroad.
(d) In so far as the satellite proceedings are in this country:

(i) If they are criminal proceedings, the court must take into account the possibility of the application being a method of by-passing the privilege against self-incrimination.
(ii) If the collateral use is for civil proceedings, the court should take into account:

(a) whether the hub proceedings and the satellite proceedings are similar in character;
(b) whether the parties in the two sets of proceedings are the same;
(c) the extent to which the party seeking relaxation of the undertaking would be able to obtain discovery by another route and, if so, which route is likely to be cheaper or quicker;
(d) whether the effect of the relaxation of the undertaking will have the effect of generating new proceedings or whether it will merely help in pursuing a claim or defence which already exists or could be run anyway;
(e) prima facie it is not in the interests of justice to hinder a party from advancing a good claim or defence in other proceedings;

[52] *Naf Naf SA v Dickens (London) Ltd* [1993] FSR 424.
[53] *Home Office v Harman* (n 9).

(f) prima facie it is not in the interests of justice to allow discovery in the hub action to be released for the purpose of supporting the initiation of contempt proceedings in the satellite action, at least if the two proceedings are 'unrelated'.

(iii) In so far as the documents are to be used in proceedings abroad:

(a) Whether those proceedings are criminal or civil;
(b) If the satellite proceedings are criminal, the court here should be wary of doing anything in this country which may subject the disclosing party to an unfair disadvantage in those proceedings;
(c) If the satellite proceedings are civil, the court should take into account whether the disclosure would put the disclosing party at a significant disadvantage in those proceedings – for example by forcing it to produce in the public domain documents which, under the local procedure, would not otherwise be made public.
(e) There does not appear to be any reason in principle why documents properly obtained as a result of an Anton Piller order should be treated differently to any other discovery documents. Once disclosed they are no more nor less protected by the implied undertaking.

The Interests of Justice

307. Whilst 'useful',[54] the guidelines in Cobra Golf were issued pre-CPR. Under the CPR the overriding principles also apply when considering whether to lift a CPR 31.22 order. In SmithKline Beecham, the Court of Appeal considered the most important of these to be the interests of justice, in particular the interests of the party seeking to use the documents and the interests of the party protected by the CPR 31.22(2) order.[55] [56]

[54] Aldous LJ in *SmithKline Beecham* (n 15).

[55] For considerations in the context of a serious fraud investigation see *Marlwood Commercial Inc v Kosemy* [2004] 3 All ER AC 289 in which the Court of Appeal said in balancing the public interest in investigating serious fraud under s 2(3) of the Criminal Justice Act 1987 (as amended) and that in maintaining the due administration of civil justice reflected in CPR 31.22, an important consideration would be the absence of any special reason for fearing injustice—, eg potential injustice in the use to which disclosure might be put or some unfairness in the foreign law involved. In principle the public interest in the investigation and prosecution of serious fraud outweighed the concern to control collateral use of documents produced compulsorily on disclosure. See also *Virgin Media Communications Ltd v British Sky Broadcasting Group Plc* [2008] 1 WLR 2854, in which the defendants applied for an order restricting inspection of documents disclosed by them to lawyers of the claimant other than those acting in the UK High Court proceedings. This was sought by the defendants because they wished to prevent those documents influencing the claimants' lawyers in two sets of parallel proceedings involving the same defendants. The Court of Appeal dismissed the defendants' appeal on the basis that the order sought would prevent the claimants from using the lawyers of their choice. It was also in the interests of justice that the knowledge of these documents should prevent the parallel proceedings being conducted on any false basis by the defendants.

[56] See also *Paul Sayers*, discussed in section entitled 'Meaning of Open Court'.

CPR 31.17 Must be Considered

308. A further material consideration put forward in *SmithKline Beecham*, pursuant to CPR31.17, is whether the documents could have been obtained under the rule enabling the Court to order disclosure from a third party if the disclosure is likely to support the party's case and is necessary in order to dispose fairly of the claim.
309. Ultimately, in *SmithKline Beecham*, in the Second Appeal, the Court ordered that the documents were to be released for use in the collateral proceedings, but subject to the protection of an order maintaining confidentiality.

Use in Foreign Proceedings

310. In *Dendron*, Laddie J revisited his decision in *Cobra Golf* and reflected on the Court of Appeal decision in *SmithKline Beecham v Generics*. An added factor that Laddie J thought should be taken into consideration was whether the release of the material from a restriction on collateral use would serve a purpose. In particular, the judge was concerned that where the intention was to place the material before a foreign court or tribunal that would not accept it or pay any attention to it, its release would be pointless. It would not serve the ends of justice.

Chapter Summary

311. Expert evidence is subject to different considerations to those governing disclosed documents when considering whether collateral use is permissible. Disclosed documents are clearly governed by CPR 31.22, but there is no express rule for expert evidence. In the absence of such a rule, regard to the pre-CPR concept of the implied undertaking may be of guidance, but is not definitive. The better view is probably that there is no implied undertaking and collateral use of such evidence is permissible, as suggested in *L'Oreal v Bellure*. However, this is not without risk and the only safe course is to seek the permission of the court.
312. Deposition evidence is subject to the rule on compulsion and, in the absence of a CPR rule to the contrary, covered by the implied undertaking. Documents referred to in an expert report are subject to a restriction on collateral use by virtue of CPR 31.22.
313. Documents and deposition evidence that is protected by a restriction and has not been referred to in open court may be sought for collateral purposes further to CPR31.22(1)(b) or, where the documents are on the court file, CPR 5.4C(2). Where documents have not been referred to in open court, and

thus are already protected from further use by CPR 31.22(1), considerations of whether it is in the interests of justice for the document to be used in collateral proceedings must be applied. In cases where the documents have been read in open court, the considerations of open justice must be at the forefront of the judge's mind when exercising his discretion whether to nonetheless protect the documents with a CPR 31.22(2) order.

13

Litigation Privilege—Competing Forces

Introduction

314. This chapter reflects on the relationship between privilege, as it applies to expert evidence, and Part 35 of the Civil Procedure Rules (CPR). Is there a smooth co-existence between the two, or are they opposing forces? If the latter, which of the opposing forces wins out? These are questions that require a look at the theory behind privilege and a consideration of how Part 35 applies to cases in reality. This chapter attempts to answer the above by briefly discussing that theory and summarising the various situations covered by this book to establish where the balance between privilege and Part 35 currently lies. First, the theory—is privilege an absolute right?

Litigation Privilege and Policy

The Rationale for Litigation Privilege

315. To address the theoretical nature and extent of litigation privilege it is sensible to begin by looking at the reason why it exists at all. In *Waugh v British Railways Board*,[1] Lord Simon of Glaisdale samples the writings of Thomas More and Samuel Johnson to assist him with an eloquent explanation of why litigation privilege is needed:

> Society provides an objective code of law and courts where civil contentions can be decided. But it contents itself with so providing a forum and a code (and nowadays some finance for those who could not otherwise get justice). Having done so much, society considers that it can safely leave each party to bring forward the evidence and argument to establish his/her case, detaching the judge from the hurly-burly of contestation and so enabling him to view the rival contentions dispassionately. It is true that this does not in itself give rise to legal professional privilege. Sir Thomas More, before his time for judicial and administrative responsibility, had a different system for the Utopians:

[1] *Waugh v British Railways Board* [1980] AC 521.

> 'For they thinke it most mete, that euery man shuld pleade his owne matter, and tell the same tale before the iudge, that he would tel to his man of lawe. So shall there be lesse circumstaunce of wordes, and the trwth shal soner cum to light; whiles the iudge with a discrete judgement doth waye the wordes of hym whom no lawier hath instruct with deceit; and whiles he helpeth and beareth out simple wittes agaynst the false and malicious circumuertions of craftie chyldren. (*Utopia*, 1516, tr. Ralph Robinson, 1551, Bk. 2, [ch. 7].)'
>
> This is all very fine; but that great moralist and master of common sense, Dr. Johnson, saw the snag. Quite apart from the descent of the judge into the arena:
>
> 'As it rarely happens that a man is fit to plead his own cause, lawyers are a class of the community, who, by study and experience, have acquired the art and power of arranging evidence, and of applying to the points at issue what the law has settled. A lawyer is to do for his client all that his client might fairly do for himself, if he could. (Boswell, *Life of Johnson*, ed. Birkbeck Hill (1950), vol. v, 26).'
>
> So the adversary system calls for legal representation if it is to operate with such justice as is vouchsafed to humankind.
>
> This system of adversary forensic procedure with legal professional advice and representation demands that communications between lawyer and client should be confidential, since the lawyer is for the purpose of litigation merely the client's alter ego. So too material which is to go into the lawyer's (i.e. the client's) brief or file for litigation. This is the basis for the privilege against disclosure of material collected by or on behalf of a client for the use of his lawyer in pending or anticipated litigation[2];

316. In the modern day, the adversarial system accepts (within limits) the 'circumuertions of craftie chyldren' on the practical and just grounds that 'it rarely happens that a man is fit to plead his own cause'. The lawyer is a mere alter ego to the party in litigation. The rationale for litigation privilege is a policy need to protect the counsel given to a party who would otherwise be unable to represent themselves. Hence, communications between a party and its lawyer are to be considered confidential as if that party were keeping its own counsel.

317. The protection of communications between a party and their lawyer is actually only one, narrow, part of the scope of such privilege—to repeat the words of Lord Simon: 'So too material which is to go into the lawyer's (i.e. the client's) brief or file for litigation' indicate that there is a broader need for litigation privilege to cover other work that is necessary for the preparation of a party's case.

In one part of his speech in the House of Lords decision in *Three Rivers (No 6)*,[3] Lord Scott of Foscote seems also to take a broad view of this right, and emphasises the flip-side of privilege; one should not have the opportunity to use a party's own advice against them:

[2] See Cotton LJ in *Southwark and Vauxhall Water Co v Quick* (1878) 3 QBD 315, 321–322; *D v National Society for the Prevention of Cruelty to Children* [1978] AC 171, 231; Law Reform Committee: Sixteenth Report on Privilege in Civil Proceedings, *The Modern Law Review*, Vol. 31, No. 2 (Mar., 1968), pp. 198–202.

[3] *Three Rivers (No 6)* [2004] 3 WLR 1274.

> Litigation privilege relates to communications at the stage when litigation is pending or in contemplation. It is based on the idea that legal proceedings take the form of a contest in which each of the opposing parties assembles his own body of evidence and uses it to try to defeat the other, with the judge or jury determining the winner. In such a system each party should be free to prepare his case as fully as possible without the risk that his opponent will be able to recover the material generated by his preparations. In the words of Justice Jackson in *Hickman v Taylor* (1947) 329 US 495,516, 'Discovery was hardly intended to enable a learned profession to perform its functions without wits or on wits borrowed from the adversary.'

Is Litigation Privilege an Absolute Right?

318. Given its broad and important role, how fundamental is this right and, ultimately based as it is on long-standing policy, to what extent can it be overridden by other matters of policy? The answer to this, at least in theory, seems to be clear to some judges. For example, in *West London Pipeline & Storage v Total UK Ltd*,[4] Beatson J reflects on the nature of legal professional privilege, generally: 'Legal professional privilege is recognised as a fundamental substantive right which prevails over the public interest in all relevant material being available to courts when deciding cases[5].'

And, in respect of litigation privilege in particular:

> Litigation privilege differs from legal advice privilege, which protects all communications to lawyers. It relates only to communications at the stage when litigation is pending or in contemplation, and only those made for the sole or dominant purpose of obtaining legal advice or conducting that litigation. The modern law on litigation privilege stems from the decision of the House of Lords in *Waugh v British Railways Board*[6], a decision in which the approach of the High Court of Australia in *Grant v Downs*[7], and in particular the formulation of Barwick CJ[8], was adopted.
>
> In *Waugh's* case Lord Edmund Davies stated that he would certainly deny a claim for privilege when litigation was merely one of several purposes of equal or similar importance intended to be served by the material sought to be withheld from disclosure. He stated[9] 'it is surely right to insist that, before the claim is conceded or upheld, such purposes must be shown to have played a paramount part' and[10]that 'the public interest is, on balance, best served by rigidly con-forming within narrow limits the cases where material relevant to litigation

[4] *West London Pipeline & Storage v Total UK Ltd* [2008] 2 CLC 258.

[5] Referring to *R v Derby Magistrates' Court, ex p B* [1996] AC 487, 507–508; *Re L (A Minor) (Police Investigation: Privilege)* [1997] AC 16, 32; *R (Morgan Grenfell & Co Ltd) v Special Commissioner of Income Tax* [2003] 1 AC 563 [7].

[6] *Waugh v British Railways Board* [1980] AC 521.

[7] *Grant v Downs* (1976) 135 CLR 674

[8] ibid 677)

[9] *Waugh v British Railways Board* (n 5) 542).

[10] ibid 543.

> may lawfully be withheld'. Lord Wilberforce said[11] that it was clear that the due administration of justice strongly required the disclosure and production of the Board's report on an accident, and that in order to override this public interest the sole or dominant purpose of the report had to be to prepare for litigation.
>
> . . . once it is established that a communication was made when litigation was contemplated or pending and for the dominant purpose of obtaining legal advice, the privilege cannot be overridden by another public interest.

Beatson J also quoted Lord Scott's speech in the House of Lords in *Three Rivers (No 6)* to support his view that privilege is an immutable right:

> If a communication or document qualifies for legal professional privilege, the privilege is absolute. It cannot be overridden by some supposedly greater public interest. It can be waived by the person, the client, entitled to it and it can be overridden by statute but it is otherwise absolute.

319. The message from Beatson J is therefore a clear one—litigation privilege, though based in public policy itself, is an absolute, inviolable right, not to be overridden by other matters of public policy. He is not alone, as this is also what Lord Scott thinks; to continue the quote from *Three Rivers (No 6)* above:

> Certainly in this country legal professional privilege, if it is attracted by a particular communication between lawyer and client or attaches to a particular document, cannot be set aside on the ground that some other higher public interest requires that to be done.

320. Beatson J's choice of *Three Rivers (No 6)* from which to seek support for the absolute nature of litigation privilege is an interesting one. First, *Three Rivers (No 6)* is of course about legal advice privilege, not litigation privilege, although the observations cited above are from a general summary of the nature of privilege as it is currently understood to apply. Secondly, however, and again obiter, a fuller reading of the decision also leaves some doubt about the correctness of the assessment of litigation privilege that Beatson J draws from it. In *Three Rivers (No 6)*, Lord Scott starts by asking why privilege is so special:

> So I must now come to policy. Why is it that the law has afforded this special privilege to communications between lawyers and their clients that it has denied to all other confidential communications? In relation to all other confidential communications, whether between doctor and patient, accountant and client, husband and wife, parent and child, priest and penitent, the common law recognises the confidentiality of the communication, will protect the confidentiality up to a point, but declines to allow the communication the absolute protection allowed to communications between lawyer and client giving or seeking legal advice. In relation to all these other confidential communications the law requires the public interest in the preservation of confidences and the private interest of the parties in

[11] ibid 531.

> maintaining the confidentiality of their communications to be balanced against the administration of justice reasons for requiring disclosure of the confidential material. There is a strong public interest that in criminal cases the innocent should be acquitted and the guilty convicted, that in civil cases the claimant should succeed if he is entitled to do so and should fail if he is not, that every trial should be a fair trial and that to provide the best chance of these desiderata being achieved all relevant material should be available to be taken into account. These are the administration of justice reasons to be placed in the balance. They will usually prevail.

Then before going on to consider legal advice privilege, he comments:

> As to the justification for litigation privilege, I would respectfully agree that the need to afford privilege to the seeking or giving of legal advice for the purposes of actual or contemplated litigation is easy to understand. I do not, however, agree that that is so in relation to those documents or communications which although having the requisite connection with litigation neither constitute nor disclose the seeking or giving of legal advice. Communications between litigant and third parties are the obvious example. This House in *In re L (A Minor) (Police Investigation: Privilege)* [1997] AC 16 restricted litigation privilege to communications or documents with the requisite connection to *adversarial* proceedings. Civil litigation conducted pursuant to the current Civil Procedure Rules is in many respects no longer adversarial. The decision in *In re L* warrants, in my opinion, a new look at the justification for litigation privilege. But that is for another day. It does not arise on this appeal.

321. Two things are apparent from what Lord Scott says in this passage: (i) that it is not clear to him why documents that do not constitute or disclose the giving of legal advice should be protected by litigation privilege, most notably those between a lawyer and a third party; and, ii) not only should litigation privilege not apply to cases in which the proceedings are non-adversarial, as exemplified by the case of *In re L*, but that this may extend to other situations under the CPR.

Point (i) is particularly relevant to privilege in expert evidence. Does Lord Scott envisage an argument that litigation privilege should not attach to elements of expert report preparation, or even to expert evidence in its entirety? Expert evidence is, after all, the work of a third party. Lord Scott's reasoning in this part of his speech appears to be that the basis for litigation privilege, and privilege as a whole, is to protect those communications with a lawyer as if he were keeping his own counsel—the narrow basis—rather than that work necessary to prepare his case—the broader basis. If so, this is at odds with the broad policy basis that he explained above. If the narrow policy objective is applied to litigation privilege then the logical conclusion is that litigation privilege does not apply to any work outside the scope of advice given by the lawyer to the client. At the very least, it would suggest that work provided by third parties that does not contain any element of advice is not covered. Even then, it is doubtful that an expert opinion could be considered as 'legal advice' so as to afford protection.

Although point (ii) is an established point of law as regards cases of the *Re L* type (see chapter 2), it is not clear from Lord Scott's reference to non-adversarial elements of the CPR whether the judge believes that the role of litigation privilege should be examined across the board of litigation, in those 'many respects no longer adversarial'. Whilst it is easy to understand that types of proceedings such as care cases should be treated differently, how can litigation privilege be adjusted to allow for the elements of the CPR that Lord Scott has in mind? In what respects can it be argued that since the introduction of the CPR and the overriding objective that proceedings are less adversarial? CPR 1 states:

> 1.1
>
> (1) These Rules are a new procedural code with the overriding objective of enabling the court to deal with cases justly.
> (2) Dealing with a case justly includes, so far as is practicable –
>
> (a) ensuring that the parties are on an equal footing;
> (b) saving expense;
> (c) dealing with the case in ways which are proportionate –
>
> (i) to the amount of money involved;
> (ii) to the importance of the case;
> (iii) to the complexity of the issues; and
> (iv) to the financial position of each party;
>
> (d) ensuring that it is dealt with expeditiously and fairly; and
> (e) allotting to it an appropriate share of the court's resources, while taking into account the need to allot resources to other cases.
>
> 1.2 Application by the court of the overriding objective
> The court must seek to give effect to the overriding objective when it –
>
> (a) exercises any power given to it by the Rules; or
> (b) interprets any rule subject to rule 76.2.
>
> 1.3 Duty of the parties
> The parties are required to help the court to further the overriding objective.
>
> 1.4 Court's duty to manage cases
>
> (1) The court must further the overriding objective by actively managing cases.
> (2) Active case management includes –
>
> (a) encouraging the parties to co-operate with each other in the conduct of the proceedings;
> (b) identifying the issues at an early stage;
> (c) deciding promptly which issues need full investigation and trial and accordingly disposing summarily of the others;
> (d) deciding the order in which issues are to be resolved;
> (e) encouraging the parties to use an alternative dispute resolution procedure if the court considers that appropriate and facilitating the use of such procedure;
> (f) helping the parties to settle the whole or part of the case;

(g) fixing timetables or otherwise controlling the progress of the case;
(h) considering whether the likely benefits of taking a particular step justify the cost of taking it;
(i) dealing with as many aspects of the case as it can on the same occasion;
(j) dealing with the case without the parties needing to attend at court;
(k) making use of technology; and
(l) giving directions to ensure that the trial of a case proceeds quickly and efficiently.

322. It is a feature of the CPR that the overriding objective should be furthered by encouraging co-operation between the parties. However, it is difficult to argue that the overriding objective goes anywhere close to removing the adversarial nature of proceedings generally. It is also patently obvious from the rules as a whole that they are intended to deal, for the most part, with adversarial proceedings. However, the imperative for the courts to ensure that parties are on an equal footing can be understood to encourage transparency. Furthermore, the court's duty to encourage parties to co-operate with each other in the conduct of proceedings is a direction to judges to see that adversarial stances do not compromise dealing with cases justly.

Whilst there is no suggestion from Lord Scott that litigation privilege should be abandoned for civil proceedings as a whole, he does imply that the application of litigation privilege to expert evidence is open to doubt and that there should be a new, more restrictive, scope of application for litigation privilege under the rules of the CPR. As chapter 3 sets out, there is plenty of support for this notion. The Access to Justice Final Report of Lord Woolf makes it clear that a number of the rules in the CPR were specifically designed to further the overriding objective by providing for greater transparency and co-operation between parties. These objectives were intended not least to apply to expert evidence.

323. Lord Woolf had originally recommended, in his Interim Report, that once an expert has been instructed to prepare a report for use by a court, any communication between the expert and the client or the client's advisers should no longer be the subject of legal privilege. Lord Woolf was eventually dissuaded from this stance, but it does say loud and clear the direction he was coming from. It also parallels the thoughts of Lord Scott.

Clearly then, the right to protect documents by privilege may not be such an absolute right at all. Senior judges foresee that the tide may have to go out on litigation privilege.

Part 35 Overriding Expert Privilege

323. That is the theory. However, this book is concerned with how litigation privilege applies in reality, under the CPR, in the important area of expert evidence. The next part of this chapter summarises some examples of where Part 35 affects the litigation privilege status of expert evidence.

The Starting Point

324. The protection of litigation privilege is established for communications and documents created between parties or their solicitors and third parties for the purpose of obtaining information or advice in connection with existing or contemplated litigation, if the following conditions are fulfilled: (a) the communications must have been made for the sole or dominant purpose of conducting that litigation; (b) the litigation must be adversarial, not investigative or inquisitional.

The starting point, as regards expert evidence, is that so long as the above conditions are satisfied, the work of an expert, as a third party communication, is protected by litigation privilege. This extends to both 'behind the scenes' expert advice and, in principle, to the draft reports of a Part 35 expert. So much is clear from the Court of Appeal decision in *Carlson v Townsend*.[12]

Similarly, in principle, the starting point for all communications with an expert that fulfil the above conditions is that they will also be subject to litigation privilege.

Instructions

325. Instructions to an expert present the first major point of contact between the general rule that litigation privilege will apply and the effect of Part 35.

As discussed in chapter 4, the regime provided by CPR 35.10(3) is specifically designed to override the application of the general rule to instructions. It directs that the substance of all material instructions must be stated in the report. If there were any doubt about the fact that privilege protection in these instructions has receded, CPR 35.10(4) makes it clear. The general rule is therefore subject to the policy need for transparency, fulfilling the imperative of Lord Woolf that forms the basis of these rules: 'it will be absolutely essential for the parties and the judge to know the basis on which the experts have been instructed'.

[12] *Carlson v Townsend* [2001] 1 WLR 2415.

Joint Experts and Discussions between Experts

326. CPR 35.7 provides that the court may direct a single joint expert to give evidence on certain issues. Where each party provides their own instructions to such an expert, CPR35.8 provides that the expert must provide a copy of those instructions to the other instructing parties. Therefore, these rules effectively oblige the parties and the expert to waive the protection of privilege in instructions that would otherwise have been so protected.

Similarly, the court will not allow one-sided conferences to take place with joint experts. Both parties and their lawyers must be present. To this extent the protection of privilege in any communications or documentation generated in, or for, such meetings is effectively waived on creation.

Discussions between unilaterally appointed experts are treated differently. Here, CPR35.12 will step in to protect the content of such discussions from being adduced at court. However, the protection does not apply to agreed discussions, which (if recorded in a statement) are open documents available to the court. Any statement produced between experts pursuant to a court order is deemed a CPR 35.12 statement. This is regardless of whether the statement was produced for use in mediation—the without prejudice status it would otherwise have enjoyed being lost if produced for mediation without the court's involvement.

Changing Experts

327. In circumstances where a party seeks to change an expert who has already been named in a court order, the cases of *Beck v Ministry of Defence*[13] and *Vasiliou Michael Vasiliou v Nicos Varnavas Hajigeorgiou*[14] indicate that permission to change expert will only be granted on the basis that the report containing the substance of the opinion of the unwanted is disclosed. The price of guaranteeing that the courts' permission to adduce expert evidence under CPR 35.4 is not abused, by expert shopping in particular, is the forced waiver of privilege in the earlier report. There is also a suggestion, as per the *Carruthers MP v Fireworks*[15] case, that the courts may go even further to require the disclosure of 'behind the scenes' advice, although there is no indication from the superior courts that they would go this far.

Use of Reports by Third Parties

328. An issue of a different nature arises when addressing what can be done with reports after they are disclosed to the other parties to proceedings. CPR

[13] *Beck v Ministry of Defence* [2005] 1 WLR 2206.
[14] *Vasiliou Michael Vasiliou v Nicos Varnavas Hajigeorgiou* [2005] EWCA Civ 236.
[15] *Carruthers MP v Fireworks* (Bristol CC 26 January 2007).

35.11 expressly provides that reports can be used by the other parties to the proceedings in which they are served, in those proceedings. However, no such clear rule exists as regards use of disclosed reports by third parties in collateral proceedings. Here the CPR is silent and, although the position is complex, the better view may be that no implied undertaking applies and such reports are available for collateral use. Thus, the protection of privilege may be lost forever. This contrasts with the position in respect of witness statements and disclosure documents.

Conclusions

329. When considering the application of litigation privilege to expert evidence, there are two forces at work that must be considered. One force is the application of privilege principles and the other is the effect of Part 35. It has been said, in some authorities, that litigation privilege is an absolute right that cannot be overridden by matters of public policy. On this view, only statute or consent of the party whose privilege it is can override the privilege. However, even looking at the subject theoretically, this is a problematic argument. Litigation privilege, for reasons that Lord Simon of Glaisdale explains in *Waugh v British Railways Board*, arises from policy—that a party should be able to treat third party counsel as if it were the party's own. Why then should it not be subject to competing imperatives of public policy?

The CPR are built on various pillars of policy, amongst them the desire for transparency and co-operation between litigating parties. Nowhere is this more obvious in the rules than in Part 35. Explored in this book, and summarised above, there are a number of areas where the general protection of litigation privilege recedes as a result of Part 35. Like a tide, it can draw back, revealing a bed of information. Furthermore, even where Part 35 does not apply directly, judges have shown their willingness to override privilege to ensure that the court's powers under the rules are not abused—nowhere is this more apparent than on the issue of changing experts, where judges may attach conditions of disclosure to granting permission for a new expert under CPR 35.4.

In *Three Rivers (No 6)*, Lord Scott says that there may need to be a reassessment of the role of litigation privilege under the CPR. Whether or not this statement reflects the mood of the judiciary as a whole on the scope of litigation privilege, it seems that it already reflects the reality, at least as far as Part 35 is concerned. Indeed this is the fulfilment of much that Lord Woolf had hoped to achieve with the CPR. The message is clear; as far as expert evidence is concerned, one cannot rely on the basic rule of litigation privilege alone. Nor can any assumptions be made based on the way disclosure documents and witness statements are treated. The rules of

Part 35 and, in certain cases, the survival of principles dating from the era of the Rules of the Supreme Court, have a direct and indirect impact on the application of privilege to expert evidence. This is apparent in the many circumstances encountered by practitioners when preparing such evidence. Litigation privilege is not absolute. We can expect judges to expand and build upon their powers under Part 35 and the protection of privilege in expert evidence may recede even further in future.

14

Practical Notes and Queries

The starting point with experts is that in all circumstances they must be instructed appropriately and with propriety. Ensure that an expert understands his or her role and duties and that both the expert and the legal team closely fulfil those duties.

From the outset with experts, always be aware of the possibility that instructions, documents or marked-up drafts, produced by or given to the expert, which are normally considered privileged and without liability of production, may nevertheless have to be produced at a later date. Also be aware from the beginning that the substance of material instructions given to the expert are not privileged against disclosure. Make sure that all the matters covered in the expert report are accurately and completely reflected in the instructions disclosed with that expert report.

When first communicating with experts, be clear with them as to why they are being engaged, or potentially will be engaged. Make sure they understand that they may ultimately be required to give evidence in court and the matters that evidence will relate to.

If the expert's views are preliminary, or based upon assumptions or limited information, make sure that is clearly recorded, even in drafts, notes or privileged material.

If possible, develop the evidence of the chosen expert as fully as possible on all the relevant issues before naming the expert in an order of the court giving permission to use that expert. Consider whether it is appropriate and acceptable to the court to name a field of expertise in such an order rather than the name of a specific expert, but note the requirement of Civil Procedure Rules (CPR) 35.4(2)(b) that the expert should be named 'where practicable'.

Careful thought needs to be given to any document referred to by the expert in their report. In particular, consider whether that document is part of the instructions or relied upon more generally. Be clear about why it is being referred to; is the content being relied upon by the expert? Is the report 'cherry-picking' the contents of that document? Is this a document that you would be happy to disclose?

Do not simply assume that copies of original documents used to assist with expert evidence, which are not privileged, will necessarily also be without protection of privilege. There may be narrow circumstances in which the copies will attract privilege. A particular example of this is where the selection of documents betrays the trend of the advice the client is being given.

Be aware that if a single joint expert is to be appointed, either by order or by agreement, then all instructions given to that expert are not privileged and must actively be shared with the other party. In addition, it will not be possible to have a one-sided conference with such an expert without the other party and their lawyers being present. Furthermore, be aware that any information that is not reasonably available to the other party may have to be shared with them.

If considering using an expert who has been appointed unilaterally by the other party, have a clear idea of what is hoped to be achieved—first, a court is unlikely to allow such an expert to be appointed jointly, and secondly, if subpoenaed, the court will be quick to prevent the expert giving evidence which is privileged to the other party.

Think very carefully before committing a third party to work akin to an experiment or survey. What is it that is hoped to be proved and will the experiment or survey realistically achieve this, or could it go wrong? There is great inconsistency in this area of law, but at the very least, if experimental evidence is to be used, the work-up experiments that laid the groundwork for that experiment must be disclosed. At worst, abandoned experiments—perhaps including experiments which have unhelpful results—may have to be disclosed too. This is particularly a concern when considering using survey evidence, where on the current cases all surveys would have to be disclosed, not just that upon which the party wishes to rely.

When thinking of using expert evidence, disclosed in one set of proceedings, in collateral proceedings, assumptions must not be made based on the rules applying to witness evidence and disclosure documents. The position in regard to expert evidence is complex, and whilst the better view may be that expert evidence (other than that taken by deposition) can be used in collateral proceedings, this is not clear cut and seeking permission from the court is the safest course.

Appendix A

Access to Justice—Final Report by the Right Honourable the Lord Woolf, Master of the Rolls, July 1996: Chapter 13 'Expert Evidence'

Introduction

1. It was a basic contention of my interim report that two of the major generators of unnecessary cost in civil litigation were uncontrolled discovery and expert evidence. No-one has seriously challenged that contention.

2. A large litigation support industry, generating a multi-million pound fee income, has grown up among professions such as accountants, architects and others, and new professions have developed such as accident reconstruction and care experts. This goes against all principles of proportionality and access to justice. In my view, its most damaging effect is that it has created an ethos of what is acceptable which has in turn filtered down to smaller cases. Many potential litigants do not even start litigation because of the advice they are given about cost, and in my view this is as great a social ill as the actual cost of pursuing litigation.

3. It was to meet these concerns that, in chapter 23 of the interim report, I recommended that the calling of expert evidence should be under the complete control of the court. Within that framework, I argued for a wider use of 'single' or 'neutral' experts who would be jointly selected and instructed by the parties, or, if the parties could not agree on a single expert, appointed by the court. I also put forward a number of other recommendations designed to achieve a more economical use of expert evidence in cases where opposing experts were involved, by narrowing the issues between them as early as possible.

4. In the second stage of the Inquiry I issued an issues paper on expert evidence, in which I reviewed the approach adopted in the interim report and its underlying objectives, and sought views as to the best way in which arrangements for experts could be improved to meet my overall aims. In particular, I invited responses from those with experience of the use of expert evidence in areas of litigation which were not considered in any detail in the interim report, such as intellectual property, housing, and construction cases, as well as of expert evidence in personal injury which was my main focus of attention in the interim report.

5. There is widespread agreement with the criticisms I made in the interim report of the way in which expert evidence is used at present, especially the point that experts sometimes take on the role of partisan advocates instead of neutral fact finders or opinion givers. My detailed proposals on experts, however, have provoked more opposition than any of my other recommendations. Most

respondents favour retaining the full-scale adversarial use of expert evidence, and resist proposals for wider use of single experts (whether court-appointed or jointly appointed by the parties) and for disclosure of communications between experts and their instructing lawyers.

Expert evidence within an adversarial framework

6. In the interim report I made it clear, in general terms, that I wanted to retain what was best in the English adversarial system. Any substantial curtailment of the parties' rights to adduce the expert evidence of their choice would certainly be a significant move away from the adversarial tradition. For that reason alone, many contributors to the Inquiry regard it as unacceptable. My concern, however, is with access to justice, and hence with reductions in cost, delay and complexity. The argument for the universal application of the full, 'red-blooded' adversarial approach is appropriate only if questions of cost and time are put aside. The present system works well for lawyers and judges, but ordinary people are being kept out of litigation. Where commercial litigants are concerned, the English courts are becoming uncompetitive because of unacceptable cost and delay.

7. The purpose of the adversarial system is to achieve just results. All too often it is used by one party or the other to achieve something which is inconsistent with justice by taking advantage of the other side's lack of resources or ignorance of relevant facts or opinions. Expert evidence is one of the principal weapons used by litigators who adopt this approach. The present system allows them to withhold from their opponents material which may be damaging to their own case or advantageous to their opponents'. This practice of non-disclosure cannot be justified, because it inevitably leads to unnecessary cost and delay, and in some cases to an unfair result.

8. The traditional English way of deciding contentious expert issues is for a judge to decide between two contrary views. This is not necessarily the best way of achieving a just result. The judge may not be sure that either side is right, especially if the issues are very technical or fall within an area in which he himself has no expertise. Nevertheless, he hopes to arrive at the right answer. Whether consciously or not, his decision may be influenced by factors such as the apparently greater authority of one side's expert, or the experts' relative fluency and persuasiveness in putting across their arguments.

9. In continental jurisdictions where neutral, court-appointed experts are the norm, there is an underlying assumption that parties' experts will tell the court only what the parties want the court to know. For the judge in an inquisitorial system, the main problem is that it may be difficult for him to know whether or not to accept a single expert's view. There is no suggestion, however, that he is inevitably less likely to reach the right answer than his English counterpart.

10. Less adversarial forms of dispute resolution are not, in any event, completely alien to our tradition. The various Ombudsman schemes have for a number of years provided a valuable service based on an impartial investigation by a neutral third party. Within the court system itself there are precedents for limiting the scope of expert evidence, in particular in the Family Division, where no expert evidence may be adduced without leave of the court and there is considerable emphasis on use of single experts.

Court control of expert evidence: a flexible approach

11. The basic premise of my new approach is that the expert's function is to assist the court. There should be no expert evidence at all unless it will help the court, and no more than one expert in any one speciality unless this is necessary for some real purpose.

12. I do not recommend a uniform solution, such as a court-appointed expert, for all cases. My overall objective is to try, from the start, to foster an approach to expert evidence which emphasises the expert's duty to help the court impartially on matters within his expertise, and encourage a more focused use of expert evidence by a variety of means. We should avoid mounting a contest between opposing experts where justice (in the widest sense) can be achieved between the parties without it. The key to achieving this is flexibility: above the fast track, there is no single answer that would apply to all cases.

13. Under the system of case management which I proposed in the interim report, the court will have complete control over the use of evidence, including expert evidence. The new rules will say that no expert evidence may be adduced without the leave of the court, which may be given as part of its own directions or specifically on application. There will be a range of options which the court will have a discretion to apply according to the type of case, or to the circumstances of an individual case. The options for limiting the scope of expert evidence will be:

(a) directing that no expert evidence is to be adduced at all, or no expert evidence of a particular type or relating to a particular issue;
(b) limiting the number of expert witnesses per party, either generally or in a given speciality;
(c) directing that evidence is to be given by one or more experts chosen by agreement between the parties or appointed by the court (this will extend the court's existing power under RSC Order 40, which permits the appointment of a court expert only on application by one of the parties);
(d) requiring expert evidence to be given in written form without the expert's attendance at court.

14. In cases where opposing experts are involved, the court already has power to direct the parties' experts to meet, before or after the experts have disclosed their reports, so as to identify and reduce areas of difference. Under the new rules the experts will be required (not simply authorised, as at present) to produce a report identifying matters agreed and outstanding areas of difference after such a meeting.

15. In fast track cases the exercise of the court's discretion will be more restricted. For the vast majority of cases falling within the financial limits of the track (that is, cases up to £10,000) the principle of proportionality of cost dictates that the scope

of expert evidence must be limited. The rules on expert evidence on the fast track will therefore limit the parties generally to one expert per side in any single speciality (with an overall limit of two per side) with no oral evidence. Single experts will be used wherever possible. These proposals are explained in greater detail in chapter 3.

Single experts

16. Since the publication of the interim report, resistance to my proposals on single experts has remained particularly strong, and it is clear that the idea is anathema to many members of the legal profession in this country who are reluctant to give up their adversarial weapons.

17. It needs to be understood that a neutral expert, under the system I am proposing, would still function within a broadly adversarial framework. Wherever possible, the expert would be chosen by agreement between the parties, not imposed by the court. Whether appointed by the parties or by the court, he or she would act on instructions from the parties. The appointment of a neutral expert would not necessarily deprive the parties of the right to cross-examine, or even to call their own experts in addition to the neutral expert if that were justified by the scale of the case. Anyone who gives expert evidence must know that he or she is at risk of being subjected to adversarial procedures, including vigorous cross-examination. This is an essential safeguard to ensure the quality and reliability of evidence.

18. The consultation process I have carried out has, at least, revealed a measure of agreement that single experts would be acceptable in certain types of cases or in certain limited circumstances, particularly on issues of quantum. Acceptance of a single expert on liability issues is generally limited to cases where the amount in issue is very small, or where there is little scope for disagreement. This is a helpful start, but without further measures it is unlikely to have any significant impact on cost.

19. I do not think it would be appropriate to specify particular areas of litigation where a single expert should or should not be used. There are in all areas some large, complex and strongly contested cases where the full adversarial system, including oral cross-examination of opposing experts on particular issues, is the best way of producing a just result. That will apply particularly to issues on which there are several tenable schools of thought, or where the boundaries of knowledge are being extended. It does not, however, apply to all cases. As a general principle, I believe that single experts should be used wherever the case (or the issue) is concerned with a substantially established area of knowledge and where it is not necessary for the court directly to sample a range of opinions. The expert's duty to the court will require him to set out in his report his view of the range of possible opinions. Too often under the present regime the experts are in fact agreed upon the range of opinion, but their reports only set out the extreme positions.

20. Given the strength of opposition to my proposals, it would not be realistic to expect a significant shift towards single experts in the short term. What is needed to initiate such a shift is a clear statement of principle in the rules, coupled with procedures to ensure that parties and procedural judges always consider whether a single expert could be appointed in a particular case (or to deal with a particular issue); and, if this is not considered appropriate, that they indicate why not.

21. A single expert is much more likely to be impartial than a party's expert can be. Appointing a single expert is likely to save time and money, and to increase the prospects of settlement. It may also be an effective way of levelling the playing field between parties of unequal resources. These are significant advantages, and there would need to be compelling reasons for not taking them up. It is certainly not sufficient to say that a party is entitled to adduce separate expert evidence provided he is willing to pay for it.

22. It has been suggested to me that by the stage at which case management starts, it will be too late for the court to control the scope of expert evidence because parties will already have appointed their own experts. There are of course circumstances in which a party will need to consult an expert before proceedings have started, sometimes even before legal action is in contemplation. It does not, however, follow that each party is entitled to rely on its own expert evidence for the purposes of litigation. Once litigation appears likely, the use of experts will be subject to different considerations: impartiality is of paramount importance, and because of the costs shifting rule, parties need to be protected against the extravagant use of experts by their opponents.

23. The use of experts before litigation has started cannot be directly controlled by the courts, but pre-action protocols of the kind that I am recommending in chapter 10 can help to encourage the parties to agree on a single expert. Failure to comply with the protocol should normally have consequences in costs. There will of course be cases where either party would be justified in not adhering to the protocol requirements, especially in relation to experts on liability rather than quantum, but the onus will be on the party to justify his decision.

24. I have said that in some cases there are good reasons for each side to appoint its own expert or experts. That need not, however, preclude a co-operative approach between the opposing experts, which should ideally start as soon as they are instructed. It should wherever possible include a joint investigation and a single report, indicating areas of disagreement where these cannot be resolved.

Impartiality

25. There is wide agreement that the expert's role should be that of an independent adviser to the court, and that lack of objectivity can be a serious problem. This may sometimes arise because of improper pressure on experts from solicitors, as was found in a survey of clinical and educational psychologists, the results of which were reported in the May 1996 issue of *The Psychologist*.

26. The present system has the effect of exaggerating the adversarial role of experts, and this helps neither the court nor the parties. As the Court of Appeal has recently remarked:

> "For whatever reason, and whether consciously or unconsciously, the fact is that expert witnesses instructed on behalf of parties to litigation often tend . . . to espouse the cause of those instructing them to a greater or lesser extent, on occasion becoming more partisan than the parties." (*Abbey National Mortgages plc v Key Surveyors Nationwide Ltd and others* [1996] EGCS 23)

27. The clear implication of this is that a new approach is required which emphasises experts' impartiality. In cases where the option of a single expert is not pursued, it is particularly important that each opposing expert's overriding duty to the court is clearly understood. This is partly a matter of good practice on the part of instructing solicitors, who may themselves need guidance as to the appropriate form of instructions to experts. In my view, clarification in the rules of court is also needed.

28. Contributions to the Inquiry from experts themselves suggest that there is a degree of uncertainty among them as to their duties, and a perceived conflict between their professional responsibilities and the demands of the client who is paying their fee. Experts would welcome some formal recognition of their role as advisers to the court rather than advocates of the parties.

29. The rules will provide that when an expert is preparing evidence for potential use in court proceedings, or is giving evidence in court, his responsibility is to help the court impartially on the matters within his expertise. This responsibility will override any duty to the client. The rule will reaffirm the duty which the courts have laid down as a matter of law in a number of cases, notably *Whitehouse v Jordan*, [1981] 1 WLR 246, when Lord Wilberforce said:

> "It is necessary that expert evidence presented to the court should be and should be seen to be the independent product of the expert uninfluenced as to form or content by the exigencies of litigation." (Cited by Cresswell J in The '*Ikarian Reefer*' [1993] 2 Lloyds Reports 68).

30. There was wide support for the proposal in my interim report that an expert's report intended for use as evidence in court proceedings should be addressed to the court. I now propose that there should be a requirement to this effect in the rules of court to apply whenever litigation is contemplated. This is a formal but important requirement. It does not imply that the expert is to be instructed by the court, but is intended to concentrate the expert's mind as he writes the report on his paramount duty to the court.

31. One of the recommendations in my interim report was that, once an expert had been instructed to prepare a report for the use of a court, any communication between the expert and the client or his advisers should no longer be the subject of legal privilege. My intention was to prevent the suppression of relevant opinions or factual material which did not support the case put forward by the party instructing the expert. There is, I believe, no disagreement with that intention, but it has been put to me very strongly that waiver of legal privilege is not the way to achieve it. The point has been made that experts must be free to submit drafts to clients and their legal advisers, so that factual misconceptions can be corrected. A further objection is that a great deal of time could be wasted if all these documents were disclosable, because the opposing party would have to comb through the various versions of a report to identify any changes, the reasons for which would not always be clear in any event. Another possibility is that lawyers and experts might begin to subvert the system by avoiding written communication in favour of off the record conversations.

32. I accept, in the light of these arguments, that it would not be realistic to make draft experts' reports disclosable. I do not, however, consider that privilege should apply to the instructions given to experts. The Chancery Working Group has pointed out that major problems can arise when opposing experts are working from different instructions, which leads to reports that are hard to compare and use. Joint or agreed instructions would meet this specific point, but even a single expert's report may be unclear or open to misinterpretation unless the instructions on which it is based are known.

33. Under the new system, transparency of instructions to experts will be particularly important. The effectiveness of pre-action protocols will depend on it. On the fast track, in cases where there are diverging opinions in two reports, it will be absolutely essential for the parties and the judge to know the basis on which the experts have been instructed. I therefore recommend that expert evidence should not be admissible unless all written instructions (including letters subsequent upon the original instructions) and a note of any oral instructions are included as an annex to the expert's report.

34. A further recommendation in the interim report was that any expert's report prepared for the purpose of giving evidence to a court should end with a declaration that it includes everything which the expert regards as being relevant to the opinion which he has expressed in his report and that he has drawn to the attention of the court any matter which would affect the validity of that opinion. That recommendation was widely supported on consultation, and I have come to the conclusion that a declaration along the lines I have proposed, coupled with the requirement for instructions to be disclosed, should be sufficient to meet my concerns about the disclosure of all relevant material.

35. The Working Group on Intellectual Property has proposed a form of declaration which would include statements that the expert:

(a) understands that his primary duty is to the court, both in preparing his report and in giving evidence;
(b) has endeavoured in his report to be accurate and complete, and to mention all matters which he regards as being material to the opinions he has expressed;
(c) has drawn the court's attention to any matter of which he is aware which might adversely affect the validity of his opinions;
(d) has indicated the source of his factual information if he has based an opinion on facts of which he has no personal knowledge;

(e) has not included anything in the report which has been suggested to him by anyone (including particularly his instructing lawyers) without forming his own independent view on the matter;
(f) will notify his instructing lawyers immediately in writing if for any reason he considers that his existing report requires any correction or qualification; and, if the correction or qualification is significant, will prepare a supplementary report as soon as possible; and
(g) understands that

(i) his report will form the evidence he will give under oath, subject to any corrections he may make before swearing as to its correctness;
(ii) he may be cross-examined on his report by a cross-examiner assisted by an expert; and
(iii) if the court concludes that he has not fairly tried to meet the standards set out in the declaration, he is likely to be the subject of public adverse criticism by the judge.

36. I should like to see added to this a statement that where there is a range of reasonable opinion, the expert has indicated the extent of that range in his report.

37. Some elements in the working group's suggested declaration may be controversial; in particular, it might be argued that a reference to the possibility of adverse criticism could deter competent experts from giving evidence. I believe, however, that the outline broadly sets out the points which should be included in an expert's declaration. It could usefully form the basis of discussion between the Law Society, the Academy of Experts and any other interested bodies, with a view to drawing up a standard declaration for use in experts' reports.

Access to evidence: inequality of resources

38. One of the fundamental principles of my approach to civil litigation is that there should, so far as possible, be a level playing field between litigants of unequal financial or other resources. A particular problem arises when one party, often the defendant or potential defendant, has an easily available source of expertise to which the other party does not have access. This happens, for example, in medical negligence, where a health authority or hospital trust can use its own doctors; or in actions against large companies with in-house technical experts. The potential claimant, on the other hand, may not even know whether he or she has a case worth pursuing without paying for an independent expert to carry out an investigation.

39. I suggested in the issues paper that one way of redressing this imbalance would be to introduce a new procedure enabling claimants to apply to the court (either before or after proceedings have started) for an order requiring the defendant to provide an in-house expert's report on a particular situation. It seemed to me that such a procedure would be particularly helpful to claimants who did not qualify for legal aid, although it could also save money for the legal aid fund. The provision of an in-house report would not prevent the opposing party from instructing his or her own expert at a later stage if it emerged that there was a case worth pursuing.

40. This proposal was generally opposed by respondents to the consultation paper. Prospective defendants considered it unfair, and claimants' representatives questioned whether an in-house report could be accepted as impartial and independent, because of the fear that an in-house expert would come under pressure to report in favour of the defendant. In the light of this reaction, I have considered whether there may be a more acceptable way of achieving my objective than a specific power to direct a prospective defendant to carry out investigations or tests.

41. I have concluded that the court should have a wide power, which could be exercised before the start of proceedings, to order that an examination or tests should be carried out in relation to any matter in issue, and a report submitted to the court. Any such order would indicate by whom the examination or tests were to be carried out, and at whose cost. This will cover a wider range of situations than I originally had in mind, and can be applied flexibly by the courts to meet particular circumstances.

Narrowing the issues: experts' meetings

42. Among the criticisms I made in my interim report was that the present system does not encourage narrowing of issues between opposing experts, or the elimination of peripheral issues. There has been widespread support for my suggestion that experts' meetings were a useful approach to narrowing the issues. In areas of litigation (such as Official Referees' business) where experts' meetings are already the usual practice, there is general agreement that they are helpful. In areas where they are not at present widely used, including medical negligence, the majority of respondents accept that they could be helpful. (This is not, however, the view of the Intellectual Property Working Group, which believes that sequential disclosure of reports may be a better way of narrowing the issues in some cases, or that each expert might usefully be asked to take the opposite side's report and underline the passages with which he or she disagrees.)

43. Two principal reservations have been expressed, even by those who support experts' meetings in principle. The first (mentioned in my interim report) is that meetings can be futile because the experts are instructed not to agree anything; or, alternatively, are told that any points of agreement must be referred back to their instructing lawyers for ratification. This subverts the judge's intention in directing the experts to meet, because the decision as to what to agree becomes a matter for the lawyers rather than the experts. I recommended in the interim report that it should be unprofessional conduct for an expert to be given or to accept instructions not to agree, and this has been widely supported.

44. On the basis of the consultation I have carried out, it is far from clear whether these are widespread problems, although there is certainly evidence that they do happen on occasions. The solution lies in a clear requirement that the experts must produce for the court, at the end of their meeting, a written list of agreed matters of professional opinion and issues still in dispute. It must be made clear that the discussion is to cover only matters within the experts' professional competence, and that it is for the parties and their legal advisers to consider the effect of any agreement or disagreement on the future conduct of the case.

45. At least in the heaviest cases where expert issues are likely to be most complex, the agenda for the experts' meeting should be set by the court. Narrowing the issues to be put before the court, including issues of expert opinion, is one of the fundamental purposes of the system of case management I have proposed. The procedural judge conducting a case management conference should not only direct an experts' meeting but define (with the help of the parties and their legal advisers) the subject matter to be covered.

46. The second reservation about the need for experts' meetings relates to cost. It is said that meetings are expensive to set up, especially if they are attended by the parties' legal advisers. My answer to this point is that, provided a clear agenda is set and the meeting is properly conducted, the investment, in the vast majority of cases, will be well worthwhile. Where the meeting does not lead directly to settlement, it will reduce the scope of further work on the case and either facilitate settlement at a later stage or ensure that the trial focuses on the essential issues. In any event, the net result should be a saving of costs.

47. It is also worth pointing out that, at least in the more straightforward cases, it may be possible to hold a 'meeting' by using telephone conferencing and video conferencing technologies, at less expense than bringing the experts physically together. The important point is that they communicate with each other.

48. It is important, too, that experts communicate at the earliest possible stage in the case, to establish that they are answering the same questions or addressing the same issues. A useful starting point for discussions between experts would be to prepare an agreed chronology and statement of facts, with a summary of important or disputed points. This should be done as soon as possible after submission of the defence, with a view to identifying non-contentious points from the outset so as to define the scope of the experts' reports. In some cases, the first meeting may be only after the exchange of experts' reports. At that stage, in any event, the reports themselves will provide a clear and agreed basis for the discussion.

49. In areas of litigation where the use of experts' meetings is well established, it seems to be accepted that there is no difficulty in allowing them to be conducted in private, with no-one present apart from the experts themselves. In other areas, it has been suggested that experts' meetings should take place only in the presence of the parties' lawyers, or of a neutral third party such as an independent lawyer or the procedural judge. In medical negligence, for example, it is thought that such an arrangement would be needed to overcome the traditional attitude of suspicion between the parties. In particular, it is said that private meetings between experts would not be acceptable to patients, because of the common perception that doctors 'hang together'.

50. In the majority of cases I see no reason why the experts should not meet alone, but I accept that there are circumstances in which this will not be appropriate. When the court directs a meeting, I suggest that the onus should be on the parties to apply for any special arrangements. In considering any such application, the court should bear in mind the expense of attendance by the parties' lawyers. When the lawyers do attend, it must also be made clear that they are present simply as observers to ensure fair play, and not to participate in the discussion or inhibit legitimate agreement between the experts.

51. Given the potential advantages, and the flexibility of the possible arrangements, it is difficult to see why there should not be at least one experts' meeting in all cases where opposing experts are involved. Certainly, I would not expect to see any substantial case come to trial under the new system without at least one such meeting having taken place.

Improving the quality of experts' reports

52. Since the publication of the interim report an appreciable level of concern has been expressed about the quality and reliability of experts' reports. This can relate to the problem of partisan reports which I have already discussed, or to the inclusion of irrelevant material, a tendency to stray beyond the expert's field of professional competence, or failure to address the real issues.

53. There are a number of ways of tackling these problems, of which training for experts is one. Some people would like to see a compulsory system of training and accreditation of experts in particular fields, along the lines of what is already provided by bodies such as the Academy of Experts. This would mean that only fully qualified and accredited experts would be permitted to appear before the courts or prepare reports for forensic use. (Special arrangements would have to be made to meet the situation in some areas of litigation such as intellectual property, where experts commonly act on a 'one-off' basis. For example, experts could be permitted to act in up to, say, three cases before accreditation was required.) Such a system would include the exercise of sanctions against experts who failed to meet the required standard.

54. I certainly support the provision of training for experts, both through attendance at courses and through the dissemination of published material such as the model form of expert's report which has been produced by the Academy of Experts. Professional people who take on responsibilities as expert witnesses need a basic understanding of the legal system and their role within it. They also need to be able to present their evidence effectively, both in written reports and orally under cross-examination. Training in presentational skills, however, should never lose sight of the fundamental point that the expert's duty is to assist the court. Otherwise it is not in the interests of justice because it may result in the truth being concealed.

55. I do not recommend an exclusive system of accreditation. Such a system could exclude potentially competent experts who choose for good reasons not to take it up. It might, in fact, narrow rather than widen the pool of available experts. It could foster an uncompetitive monopoly, and might encourage the development of 'professional experts' who were out of touch with current practice in their field of experience.

56. Another way of improving the quality of experts' reports is by ensuring that experts are given adequate instructions. From the comments I have received on this point it appears that solicitors' instructions vary from detailed to perfunctory. "Please provide your usual report" is an example that has been mentioned to me, and it may well be that this is adequate for an experienced expert who is frequently instructed by the same solicitor. Many experts have, however, indicated that they would welcome more detailed and explicit instructions, and I have no doubt that solicitors would benefit from guidance in this area.

57. The Law Society has already published pro forma instructions in its *Directory of Experts*, and, jointly with the British Orthopaedic Association, a model letter of instruction to medical experts. A number of other initiatives which have begun in the course of the Inquiry will help to take this work forward under the new system. These include a working group set up by the ABI to develop a protocol for the instruction of experts, and an APIL/ABI working party on pre-action protocols for the fast track which has produced a model letter of instruction.

Expert assessors

58. In the interim report I recommended that the courts should make wider use of their powers to appoint expert assessors to assist the judge in complex litigation and, in appropriate cases, to preside over meetings between the parties' experts and help them to reach agreement.

59. There has been some resistance to these proposals, largely on the grounds that an assessor would usurp the role of the judge. I do not agree that this would necessarily be the case: where there are complex technical issues the assessor's function would be to 'educate' the judge to enable him to reach a properly informed decision. In the most complex cases this function could be performed by two assessors, one instructed by each party.

60. Clearly the use of an independent assessor in addition to the parties' experts and the judge will not be cost-effective except in the heaviest cases. In smaller cases, such as boundary disputes or complaints about domestic appliances, there may also be technical issues which are not agreed between the parties. In these circumstances I see no objection to appointing an independent expert as adjudicator. This may well be the most economical way of disposing of the case, and the result is no less likely to be satisfactory to the parties than a decision by a judge who has little or no expertise in the subject matter of the dispute. The county courts already have a power (albeit rarely used) to appoint outside arbitrators for small claims.

Recommendations

My main recommendations are as follows.

(1) As a general principle, single experts should be used wherever the case (or the issue) is concerned with a substantially established area of knowledge and where it is not necessary for the court directly to sample a range of opinions.

(2) Parties and procedural judges should always consider whether a single expert could be appointed in a particular case (or to deal with a particular issue); and, if this is not considered appropriate, indicate why not.
(3) Where opposing experts are appointed they should adopt a co-operative approach. Wherever possible this should include a joint investigation and a single report, indicating areas of disagreement which cannot be resolved.
(4) Expert evidence should not be admissible unless all written instructions (including letters subsequent upon the original instructions) and a note of any oral instructions are included as an annex to the expert's report.
(5) The court should have a wide power, which could be exercised before the start of proceedings, to order that an examination or tests should be carried out in relation to any matter in issue, and a report submitted to the court.
(6) Experts' meetings should normally be held in private. When the court directs a meeting, the parties should be able to apply for any special arrangements such as attendance by the parties' legal advisers.
(7) Training courses and published material should provide expert witnesses with a basic understanding of the legal system and their role within it, focusing on the expert's duty to the court, and enable them to present written and oral evidence effectively. Training should not be compulsory.

Appendix B

PART 35
EXPERTS AND ASSESSORS

35.1 Duty to restrict expert evidence

Expert evidence shall be restricted to that which is reasonably required to resolve the proceedings.

35.2 Interpretation and definitions

(1) A reference to an 'expert' in this Part is a reference to a person who has been instructed to give or prepare expert evidence for the purpose of proceedings.
(2) 'Single joint expert' means an expert instructed to prepare a report for the court on behalf of two or more of the parties (including the claimant) to the proceedings.

35.3 Experts—overriding duty to the court

(1) It is the duty of experts to help the court on matters within their expertise.
(2) This duty overrides any obligation to the person from whom experts have received instructions or by whom they are paid.

35.4 Court's power to restrict expert evidence

(1) No party may call an expert or put in evidence an expert's report without the court's permission.
(2) When parties apply for permission they must identify –

(a) the field in which expert evidence is required; and
(b) where practicable, the name of the proposed expert.

(3) If permission is granted it shall be in relation only to the expert named or the field identified under paragraph (2).
(3A) Where a claim has been allocated to the small claims track or the fast track, if permission is given for expert evidence, it will normally be given for evidence from only one expert on a particular issue.

(Paragraph 7 of practice direction 35 sets out some of the circumstances the court will consider when deciding whether expert evidence should be given by a single joint expert.)

(4) The court may limit the amount of a party's expert's fees and expenses that may be recovered from any other party.

35.5 General requirement for expert evidence to be given in a written report

(1) Expert evidence is to be given in a written report unless the court directs otherwise.

(2) If a claim is on the small claims track or the fast track, the court will not direct an expert to attend a hearing unless it is necessary to do so in the interests of justice.

35.6 Written questions to experts

(1) A party may put written questions about an expert's report (which must be proportionate) to –

(a) an expert instructed by another party; or
(b) a single joint expert appointed under rule 35.7.

(2) Written questions under paragraph (1) –

(a) may be put once only;
(b) must be put within 28 days of service of the expert's report; and
(c) must be for the purpose only of clarification of the report,

unless in any case –

(i) the court gives permission; or
(ii) the other party agrees.

(3) An expert's answers to questions put in accordance with paragraph (1) shall be treated as part of the expert's report.

(4) Where –

(a) a party has put a written question to an expert instructed by another party; and
(b) the expert does not answer that question,

the court may make one or both of the following orders in relation to the party who instructed the expert –

(i) that the party may not rely on the evidence of that expert; or
(ii) that the party may not recover the fees and expenses of that expert from any other party.

35.7 Court's power to direct that evidence is to be given by a single joint expert

(1) Where two or more parties wish to submit expert evidence on a particular issue, the court may direct that the evidence on that issue is to be given by a single joint expert.

(2) Where the parties who wish to submit the evidence ('the relevant parties') cannot agree who should be the single joint expert, the court may –

(a) select the expert from a list prepared or identified by the relevant parties; or
(b) direct that the expert be selected in such other manner as the court may direct.

35.8 Instructions to a single joint expert

(1) Where the court gives a direction under rule 35.7 for a single joint expert to be used, any relevant party may give instructions to the expert.

(2) When a party gives instructions to the expert that party must, at the same time, send a copy to the other relevant parties.

(3) The court may give directions about –

(a) the payment of the expert's fees and expenses; and

(b) any inspection, examination or experiments which the expert wishes to carry out.

(4) The court may, before an expert is instructed –

(a) limit the amount that can be paid by way of fees and expenses to the expert; and

(b) direct that some or all of the relevant parties pay that amount into court.

(5) Unless the court otherwise directs, the relevant parties are jointly and severally liable for the payment of the expert's fees and expenses.

35.9 Power of court to direct a party to provide information

Where a party has access to information which is not reasonably available to another party, the court may direct the party who has access to the information to –

(a) prepare and file a document recording the information; and

(b) serve a copy of that document on the other party.

35.10 Contents of report

(1) An expert's report must comply with the requirements set out in practice direction 35.

(2) At the end of an expert's report there must be a statement that the expert understands and has complied with their duty to the court.

(3) The expert's report must state the substance of all material instructions, whether written or oral, on the basis of which the report was written.

(4) The instructions referred to in paragraph (3) shall not be privileged(GL) against disclosure but the court will not, in relation to those instructions –

(a) order disclosure of any specific document; or

(b) permit any questioning in court, other than by the party who instructed the expert,

unless it is satisfied that there are reasonable grounds to consider the statement of instructions given under paragraph (3) to be inaccurate or incomplete.

35.11 Use by one party of expert's report disclosed by another

Where a party has disclosed an expert's report, any party may use that expert's report as evidence at the trial.

35.12 Discussions between experts

(1) The court may, at any stage, direct a discussion between experts for the purpose of requiring the experts to –

(a) identify and discuss the expert issues in the proceedings; and
(b) where possible, reach an agreed opinion on those issues.

(2) The court may specify the issues which the experts must discuss.
(3) The court may direct that following a discussion between the experts they must prepare a statement for the court setting out those issues on which –

(a) they agree; and
(b) they disagree, with a summary of their reasons for disagreeing.

(4) The content of the discussion between the experts shall not be referred to at the trial unless the parties agree.
(5) Where experts reach agreement on an issue during their discussions, the agreement shall not bind the parties unless the parties expressly agree to be bound by the agreement.

35.13 Consequence of failure to disclose expert's report

A party who fails to disclose an expert's report may not use the report at the trial or call the expert to give evidence orally unless the court gives permission.

35.14 Expert's right to ask court for directions

(1) Experts may file written requests for directions for the purpose of assisting them in carrying out their functions.
(2) Experts must, unless the court orders otherwise, provide copies of the proposed requests for directions under paragraph (1) –

(a) to the party instructing them, at least 7 days before they file the requests; and
(b) to all other parties, at least 4 days before they file them.

(3) The court, when it gives directions, may also direct that a party be served with a copy of the directions.

35.15 Assessors

(1) This rule applies where the court appoints one or more persons under section 70 of the Senior Courts Act 1981[1] or section 63 of the County Courts Act 1984[2] as an assessor.
(2) An assessor will assist the court in dealing with a matter in which the assessor has skill and experience.

1 1981 c. 54.
2 1984 c. 28.

(3) An assessor will take such part in the proceedings as the court may direct and in particular the court may direct an assessor to –

(a) prepare a report for the court on any matter at issue in the proceedings; and
(b) attend the whole or any part of the trial to advise the court on any such matter.

(4) If an assessor prepares a report for the court before the trial has begun –

(a) the court will send a copy to each of the parties; and
(b) the parties may use it at trial.

(5) The remuneration to be paid to an assessor is to be determined by the court and will form part of the costs of the proceedings.
(6) The court may order any party to deposit in the court office a specified sum in respect of an assessor's fees and, where it does so, the assessor will not be asked to act until the sum has been deposited.
(7) Paragraphs (5) and (6) do not apply where the remuneration of the assessor is to be paid out of money provided by Parliament.

Appendix C

PRACTICE DIRECTION 35 – EXPERTS AND ASSESSORS
This Practice Direction Supplements CPR Part 35

Introduction
1 Part 35 is intended to limit the use of oral expert evidence to that which is reasonably required. In addition, where possible, matters requiring expert evidence should be dealt with by only one expert. Experts and those instructing them are expected to have regard to the guidance contained in the Protocol for the Instruction of Experts to give Evidence in Civil Claims annexed to this practice direction. (Further guidance on experts is contained in Annex C to the Practice Direction (Pre-Action Conduct)).

Expert Evidence – General Requirements
2.1 Expert evidence should be the independent product of the expert uninfluenced by the pressures of litigation.
2.2 Experts should assist the court by providing objective, unbiased opinions on matters within their expertise, and should not assume the role of an advocate.
2.3 Experts should consider all material facts, including those which might detract from their opinions.
2.4 Experts should make it clear –

(a) when a question or issue falls outside their expertise; and
(b) when they are not able to reach a definite opinion, for example because they have insufficient information.

2.5 If, after producing a report, an expert's view changes on any material matter, such change of view should be communicated to all the parties without delay, and when appropriate to the court.

Form and Content of an Expert's Report
3.1 An expert's report should be addressed to the court and not to the party from whom the expert has received instructions.
3.2 An expert's report must:

(1) give details of the expert's qualifications;
(2) give details of any literature or other material which has been relied on in making the report;
(3) contain a statement setting out the substance of all facts and instructions

which are material to the opinions expressed in the report or upon which those opinions are based;

(4) make clear which of the facts stated in the report are within the expert's own knowledge;

(5) say who carried out any examination, measurement, test or experiment which the expert has used for the report, give the qualifications of that person, and say whether or not the test or experiment has been carried out under the expert's supervision;

(6) where there is a range of opinion on the matters dealt with in the report –

(a) summarise the range of opinions; and

(b) give reasons for the expert's own opinion;

(7) contain a summary of the conclusions reached;

(8) if the expert is not able to give an opinion without qualification, state the qualification; and

(9) contain a statement that the expert –

(a) understands their duty to the court, and has complied with that duty; and

(b) is aware of the requirements of Part 35, this practice direction and the Protocol for Instruction of Experts to give Evidence in Civil Claims.

3.3 An expert's report must be verified by a statement of truth in the following form –

> I confirm that I have made clear which facts and matters referred to in this report are within my own knowledge and which are not. Those that are within my own knowledge I confirm to be true. The opinions I have expressed represent my true and complete professional opinions on the matters to which they refer.'

(Part 22 deals with statements of truth. Rule 32.14 sets out the consequences of verifying a document containing a false statement without an honest belief in its truth.)

Information

4 Under rule 35.9 the court may direct a party with access to information, which is not reasonably available to another party to serve on that other party a document, which records the information. The document served must include sufficient details of all the facts, tests, experiments and assumptions which underlie any part of the information to enable the party on whom it is served to make, or to obtain, a proper interpretation of the information and an assessment of its significance.

Instructions

5 Cross-examination of experts on the contents of their instructions will not be allowed unless the court permits it (or unless the party who gave the instructions consents). Before it gives permission the court must be satisfied that there are reasonable grounds to consider that the statement in the report of the substance of the instructions is inaccurate or incomplete. If the court is so satisfied, it will allow the cross-examination where it appears to be in the interests of justice.

Questions to Experts

6.1 Where a party sends a written question or questions under rule 35.6 direct to an expert, a copy of the questions must, at the same time, be sent to the other party or parties.

6.2 The party or parties instructing the expert must pay any fees charged by that expert for answering questions put under rule 35.6. This does not affect any decision of the court as to the party who is ultimately to bear the expert's fees.

Single joint expert

7 When considering whether to give permission for the parties to rely on expert evidence and whether that evidence should be from a single joint expert the court will take into account all the circumstances in particular, whether:

(a) it is proportionate to have separate experts for each party on a particular issue with reference to –

(i) the amount in dispute;
(ii) the importance to the parties; and
(iii) the complexity of the issue;

(b) the instruction of a single joint expert is likely to assist the parties and the court to resolve the issue more speedily and in a more cost-effective way than separately instructed experts;
(c) expert evidence is to be given on the issue of liability, causation or quantum;
(d) the expert evidence falls within a substantially established area of knowledge which is unlikely to be in dispute or there is likely to be a range of expert opinion;
(e) a party has already instructed an expert on the issue in question and whether or not that was done in compliance with any practice direction or relevant pre-action protocol;
(f) questions put in accordance with rule 35.6 are likely to remove the need for the other party to instruct an expert if one party has already instructed an expert;
(g) questions put to a single joint expert may not conclusively deal with all issues that may require testing prior to trial;
(h) a conference may be required with the legal representatives, experts and other witnesses which may make instruction of a single joint expert impractical; and
(i) a claim to privilege makes the instruction of any expert as a single joint expert inappropriate.

Orders

8 Where an order requires an act to be done by an expert, or otherwise affects an expert, the party instructing that expert must serve a copy of the order on the expert. The claimant must serve the order on a single joint expert.

Discussions between experts

9.1 Unless directed by the court discussions between experts are not mandatory. Parties must consider, with their experts, at an early stage, whether there is likely to be any useful purpose in holding an experts' discussion and if so when.

9.2 The purpose of discussions between experts is not for experts to settle cases but to agree and narrow issues and in particular to identify:

(i) the extent of the agreement between them;
(ii) the points of and short reasons for any disagreement;
(iii) action, if any, which may be taken to resolve any outstanding points of disagreement; and
(iv) any further material issues not raised and the extent to which these issues are agreed.

9.3 Where the experts are to meet, the parties must discuss and if possible agree whether an agenda is necessary, and if so attempt to agree one that helps the experts to focus on the issues which need to be discussed. The agenda must not be in the form of leading questions or hostile in tone.

9.4 Unless ordered by the court, or agreed by all parties, and the experts, neither the parties nor their legal representatives may attend experts discussions.

9.5 If the legal representatives do attend –

(i) they should not normally intervene in the discussion, except to answer questions put to them by the experts or to advise on the law; and
(ii) the experts may if they so wish hold part of their discussions in the absence of the legal representatives.

9.6 A statement must be prepared by the experts dealing with paragraphs 9.2(i)–(iv) above. Individual copies of the statements must be signed by the experts at the conclusion of the discussion, or as soon thereafter as practicable, and in any event within 7 days. Copies of the statements must be provided to the parties no later than 14 days after signing.

9.7 Experts must give their own opinions to assist the court and do not require the authority of the parties to sign a joint statement.

9.8 If an expert significantly alters an opinion, the joint statement must include a note or addendum by that expert explaining the change of opinion.

Assessors

10.1 An assessor may be appointed to assist the court under rule 35.15. Not less than 21 days before making any such appointment, the court will notify each party in writing of the name of the proposed assessor, of the matter in respect of which the assistance of the assessor will be sought and of the qualifications of the assessor to give that assistance.

10.2 Where any person has been proposed for appointment as an assessor, any party may object to that person either personally or in respect of that person's qualification.

10.3 Any such objection must be made in writing and filed with the court within 7 days of receipt of the notification referred to in paragraph 10.1 and will be taken into account by the court in deciding whether or not to make the appointment.

10.4 Copies of any report prepared by the assessor will be sent to each of the parties but the assessor will not give oral evidence or be open to cross-examination or questioning.

Appendix D

Protocol for the Instruction of Experts to give Evidence in Civil Claims
Civil Justice Council, June 2005, amended October 2009

1. Introduction

Expert witnesses perform a vital role in civil litigation. It is essential that both those who instruct experts and experts themselves are given clear guidance as to what they are expected to do in civil proceedings. The purpose of this Protocol is to provide such guidance. It has been drafted by the Civil Justice Council and reflects the rules and practice directions current [in June 2005], replacing the Code of Guidance on Expert Evidence. The authors of the Protocol wish to acknowledge the valuable assistance they obtained by drawing on earlier documents produced by the Academy of Experts and the Expert Witness Institute, as well as suggestions made by the Clinical Dispute Forum. The Protocol has been approved by the Master of the Rolls.

2. Aims of Protocol

2.1 This Protocol offers guidance to experts and to those instructing them in the interpretation of and compliance with Part 35 of the Civil Procedure Rules (CPR 35) and its associated Practice Direction (PD 35) and to further the objectives of the Civil Procedure Rules in general. It is intended to assist in the interpretation of those provisions in the interests of good practice but it does not replace them. It sets out standards for the use of experts and the conduct of experts and those who instruct them. The existence of this Protocol does not remove the need for experts and those who instruct them to be familiar with CPR35 and PD35.

2.2 Experts and those who instruct them should also bear in mind para 1.4 of the Practice Direction on Protocols which contains the following objectives, namely to:

(a) encourage the exchange of early and full information about the expert issues involved in a prospective legal claim;
(b) enable the parties to avoid or reduce the scope of litigation by agreeing the whole or part of an expert issue before commencement of proceedings; and
(c) support the efficient management of proceedings where litigation cannot be avoided.

3. Application

3.1 This Protocol applies to any steps taken for the purpose of civil proceedings by experts or those who instruct them on or after 5th September 2005.

3.2 It applies to all experts who are, or who may be, governed by CPR Part 35 and to those who instruct them. Experts are governed by Part 35 if they are or have been instructed to give or prepare evidence for the purpose of civil proceedings in a court in England and Wales (CPR 35.2).
3.3 Experts, and those instructing them, should be aware that some cases may be "specialist proceedings" (CPR 49) where there are modifications to the Civil Procedure Rules. Proceedings may also be governed by other Protocols. Further, some courts have published their own Guides which supplement the Civil Procedure Rules for proceedings in those courts. They contain provisions affecting expert evidence. Expert witnesses and those instructing them should be familiar with them when they are relevant.
3.4 Courts may take into account any failure to comply with this Protocol when making orders in relation to costs, interest, time limits, the stay of proceedings and whether to order a party to pay a sum of money into court.

Limitation
3.5 If, as a result of complying with any part of this Protocol, claims would or might be time barred under any provision in the Limitation Act 1980, or any other legislation that imposes a time limit for the bringing an action, claimants may commence proceedings without complying with this Protocol. In such circumstances, claimants who commence proceedings without complying with all, or any part, of this Protocol must apply, giving notice to all other parties, to the court for directions as to the timetable and form of procedure to be adopted, at the same time as they request the court to issue proceedings. The court may consider whether to order a stay of the whole or part of the proceedings pending compliance with this Protocol and may make orders in relation to costs.

4. Duties of experts
4.1 Experts always owe a duty to exercise reasonable skill and care to those instructing them, and to comply with any relevant professional code of ethics. However when they are instructed to give or prepare evidence for the purpose of civil proceedings in England and Wales they have an overriding duty to help the court on matters within their expertise (CPR 35.3). This duty overrides any obligation to the person instructing or paying them. Experts must not serve the exclusive interest of those who retain them.
4.2 Experts should be aware of the overriding objective that courts deal with cases justly. This includes dealing with cases proportionately, expeditiously and fairly (CPR 1.1). Experts are under an obligation to assist the court so as to enable them to deal with cases in accordance with the overriding objective. However the overriding objective does not impose on experts any duty to act as mediators between the parties or require them to trespass on the role of the court in deciding facts.
4.3 Experts should provide opinions which are independent, regardless of the pressures of litigation. In this context, a useful test of 'independence' is that the expert would express the same opinion if given the same instructions by an

opposing party. Experts should not take it upon themselves to promote the point of view of the party instructing them or engage in the role of advocates.
4.4 Experts should confine their opinions to matters which are material to the disputes between the parties and provide opinions only in relation to matters which lie within their expertise. Experts should indicate without delay where particular questions or issues fall outside their expertise.
4.5 Experts should take into account all material facts before them at the time that they give their opinion. Their reports should set out those facts and any literature or any other material on which they have relied in forming their opinions. They should indicate if an opinion is provisional, or qualified, or where they consider that further information is required or if, for any other reason, they are not satisfied that an opinion can be expressed finally and without qualification.
4.6 Experts should inform those instructing them without delay of any change in their opinions on any material matter and the reason for it.
4.7 Experts should be aware that any failure by them to comply with the Civil Procedure Rules or court orders or any excessive delay for which they are responsible may result in the parties who instructed them being penalised in costs and even, in extreme cases, being debarred from placing the experts' evidence before the court. In *Phillips v Symes*[1] Peter Smith J held that courts may also make orders for costs (under section 51 of the Supreme Court Act 1981) directly against expert witnesses who by their evidence cause significant expense to be incurred, and do so in flagrant and reckless disregard of their duties to the Court.

5. Conduct of Experts instructed only to advise

5.1 Part 35 only applies where experts are instructed to give opinions which are relied on for the purposes of court proceedings. Advice which the parties do not intend to adduce in litigation is likely to be confidential; the Protocol does not apply in these circumstances[2],[3].
5.2 The same applies where, after the commencement of proceedings, experts are instructed only to advise (e.g. to comment upon a single joint expert's report) and not to give or prepare evidence for use in the proceedings.
5.3 However this Protocol does apply if experts who were formerly instructed only to advise are later instructed to give or prepare evidence for the purpose of civil proceedings.

6. The Need for Experts

6.1 Those intending to instruct experts to give or prepare evidence for the purpose of civil proceedings should consider whether expert evidence is appropriate, taking account of the principles set out in CPR Parts 1 and 35, and in particular whether:

(a) it is relevant to a matter which is in dispute between the parties.
(b) it is reasonably required to resolve the proceedings (CPR 35.1);

[1] [2004] EWHC 2330 (Ch)
[2] *Carlson v Townsend* [2001] 1 WLR 2415
[3] *Jackson v Marley Davenport* [2004] 1 WLR 2926

(c) the expert has expertise relevant to the issue on which an opinion is sought;
(d) the expert has the experience, expertise and training appropriate to the value complexity and importance of the case; and whether
(e) these objects can be achieved by the appointment of a single joint expert (see section 17 below).

6.2 Although the court's permission is not generally required to instruct an expert, the court's permission is required before experts can be called to give evidence or their evidence can be put in (CPR 35.4).

7. The appointment of experts

7.1 Before experts are formally instructed or the court's permission to appoint named experts is sought, the following should be established:

(a) that they have the appropriate expertise and experience;
(b) that they are familiar with the general duties of an expert;
(c) that they can produce a report, deal with questions and have discussions with other experts within a reasonable time and at a cost proportionate to the matters in issue;
(d) a description of the work required;
(e) whether they are available to attend the trial, if attendance is required; and
(f) there is no potential conflict of interest.

7.2 Terms of appointment should be agreed at the outset and should normally include:

(a) the capacity in which the expert is to be appointed (e.g. party appointed expert, single joint expert or expert advisor);
(b) the services required of the expert (e.g. provision of expert's report, answering questions in writing, attendance at meetings and attendance at court);
(c) time for delivery of the report;
(d) the basis of the expert's charges (either daily or hourly rates and an estimate of the time likely to be required, or a total fee for the services);
(e) travelling expenses and disbursements;
(f) cancellation charges;
(g) any fees for attending court;
(h) time for making the payment; and
(i) whether fees are to be paid by a third party.
(j) if a party is publicly funded, whether or not the expert's charges will be subject to assessment by a costs officer.

7.3 As to the appointment of single joint experts, see section 17 below.
7.4 When necessary, arrangements should be made for dealing with questions to experts and discussions between experts, including any directions given by the court, and provision should be made for the cost of this work.
7.5 Experts should be informed regularly about deadlines for all matters concerning them. Those instructing experts should promptly send them copies of all court

orders and directions which may affect the preparation of their reports or any other matters concerning their obligations.

Conditional and Contingency Fees

7.6 Payments contingent upon the nature of the expert evidence given in legal proceedings, or upon the outcome of a case, must not be offered or accepted. To do so would contravene experts' overriding duty to the court and compromise their duty of independence.

7.7 Agreement to delay payment of experts' fees until after the conclusion of cases is permissible as long as the amount of the fee does not depend on the outcome of the case.

8. Instructions

8.1 Those instructing experts should ensure that they give clear instructions, including the following:

(a) basic information, such as names, addresses, telephone numbers, dates of birth and dates of incidents;

(b) the nature and extent of the expertise which is called for;

(c) the purpose of requesting the advice or report, a description of the matter(s) to be investigated, the principal known issues and the identity of all parties;

(d) the statement(s) of case (if any), those documents which form part of standard disclosure and witness statements which are relevant to the advice or report;

(e) where proceedings have not been started, whether proceedings are being contemplated and, if so, whether the expert is asked only for advice;

(f) an outline programme, consistent with good case management and the expert's availability, for the completion and delivery of each stage of the expert's work; and

(g) where proceedings have been started, the dates of any hearings (including any Case Management Conferences and/or Pre-Trial Reviews), the name of the court, the claim number and the track to which the claim has been allocated.

8.2 Experts who do not receive clear instructions should request clarification and may indicate that they are not prepared to act unless and until such clear instructions are received.

8.3 As to the instruction of single joint experts, see section 17 below.

9. Experts' Acceptance of Instructions

9.1 Experts should confirm without delay whether or not they accept instructions. They should also inform those instructing them (whether on initial instruction or at any later stage) without delay if:

(a) instructions are not acceptable because, for example, they require work that falls outside their expertise, impose unrealistic deadlines, or are insufficiently clear;

(b) they consider that instructions are or have become insufficient to complete the work;
(c) they become aware that they may not be able to fulfil any of the terms of appointment;
(d) the instructions and/or work have, for any reason, placed them in conflict with their duties as an expert; or
(e) they are not satisfied that they can comply with any orders that have been made. 9.2 Experts must neither express an opinion outside the scope of their field of expertise, nor accept any instructions to do so.

10. Withdrawal
10.1 Where experts' instructions remain incompatible with their duties, whether through incompleteness, a conflict between their duty to the court and their instructions, or for any other substantial and significant reason, they may consider withdrawing from the case. However, experts should not withdraw without first discussing the position fully with those who instruct them and considering carefully whether it would be more appropriate to make a written request for directions from the court. If experts do withdraw, they must give formal written notice to those instructing them.

11. Experts' Right to ask Court for Directions
11.1 Experts may request directions from the court to assist them in carrying out their functions as experts. Experts should normally discuss such matters with those who instruct them before making any such request. Unless the court otherwise orders, any proposed request for directions should be copied to the party instructing the expert at least seven days before filing any request to the court, and to all other parties at least four days before filing it. (CPR 35.14).
11.2 Requests to the court for directions should be made by letter, containing.

(a) the title of the claim;
(b) the claim number of the case;
(c) the name of the expert;
(d) full details of why directions are sought; and
(e) copies of any relevant documentation.

12. Power of the Court to Direct a Party to Provide Information
12.1 If experts consider that those instructing them have not provided information which they require, they may, after discussion with those instructing them and giving notice, write to the court to seek directions (CPR 35.14).
12.2 Experts and those who instruct them should also be aware of CPR 35.9. This provides that where one party has access to information which is not readily available to the other party, the court may direct the party who has access to the information to prepare, file and copy to the other party a document recording the information. If experts require such information which has not been disclosed, they

should discuss the position with those instructing them without delay, so that a request for the information can be made, and, if not forthcoming, an application can be made to the court. Unless a document appears to be essential, experts should assess the cost and time involved in the production of a document and whether its provision would be proportionate in the context of the case.

13. Contents of Experts' Reports

13.1 The content and extent of experts' reports should be governed by the scope of their instructions and general obligations, the contents of CPR 35 and PD35 and their overriding duty to the court.

13.2 In preparing reports, experts should maintain professional objectivity and impartiality at all times.

13.3 PD 35, para 2 provides that experts' reports should be addressed to the court and gives detailed directions about the form and content of such reports. All experts and those who instruct them should ensure that they are familiar with these requirements.

13.4 Model forms of Experts' Reports are available from bodies such as the Academy of Experts or the Expert Witness Institute.

13.5 Experts' reports must contain statements that they—

(i) understand their duty to the court and have complied and will continue to comply with it; and

(ii) are aware of the requirements of Part 35 and practice direction 35, this protocol and the practice direction on pre-action conduct. Experts' reports must also be verified by a statement of truth. The form of the statement of truth is as follows—" I confirm that I have made clear which facts and matters referred to in thisreport are within my own knowledge and which are not. Those that are within my own knowledge I confirm to be true. The opinions I have expressed represent my true and complete professional opinions on the matters to which they refer." This wording is mandatory and must not be modified.

Qualifications

13.6 The details of experts' qualifications to be given in reports should be commensurate with the nature and complexity of the case. It may be sufficient merely to state academic and professional qualifications. However, where highly specialized expertise is called for, experts should include the detail of particular training and/or experience that qualifies them to provide that highly specialised evidence.

Tests

13.7 Where tests of a scientific or technical nature have been carried out, experts should state:

(a) the methodology used; and

(b) by whom the tests were undertaken and under whose supervision, summarizing their respective qualifications and experience.

Reliance on the work of others

13.8 Where experts rely in their reports on literature or other material and cite the opinions of others without having verified them, they must give details of those opinions relied on. It is likely to assist the court if the qualifications of the originator(s) are also stated.

Facts

13.9 When addressing questions of fact and opinion, experts should keep the two separate and discrete.

13.10 Experts must state those facts (whether assumed or otherwise) upon which their opinions are based. They must distinguish clearly between those facts which experts know to be true and those facts which they assume.

13.11 Where there are material facts in dispute experts should express separate opinions on each hypothesis put forward. They should not express a view in favour of one or other disputed version of the facts unless, as a result of particular expertise and experience, they consider one set of facts as being improbable or less probable, in which case they may express that view, and should give reasons for holding it.

Range of opinion

13.12 If the mandatory summary of the range of opinion is based on published sources, experts should explain those sources and, where appropriate, state the qualifications of the originator(s) of the opinions from which they differ, particularly if such opinions represent a well-established school of thought.

13.13 Where there is no available source for the range of opinion, experts may need to express opinions on what they believe to be the range which other experts would arrive at if asked. In those circumstances, experts should make it clear that the range that they summarise is based on their own judgement and explain the basis of that judgement.

Conclusions

13.14 A summary of conclusions is mandatory. The summary should be at the end of the report after all the reasoning. There may be cases, however, where the benefit to the court is heightened by placing a short summary at the beginning of the report whilst giving the full conclusions at the end. For example, it can assist with the comprehension of the analysis and with the absorption of the detailed facts if the court is told at the outset of the direction in which the report's logic will flow in cases involving highly complex matters which fall outside the general knowledge of the court.

Basis of report: material instructions

13.15 The mandatory statement of the substance of all material instructions should not be incomplete or otherwise tend to mislead. The imperative is transparency. The term "instructions" includes all material which solicitors place in front of experts in order to gain advice. The omission from the statement of 'off-the-record' oral instructions is not permitted. Courts may allow cross-examination about the instructions if there are reasonable grounds to consider that the statement may be inaccurate or incomplete.

14. After receipt of experts' reports

14.1 Following the receipt of experts' reports, those instructing them should advise the experts as soon as reasonably practicable whether, and if so when, the report will be disclosed to other parties; and, if so disclosed, the date of actual disclosure.

14.2 If experts' reports are to be relied upon, and if experts are to give oral evidence, those instructing them should give the experts the opportunity to consider and comment upon other reports within their area of expertise and which deal with relevant issues at the earliest opportunity.

14.3 Those instructing experts should keep experts informed of the progress of cases, including amendments to statements of case relevant to experts' opinion.

14.4 If those instructing experts become aware of material changes in circumstances or that relevant information within their control was not previously provided to experts, they should without delay instruct experts to review, and if necessary, update the contents of their reports.

15. Amendment of reports

15.1 It may become necessary for experts to amend their reports:

(a) as a result of an exchange of questions and answers;
(b) following agreements reached at meetings between experts; or
(c) where further evidence or documentation is disclosed.

15.2 Experts should not be asked to, and should not, amend, expand or alter any parts of reports in a manner which distorts their true opinion, but may be invited to amend or expand reports to ensure accuracy, internal consistency, completeness and relevance to the issues and clarity. Although experts should generally follow the recommendations of solicitors with regard to the form of reports, they should form their own independent views as to the opinions and contents expressed in their reports and exclude any suggestions which do not accord with their views.

15.3 Where experts change their opinion following a meeting of experts, a simple signed and dated addendum or memorandum to that effect is generally sufficient. In some cases, however, the benefit to the court of having an amended report may justify the cost of making the amendment.

15.4 Where experts significantly alter their opinion, as a result of new evidence or because evidence on which they relied has become unreliable, or for any other reason, they should amend their reports to reflect that fact. Amended reports should include reasons for amendments. In such circumstances those instructing experts should inform other parties as soon as possible of any change of opinion.

15.5 When experts intend to amend their reports, they should inform those instructing them without delay and give reasons. They should provide the amended version (or an addendum or memorandum) clearly marked as such as quickly as possible.

16. Written Questions to Experts

16.1 The procedure for putting written questions to experts (CPR 35.6) is intended to facilitate the clarification of opinions and issues after experts' reports have been served. Experts have a duty to provide answers to questions properly put. Where they fail to do so, the court may impose sanctions against the party instructing the expert, and, if, there is continued non-compliance, debar a party from relying on the report. Experts should copy their answers to those instructing them.

16.2 Experts' answers to questions automatically become part of their reports. They are covered by the statement of truth and form part of the expert evidence.

16.3 Where experts believe that questions put are not properly directed to the clarification of the report, or are disproportionate, or have been asked out of time, they should discuss the questions with those instructing them and, if appropriate, those asking the questions. Attempts should be made to resolve such problems without the need for an application to the court for directions.

Written requests for directions in relation to questions

16.4 If those instructing experts do not apply to the court in respect of questions, but experts still believe that questions are improper or out of time, experts may file written requests with the court for directions to assist in carrying out their functions as experts (CPR 35.14). See Section 11 above.

17. Single Joint Experts

17.1 CPR 35 and PD35 deal extensively with the instruction and use of joint experts by the parties and the powers of the court to order their use (see CPR 35.7 and 35.8, PD35, para 5).

17.2 The Civil Procedure Rules encourage the use of joint experts. Wherever possible a joint report should be obtained. Consideration should therefore be given by all parties to the appointment of single joint experts in all cases where a court might direct such an appointment. Single joint experts are the norm in cases allocated to the small claims track and the fast track.

17.3 Where, in the early stages of a dispute, examinations, investigations, tests, site inspections, experiments, preparation of photographs, plans or other similar preliminary expert tasks are necessary, consideration should be given to the instruction of a single joint expert, especially where such matters are not, at that stage, expected to be contentious as between the parties. The objective of such an appointment should be to agree or to narrow issues.

17.4 Experts who have previously advised a party (whether in the same case or otherwise) should only be proposed as single joint experts if other parties are given all relevant information about the previous involvement.

17.5 The appointment of a single joint expert does not prevent parties from instructing their own experts to advise (but the costs of such expert advisers may not be recoverable in the case).

Joint instructions

17.6 The parties should try to agree joint instructions to single joint experts, but, in default of agreement, each party may give instructions. In particular, all parties should try to agree what documents should be included with instructions and what assumptions single joint experts should make.

17.7 Where the parties fail to agree joint instructions, they should try to agree where the areas of disagreement lie and their instructions should make this clear. If separate instructions are given, they should be copied at the same time to the other instructing parties.

17.8 Where experts are instructed by two or more parties, the terms of appointment should, unless the court has directed otherwise, or the parties have agreed otherwise, include:

(a) a statement that all the instructing parties are jointly and severally liable to pay the experts' fees and, accordingly, that experts' invoices should be sent simultaneously to all instructing parties or their solicitors (as appropriate); and
(b) a statement as to whether any order has been made limiting the amount of experts' fees and expenses (CPR 35.8(4)(a)).

17.9 Where instructions have not been received by the expert from one or more of the instructing parties the expert should give notice (normally at least 7 days) of a deadline to all instructing parties for the receipt by the expert of such instructions. Unless the instructions are received within the deadline the expert may begin work. In the event that instructions are received after the deadline but before the signing off of the report the expert should consider whether it is practicable to comply with those instructions without adversely affecting the timetable set for delivery of the report and in such a manner as to comply with the proportionality principle. An expert who decides to issue a report without taking into account instructions received after the deadline should inform the parties who may apply to the court for directions. In either event the report must show clearly that the expert did not receive instructions within the deadline, or, as the case may be, at all.

Conduct of the single joint expert

17.10 Single joint experts should keep all instructing parties informed of any material steps that they may be taking by, for example, copying all correspondence to those instructing them.

17.11 Single joint experts are Part 35 experts and so have an overriding duty to the court. They are the parties' appointed experts and therefore owe an equal duty to all parties. They should maintain independence, impartiality and transparency at all times.

17.12 Single joint experts should not attend any meeting or conference which is not a joint one, unless all the parties have agreed in writing or the court has directed that such a meeting may be held[4] and who is to pay the experts' fees for the meeting.

[4] *Peet v Mid Kent Area Healthcare NHS Trust* [2002] 1 WLR 210

17.13 Single joint experts may request directions from the court—see Section 11 above.

17.14 Single joint experts should serve their reports simultaneously on all instructing parties. They should provide a single report even though they may have received instructions which contain areas of conflicting fact or allegation. If conflicting instructions lead to different opinions (for example, because the instructions require experts to make different assumptions of fact), reports may need to contain more than one set of opinions on any issue. It is for the court to determine the facts.

Cross-examination

17.15 Single joint experts do not normally give oral evidence at trial but if they do, all parties may cross-examine them. In general written questions (CPR 35.6) should be put to single joint experts before requests are made for them to attend court for the purpose of cross-examination[5].

18. Discussions between Experts

18.1 The court has powers to direct discussions between experts for the purposes set out in the Rules (CPR 35.12). Parties may also agree that discussions take place between their experts.

18.2 Where single joint experts have been instructed but parties have, with the permission of the court, instructed their own additional Part 35 experts, there may, if the court so orders or the parties agree, be discussions between the single joint experts and the additional Part 35 experts. Such discussions should be confined to those matters within the remit of the additional Part 35 experts or as ordered by the court.

18.3 The purpose of discussions between experts should be, wherever possible, to:

(a) identify and discuss the expert issues in the proceedings;

(b) reach agreed opinions on those issues, and, if that is not possible, to narrow the issues in the case;

(c) identify those issues on which they agree and disagree and summarise their reasons for disagreement on any issue; and

(d) identify what action, if any, may be taken to resolve any of the outstanding issues between the parties.

Arrangements for discussions between experts

18.4 Arrangements for discussions between experts should be proportionate to the value of cases. In small claims and fast-track cases there should not normally be meetings between experts. Where discussion is justified in such cases, telephone discussion or an exchange of letters should, in the interests of proportionality, usually suffice. In multi-track cases, discussion may be face to face, but the practicalities or the proportionality principle may require discussions to be by telephone or video conference.

[5] *Daniels v Walker* [2000] 1 WLR 1382

18.5 The parties, their lawyers and experts should co-operate to produce the agenda for any discussion between experts, although primary responsibility for preparation of the agenda should normally lie with the parties' solicitors.
18.6 The agenda should indicate what matters have been agreed and summarise concisely those which are in issue. It is often helpful for it to include questions to be answered by the experts. If agreement cannot be reached promptly or a party is unrepresented, the court may give directions for the drawing up of the agenda. The agenda should be circulated to experts and those instructing them to allow sufficient time for the experts to prepare for the discussion.
18.7 Those instructing experts must not instruct experts to avoid reaching agreement (or to defer doing so) on any matter within the experts' competence. Experts are not permitted to accept such instructions.
18.8 The parties' lawyers may only be present at discussions between experts if all the parties agree or the court so orders. If lawyers do attend, they should not normally intervene except to answer questions put to them by the experts or to advise about the law[6]
18.9 The content of discussions between experts should not be referred to at trial unless the parties agree (CPR 35.12(4)). It is good practice for any such agreement to be in writing.
18.10 At the conclusion of any discussion between experts, a statement should be prepared setting out:

(a) a list of issues that have been agreed, including, in each instance, the basis of agreement;
(b) a list of issues that have not been agreed, including, in each instance, the basis of disagreement;
(c) a list of any further issues that have arisen that were not included in the original agenda for discussion;
(d) a record of further action, if any, to be taken or recommended, including as appropriate the holding of further discussions between experts.

18.11 The statement should be agreed and signed by all the parties to the discussion as soon as may be practicable.
18.12 Agreements between experts during discussions do not bind the parties unless the parties expressly agree to be bound by the agreement (CPR 35.12(5)). However, in view of the overriding objective, parties should give careful consideration before refusing to be bound by such an agreement and be able to explain their refusal should it become relevant to the issue of costs.

19. Attendance of Experts at Court

19.1 Experts instructed in cases have an obligation to attend court if called upon to do so and accordingly should ensure that those instructing them are always aware of their dates to be avoided and take all reasonable steps to be available.

[6] *Hubbard v Lambeth, Southwark and Lewisham HA* [2001] EWCA 1455

19.2 Those instructing experts should:

(a) ascertain the availability of experts before trial dates are fixed;
(b) keep experts updated with timetables (including the dates and times experts are to attend) and the location of the court;
(c) give consideration, where appropriate, to experts giving evidence via a video-link.
(d) inform experts immediately if trial dates are vacated.

19.3 Experts should normally attend court without the need for the service of witness summonses, but on occasion they may be served to require attendance (CPR 34). The use of witness summonses does not affect the contractual or other obligations of the parties to pay experts' fees.

Appendix E

PART 31
DISCLOSURE AND INSPECTION OF DOCUMENTS

31.1 Scope of this Part
(1) This Part sets out rules about the disclosure and inspection of documents.
(2) This Part applies to all claims except a claim on the small claims track.

31.2 Meaning of disclosure
A party discloses a document by stating that the document exists or has existed.

31.3 Right of inspection of a disclosed document
(1) A party to whom a document has been disclosed has a right to inspect that document except where –

(a) the document is no longer in the control of the party who disclosed it;
(b) the party disclosing the document has a right or a duty to withhold inspection of it; or
(c) paragraph (2) applies.

(Rule 31.8 sets out when a document is in the control of a party)
(Rule 31.19 sets out the procedure for claiming a right or duty to withhold inspection)
(2) Where a party considers that it would be disproportionate to the issues in the case to permit inspection of documents within a category or class of document disclosed under rule 31.6(b) –

(a) he is not required to permit inspection of documents within that category or class; but
(b) he must state in his disclosure statement that inspection of those documents will not be permitted on the grounds that to do so would be disproportionate.

(Rule 31.6 provides for standard disclosure)
(Rule 31.10 makes provision for a disclosure statement)
(Rule 31.12 provides for a party to apply for an order for specific inspection of documents)

31.4 Meaning of document

In this Part –

'document' means anything in which information of any description is recorded; and

'copy', in relation to a document, means anything onto which information recorded in the document has been copied, by whatever means and whether directly or indirectly.

31.5 Disclosure limited to standard disclosure

(1) An order to give disclosure is an order to give standard disclosure unless the court directs otherwise.

(2) The court may dispense with or limit standard disclosure.

(3) The parties may agree in writing to dispense with or to limit standard disclosure.

(The court may make an order requiring standard disclosure under rule 28.3 which deals with directions in relation to cases on the fast track and under rule 29.2 which deals with case management in relation to cases on the multi-track)

31.6 Standard disclosure—what documents are to be disclosed

Standard disclosure requires a party to disclose only –

(a) the documents on which he relies; and
(b) the documents which –
  (i) adversely affect his own case;
  (ii) adversely affect another party's case; or
  (iii) support another party's case; and
(c) the documents which he is required to disclose by a relevant practice direction.

31.7 Duty of search

(1) When giving standard disclosure, a party is required to make a reasonable search for documents falling within rule 31.6(b) or (c).

(2) The factors relevant in deciding the reasonableness of a search include the following –

(a) the number of documents involved;
(b) the nature and complexity of the proceedings;
(c) the ease and expense of retrieval of any particular document; and
(d) the significance of any document which is likely to be located during the search.

(3) Where a party has not searched for a category or class of document on the grounds that to do so would be unreasonable, he must state this in his disclosure statement and identify the category or class of document.

(Rule 31.10 makes provision for a disclosure statement)

31.8 Duty of disclosure limited to documents which are or have been in a party's control

(1) A party's duty to disclose documents is limited to documents which are or have been in his control.

(2) For this purpose a party has or has had a document in his control if –

(a) it is or was in his physical possession;
(b) he has or has had a right to possession of it; or
(c) he has or has had a right to inspect or take copies of it.

31.9 Disclosure of copies

(1) A party need not disclose more than one copy of a document.

(2) A copy of a document that contains a modification, obliteration or other marking or feature –

(a) on which a party intends to rely; or
(b) which adversely affects his own case or another party's case or supports another party's case;

shall be treated as a separate document.

(Rule 31.4 sets out the meaning of a copy of a document)

31.10 Procedure for standard disclosure

(1) The procedure for standard disclosure is as follows.

(2) Each party must make and serve on every other party, a list of documents in the relevant practice form.

(3) The list must identify the documents in a convenient order and manner and as concisely as possible.

(4) The list must indicate –

(a) those documents in respect of which the party claims a right or duty to withhold inspection; and
(b)
  (i) those documents which are no longer in the party's control; and
  (ii) what has happened to those documents.

(Rule 31.19 (3) and (4) require a statement in the list of documents relating to any documents inspection of which a person claims he has a right or duty to withhold)

(5) The list must include a disclosure statement.

(6) A disclosure statement is a statement made by the party disclosing the documents –

(a) setting out the extent of the search that has been made to locate documents which he is required to disclose;
(b) certifying that he understands the duty to disclose documents; and
(c) certifying that to the best of his knowledge he has carried out that duty.

(7) Where the party making the disclosure statement is a company, firm, association or other organisation, the statement must also –

(a) identify the person making the statement; and
(b) explain why he is considered an appropriate person to make the statement.

(8) The parties may agree in writing –

(a) to disclose documents without making a list; and
(b) to disclose documents without the disclosing party making a disclosure statement.

(9) A disclosure statement may be made by a person who is not a party where this is permitted by a relevant practice direction.

31.11 Duty of disclosure continues during proceedings
(1) Any duty of disclosure continues until the proceedings are concluded.
(2) If documents to which that duty extends come to a party's notice at any time during the proceedings, he must immediately notify every other party.

31.12 Specific disclosure or inspection
(1) The court may make an order for specific disclosure or specific inspection.
(2) An order for specific disclosure is an order that a party must do one or more of the following things –

(a) disclose documents or classes of documents specified in the order;
(b) carry out a search to the extent stated in the order;
(c) disclose any documents located as a result of that search.

(3) An order for specific inspection is an order that a party permit inspection of a document referred to in rule 31.3(2).
(Rule 31.3(2) allows a party to state in his disclosure statement that he will not permit inspection of a document on the grounds that it would be disproportionate to do so)

31.13 Disclosure in stages
The parties may agree in writing, or the court may direct, that disclosure or inspection or both shall take place in stages.

31.14 Documents referred to in statements of case etc.
(1) A party may inspect a document mentioned in –

(a) a statement of case;
(b) a witness statement;
(c) a witness summary; or
(d) an affidavit[(GL)].
(e) Revoked.

(2) Subject to rule 35.10(4), a party may apply for an order for inspection of any document mentioned in an expert's report which has not already been disclosed in the proceedings.
(Rule 35.10(4) makes provision in relation to instructions referred to in an expert's report)

31.15 Inspection and copying of documents
Where a party has a right to inspect a document –

(a) that party must give the party who disclosed the document written notice of his wish to inspect it;
(b) the party who disclosed the document must permit inspection not more than 7 days after the date on which he received the notice; and
(c) that party may request a copy of the document and, if he also undertakes to pay reasonable copying costs, the party who disclosed the document must supply him with a copy not more than 7 days after the date on which he received the request.

(Rule 31.3 and 31.14 deal with the right of a party to inspect a document)

31.16 Disclosure before proceedings start
(1) This rule applies where an application is made to the court under any Act for disclosure before proceedings have started[1].
(2) The application must be supported by evidence.
(3) The court may make an order under this rule only where –

(a) the respondent is likely to be a party to subsequent proceedings;
(b) the applicant is also likely to be a party to those proceedings;
(c) if proceedings had started, the respondent's duty by way of standard disclosure, set out in rule 31.6, would extend to the documents or classes of documents of which the applicant seeks disclosure; and
(d) disclosure before proceedings have started is desirable in order to –

(i) dispose fairly of the anticipated proceedings;
(ii) assist the dispute to be resolved without proceedings; or
(iii) save costs.

(4) An order under this rule must –

(a) specify the documents or the classes of documents which the respondent must disclose; and
(b) require him, when making disclosure, to specify any of those documents –

(i) which are no longer in his control; or
(ii) in respect of which he claims a right or duty to withhold inspection.

(5) Such an order may –
(a) require the respondent to indicate what has happened to any documents which are no longer in his control; and

(b) specify the time and place for disclosure and inspection.

31.17 Orders for disclosure against a person not a party

(1) This rule applies where an application is made to the court under any Act for disclosure by a person who is not a party to the proceedings.
(2) The application must be supported by evidence.
(3) The court may make an order under this rule only where –

(a) the documents of which disclosure is sought are likely to support the case of the applicant or adversely affect the case of one of the other parties to the proceedings; and
(b) disclosure is necessary in order to dispose fairly of the claim or to save costs.

(4) An order under this rule must –

(a) specify the documents or the classes of documents which the respondent must disclose; and
(b) require the respondent, when making disclosure, to specify any of those documents –

(i) which are no longer in his control; or
(ii) in respect of which he claims a right or duty to withhold inspection.

(5) Such an order may –

(a) require the respondent to indicate what has happened to any documents which are no longer in his control; and
(b) specify the time and place for disclosure and inspection.

31.18 Rules not to limit other powers of the court to order disclosure

Rules 31.16 and 31.17 do not limit any other power which the court may have to order –

(a) disclosure before proceedings have started; and
(b) disclosure against a person who is not a party to proceedings.

31.19 Claim to withhold inspection or disclosure of a document

(1) A person may apply, without notice, for an order permitting him to withhold disclosure of a document on the ground that disclosure would damage the public interest.
(2) Unless the court orders otherwise, an order of the court under paragraph (1) –

(a) must not be served on any other person; and
(b) must not be open to inspection by any person.

(3) A person who wishes to claim that he has a right or a duty to withhold inspection of a document, or part of a document, must state in writing –

(a) that he has such a right or duty; and
(b) the grounds on which he claims that right or duty.

(4) The statement referred to in paragraph (3) must be made –

(a) in the list in which the document is disclosed; or
(b) if there is no list, to the person wishing to inspect the document.

(5) A party may apply to the court to decide whether a claim made under paragraph (3) should be upheld.
(6) For the purpose of deciding an application under paragraph (1) (application to withhold disclosure) or paragraph (3) (claim to withhold inspection) the court may –

(a) require the person seeking to withhold disclosure or inspection of a document to produce that document to the court; and
(b) invite any person, whether or not a party, to make representations.

(7) An application under paragraph (1) or paragraph (5) must be supported by evidence.
(8) This Part does not affect any rule of law which permits or requires a document to be withheld from disclosure or inspection on the ground that its disclosure or inspection would damage the public interest.

31.20 Restriction on use of a privileged document inspection of which has been inadvertently allowed
Where a party inadvertently allows a privileged[GL] document to be inspected, the party who has inspected the document may use it or its contents only with the permission of the court.

31.21 Consequence of failure to disclose documents or permit inspection
A party may not rely on any document which he fails to disclose or in respect of which he fails to permit inspection unless the court gives permission.

31.22 Subsequent use of disclosed documents
(1) A party to whom a document has been disclosed may use the document only for the purpose of the proceedings in which it is disclosed, except where –

(a) the document has been read to or by the court, or referred to, at a hearing which has been held in public;
(b) the court gives permission; or
(c) the party who disclosed the document and the person to whom the document belongs agree.

(2) The court may make an order restricting or prohibiting the use of a document which has been disclosed, even where the document has been read to or by the court, or referred to, at a hearing which has been held in public.
(3) An application for such an order may be made –

(a) by a party; or
(b) by any person to whom the document belongs.

31.23 False disclosure statements

(1) Proceedings for contempt of court may be brought against a person if he makes, or causes to be made, a false disclosure statement, without an honest belief in its truth.

(2) Proceedings under this rule may be brought only –

(a) by the Attorney General; or
(b) with the permission of the court.

1. An application for disclosure before proceedings have started is permitted under section 33 of the Supreme Court Act 1981 (c.54) or section 52 of the County Courts Act 1984 (c.28).

2. An application for disclosure against a person who is not a party to proceedings is permitted under section 34 of the Supreme Court Act 1981 (c.54) or section 53 of the County Courts Act 1984 (c.28).

Appendix F

PRACTICE DIRECTION 31 – DISCLOSURE AND INSPECTION
This Practice Direction Supplements CPR Part 31

General

1.1 The normal order for disclosure will be an order that the parties give standard disclosure.

1.2 In order to give standard disclosure the disclosing party must make a reasonable search for documents falling within the paragraphs of rule 31.6.

1.3 Having made the search the disclosing party must (unless rule 31.10(8) applies) make a list of the documents of whose existence the party is aware that fall within those paragraphs and which are or have been in the party's control (see rule 31.8).

1.4 The obligations imposed by an order for standard disclosure may be dispensed with or limited either by the court or by written agreement between the parties. Any such written agreement should be lodged with the court.

The search

2 The extent of the search which must be made will depend upon the circumstances of the case including, in particular, the factors referred to in rule 31.7(2). The parties should bear in mind the overriding principle of proportionality (see rule 1.1(2)(c)). It may, for example, be reasonable to decide not to search for documents coming into existence before some particular date, or to limit the search to documents in some particular place or places, or to documents falling into particular categories.

Electronic disclosure

2A.1 Rule 31.4 contains a broad definition of a document. This extends to electronic documents, including e-mail and other electronic communications, word processed documents and databases. In addition to documents that are readily accessible from computer systems and other electronic devices and media, the definition covers those documents that are stored on servers and back-up systems and electronic documents that have been 'deleted'. It also extends to additional information stored and associated with electronic documents known as metadata.

2A.2 The parties should, prior to the first Case Management Conference, discuss any issues that may arise regarding searches for and the preservation of electronic documents. This may involve the parties providing information about the categories of electronic documents within their control, the computer systems, electronic devices and media on which any relevant documents may be held, the storage systems maintained by the parties and their document retention policies. In the case of difficulty or disagreement, the matter should be referred to a judge for directions at the earliest practical date, if possible at the first Case Management Conference.

2A.3 The parties should co-operate at an early stage as to the format in which electronic copy documents are to be provided on inspection. In the case of difficulty or disagreement, the matter should be referred to a Judge for directions at the earliest practical date, if possible at the first Case Management Conference.

2A.4 The existence of electronic documents impacts upon the extent of the reasonable search required by Rule 31.7 for the purposes of standard disclosure. The factors that may be relevant in deciding the reasonableness of a search for electronic documents include (but are not limited to) the following:–

(a) The number of documents involved.
(b) The nature and complexity of the proceedings.
(c) The ease and expense of retrieval of any particular document. This includes:
  (i) The accessibility of electronic documents or data including e-mail communications on computer systems, servers, back-up systems and other electronic devices or media that may contain such documents taking into account alterations or developments in hardware or software systems used by the disclosing party and/or available to enable access to such documents.
  (ii) The location of relevant electronic documents, data, computer systems, servers, back-up systems and other electronic devices or media that may contain such documents.
  (iii) The likelihood of locating relevant data.
  (iv) The cost of recovering any electronic documents.
  (v) The cost of disclosing and providing inspection of any relevant electronic documents.
  (vi) The likelihood that electronic documents will be materially altered in the course of recovery, disclosure or inspection.
(d) The significance of any document which is likely to be located during the search.

2A.5 It may be reasonable to search some or all of the parties' electronic storage systems. In some circumstances, it may be reasonable to search for electronic documents by means of keyword searches (agreed as far as possible between the parties) even where a full review of each and every document would be unreasonable. There may be other forms of electronic search that may be appropriate in particular circumstances.

The list

3.1 The list should be in Form N265.

3.2 In order to comply with rule 31.10(3) it will normally be necessary to list the documents in date order, to number them consecutively and to give each a concise

description (e.g. letter, claimant to defendant). Where there is a large number of documents all falling into a particular category the disclosing party may list those documents as a category rather than individually e.g. 50 bank statements relating to account number _ at _ Bank, _20_ to _20_; or, 35 letters passing between _ and _ between _20_ and _20_.
3.3 The obligations imposed by an order for disclosure will continue until the proceedings come to an end. If, after a list of documents has been prepared and served, the existence of further documents to which the order applies comes to the attention of the disclosing party, the party must prepare and serve a supplemental list.

Disclosure statement
4.1 A list of documents must (unless rule 31.10(8)(b) applies) contain a disclosure statement complying with rule 31.10. The form of disclosure statement is set out in the Annex to this practice direction.
4.2 The disclosure statement should:

(1) expressly state that the disclosing party believes the extent of the search to have been reasonable in all the circumstances, and
(2) in setting out the extent of the search (see rule 31.10(6)) draw attention to any particular limitations on the extent of the search which were adopted for proportionality reasons and give the reasons why the limitations were adopted, e.g. the difficulty or expense that a search not subject to those limitations would have entailed or the marginal relevance of categories of documents omitted from the search.

4.3 Where rule 31.10(7) applies, the details given in the disclosure statement about the person making the statement must include his name and address and the office or position he holds in the disclosing party or the basis upon which he makes the statement on behalf of the party.
4.4 If the disclosing party has a legal representative acting for him, the legal representative must endeavour to ensure that the person making the disclosure statement (whether the disclosing party or, in a case to which rule 31.10(7) applies, some other person) understands the duty of disclosure under Part 31.
4.5 If the disclosing party wishes to claim that he has a right or duty to withhold a document, or part of a document, in his list of documents from inspection (see rule 31.19(3)), he must state in writing:

(1) that he has such a right or duty, and
(2) the grounds on which he claims that right or duty.

4.6 The statement referred to in paragraph 4.5 above should normally be included in the disclosure statement and must indicate the document, or part of a document, to which the claim relates.
4.7 An insurer or the Motor Insurers' Bureau may sign a disclosure statement on behalf of a party where the insurer or the Motor Insurers' Bureau has a financial

interest in the result of proceedings brought wholly or partially by or against that party. Rule 31.10(7) and paragraph 4.3 above shall apply to the insurer or the Motor Insurers' Bureau making such a statement.

Specific disclosure

5.1 If a party believes that the disclosure of documents given by a disclosing party is inadequate he may make an application for an order for specific disclosure (see rule 31.12).

5.2 The application notice must specify the order that the applicant intends to ask the court to make and must be supported by evidence (see rule 31.12(2) which describes the orders the court may make).

5.3 The grounds on which the order is sought may be set out in the application notice itself but if not there set out must be set out in the evidence filed in support of the application.

5.4 In deciding whether or not to make an order for specific disclosure the court will take into account all the circumstances of the case and, in particular, the overriding objective described in Part 1. But if the court concludes that the party from whom specific disclosure is sought has failed adequately to comply with the obligations imposed by an order for disclosure (whether by failing to make a sufficient search for documents or otherwise) the court will usually make such order as is necessary to ensure that those obligations are properly complied with.

5.5 An order for specific disclosure may in an appropriate case direct a party to –

(1) carry out a search for any documents which it is reasonable to suppose may contain information which may –

(a) enable the party applying for disclosure either to advance his own case or to damage that of the party giving disclosure; or

(b) lead to a train of enquiry which has either of those consequences; and

(2) disclose any documents found as a result of that search.

Claims to withhold disclosure or inspection of a document

6.1 A claim to withhold inspection of a document, or part of a document, disclosed in a list of documents does not require an application to the court. Where such a claim has been made, a party who wishes to challenge it must apply to the court (see rule 31.19(5)).

6.2 Rule 31.19(1) and (6) provide a procedure enabling a party to apply for an order permitting disclosure of the existence of a document to be withheld.

Inspection of documents mentioned in expert's report (Rule 31.14(2))

7.1 If a party wishes to inspect documents referred to in the expert report of another party, before issuing an application he should request inspection of the documents informally, and inspection should be provided by agreement unless the request is unreasonable.

7.2 Where an expert report refers to a large number or volume of documents and it would be burdensome to copy or collate them, the court will only order inspection of such documents if it is satisfied that it is necessary for the just disposal of the proceedings and the party cannot reasonably obtain the documents from another source.

False disclosure statement

8 Attention is drawn to rule 31.23 which sets out the consequences of making a false disclosure statement without an honest belief in its truth, and to the procedures set out in paragraphs 28.1 – 28.3 of the practice direction supplementing Part 32.

Annex

Disclosure statement

I, the above named claimant [or defendant] [if party making disclosure is a company, firm or other organisation identify here who the person making the disclosure statement is and why he is the appropriate person to make it] state that I have carried out a reasonable and proportionate search to locate all the documents which I am required to disclose under the order made by the court on day of . I did not search:

(1) for documents predating ....,
(2) for documents located elsewhere than ....,
(3) for documents in categories other than ....
(4) for electronic documents

I carried out a search for electronic documents contained on or created by the following:

[list what was searched and extent of search]
I did not search for the following:

(1) documents created before..........,
(2) documents contained on or created by the Claimant's/Defendant's PCs/ portable data storage media/databases/servers/back-up tapes/off-site storage/ mobile phones/laptops/notebooks/handheld devices/PDA devices (delete as appropriate),
(3) documents contained on or created by the Claimant's/Defendant's mail files/ document files/calendar files/spreadsheet files/graphic and presentation files/web-based applications (delete as appropriate),
(4) documents other than by reference to the following keyword(s)/concepts.......... (delete if your search was not confined to specific keywords or concepts).
I certify that I understand the duty of disclosure and to the best of my knowledge I have carried out that duty. I certify that the list above is a complete list of all documents which are or have been in my control and which I am obliged under the said order to disclose.

Appendix G

PART 5
COURT DOCUMENTS

5.1 Scope of this Part

This part contains general provisions about –

(a) documents used in court proceedings; and
(b) the obligations of a court officer in relation to those documents.

5.2 Preparation of documents

(1) Where under these Rules, a document is to be prepared by the court, the document may be prepared by the party whose document it is, unless –

(a) a court officer otherwise directs; or
(b) it is a document to which –

(i) Revoked
(ii) CCR Order 25, rule 8(9) (reissue of warrant where condition upon which warrant was suspended has not been complied with); or
(iii) CCR Order 28, rule 11(1) (issue of warrant of committal),

applies.
(2) Nothing in this rule shall require a court officer to accept a document which is illegible, has not been duly authorised, or is unsatisfactory for some other similar reason.

5.3 Signature of documents by mechanical means

Where any of these Rules or any practice direction requires a document to be signed, that requirement shall be satisfied if the signature is printed by computer or other mechanical means.

5.4 Register of claims

(1) A court or court office may keep a publicly accessible register of claims which have been issued out of that court or court office.
(2) Any person who pays the prescribed fee may, during office hours, search any available register of claims.
(The practice direction contains details of available registers).

5.4A Supply of documents to Attorney-General from court records
(1) The Attorney-General may search for, inspect and take a copy of any documents within a court file for the purpose of preparing an application or considering whether to make an application under section 42 of the Supreme Court Act 1981 or section 33 of the Employment Tribunals Act 1996 (restriction of vexatious proceedings).
(2) The Attorney-General must, when exercising the right under paragraph (1) –

(a) pay any prescribed fee; and
(b) file a written request, which must –

(i) confirm that the request is for the purpose of preparing an application or considering whether to make an application mentioned in paragraph (1); and
(ii) name the person who would be the subject of the application.

5.4B Supply of documents to a party from court records
(1) A party to proceedings may, unless the court orders otherwise, obtain from the records of the court a copy of any document listed in paragraph 4.2A of the Practice Direction.
(2) A party to proceedings may, if the court gives permission, obtain from the records of the court a copy of any other document filed by a party or communication between the court and a party or another person.

5.4C Supply of documents to a non-party from court records
(1) The general rule is that a person who is not a party to proceedings may obtain from the court records a copy of –

(a) a statement of case, but not any documents filed with or attached to the statement of case, or intended by the party whose statement it is to be served with it;
(b) a judgment or order given or made in public (whether made at a hearing or without a hearing).

(1A) Where a non-party seeks to obtain a copy of a statement of case filed before 2nd October 2006 –

(a) this rule does not apply; and
(b) the rules of court relating to access by a non-party to statements of case in force immediately before 2nd October 2006 apply as if they had not been revoked.

(The rules relating to access by a non-party to statements of case in force immediately before 2nd October 2006 were contained in the former rule 5.4(5) to 5.4(9). The Practice Direction to this Part sets out the relevant provisions as they applied to statements of case.)

(2) A non-party may, if the court gives permission, obtain from the records of the court a copy of any other document filed by a party, or communication between the court and a party or another person.
(3) A non-party may obtain a copy of a statement of case or judgment or order under paragraph (1) only if –

(a) where there is one defendant, the defendant has filed an acknowledgment of service or a defence;
(b) where there is more than one defendant, either –

(i) all the defendants have filed an acknowledgment of service or a defence;
(ii) at least one defendant has filed an acknowledgment of service or a defence, and the court gives permission;

(c) the claim has been listed for a hearing; or
(d) judgment has been entered in the claim.

(4) The court may, on the application of a party or of any person identified in a statement of case –

(a) order that a non-party may not obtain a copy of a statement of case under paragraph (1);
(b) restrict the persons or classes of persons who may obtain a copy of a statement of case;
(c) order that persons or classes of persons may only obtain a copy of a statement of case if it is edited in accordance with the directions of the court; or
(d) make such other order as it thinks fit.

(5) A person wishing to apply for an order under paragraph (4) must file an application notice in accordance with Part 23.
(6) Where the court makes an order under paragraph (4), a non-party who wishes to obtain a copy of the statement of case, or to obtain an unedited copy of the statement of case, may apply on notice to the party or person identified in the statement of case who requested the order, for permission.

5.4D Supply of documents from court records—general
(1) A person wishing to obtain a copy of a document under rule 5.4B or rule 5.4C must pay any prescribed fee and –

(a) if the court's permission is required, file an application notice in accordance with Part 23; or
(b) if permission is not required, file a written request for the document.

(2) An application for an order under rule 5.4C(4) or for permission to obtain a copy of a document under rule 5.4B or rule 5.4C (except an application for permission under rule 5.4C(6)) may be made without notice, but the court may direct notice to be given to any person who would be affected by its decision.

(3) Rules 5.4, 5.4B and 5.4C do not apply in relation to any proceedings in respect of which a rule or practice direction makes different provision.

5.5 Filing and sending documents

(1) A practice direction may make provision for documents to be filed or sent to the court by –

(a) facsimile; or
(b) other electronic means.

(2) Any such practice direction may –

(a) provide that only particular categories of documents may be filed or sent to the court by such means;
(b) provide that particular provisions only apply in specific courts; and
(c) specify the requirements that must be fulfilled for any document filed or sent to the court by such means.

1. 1981 c.54.
2. 1996 c.17.

Appendix H

PRACTICE DIRECTION 5A—COURT DOCUMENTS
This Practice Direction Supplements CPR Part 5

Signature of Documents by mechanical means

1 Where, under rule 5.3, a replica signature is printed electronically or by other mechanical means on any document, the name of the person whose signature is printed must also be printed so that the person may be identified. This paragraph does not apply to claim forms issued through the Claims Production Centre.

Form of Documents

2.1 Statements of case and other documents drafted by a legal representative should bear his/her signature and if they are drafted by a legal representative as a member or employee of a firm they should be signed in the name of the firm.

2.2 Every document prepared by a party for filing or use at the Court must –

(1) Unless the nature of the document renders it impracticable, be on A4 paper of durable quality having a margin, not less than 3.5 centimetres wide,
(2) be fully legible and should normally be typed,
(3) where possible be bound securely in a manner which would not hamper filing or otherwise each page should be endorsed with the case number,
(4) have the pages numbered consecutively,
(5) be divided into numbered paragraphs,
(6) have all numbers, including dates, expressed as figures, and
(7) give in the margin the reference of every document mentioned that has already been filed.

2.3 A document which is a copy produced by a colour photostat machine or other similar device may be filed at the court office provided that the coloured date seal of the Court is not reproduced on the copy.

Supply of Documents to New Parties

3.1 Where a party is joined to existing proceedings, the party joined shall be entitled to require the party joining him to supply, without charge, copies of all statements of case, written evidence and any documents appended or exhibited to them which have been served in the proceedings by or upon the joining party which relate to any issues between the joining party and the party joined, and copies of all orders made in those proceedings. The documents must be supplied within 48 hours after a written request for them is received.

3.2 If the party joined is not supplied with copies of the documents requested under paragraph 3.1 within 48 hours, he may apply under Part 23 for an order that they be supplied.
3.3 The party by whom a copy is supplied under paragraph 3.1 or, if he is acting by a solicitor, his solicitor, shall be responsible for it being a true copy.

Supply of documents from court records
4.1 Registers of claims which have been issued are available for inspection at the following offices of the High Court at the Royal Courts of Justice:

(1) the Central Office of the Queen's Bench Division;
(2) Chancery Chambers;
(3) the Admiralty and Commercial Court Registry.

4.2 No registers of claims are at present available for inspection in county courts or in district registries or other offices of the High Court.
4.2A A party to proceedings may, unless the court orders otherwise, obtain from the records of the court a copy of –

(a) a certificate of suitability of a litigation friend;
(b) a notice of funding;
(c) a claim form or other statement of case together with any documents filed with or attached to or intended by the claimant to be served with such claim form;
(d) an acknowledgment of service together with any documents filed with or attached to or intended by the party acknowledging service to be served with such acknowledgement of service;
(e) a certificate of service, other than a certificate of service of an application notice or order in relation to a type of application mentioned in sub-paragraph (h)(i) or (ii);
(f) a notice of non-service;
(g) an allocation questionnaire;
(h) an application notice, other than in relation to –

 (i) an application by a solicitor for an order declaring that he has ceased to be the solicitor acting for a party; or
 (ii) an application for an order that the identity of a party or witness should not be disclosed;

(i) any written evidence filed in relation to an application, other than a type of application mentioned in sub-paragraph (h)(i) or (ii);
(j) a judgment or order given or made in public (whether made at a hearing or without a hearing);
(k) a statement of costs;
(l) a list of documents;
(m) a notice of payment into court;
(n) a notice of discontinuance;

(o) a notice of change; or
(p) an appellant's or respondent's notice of appeal.

4.3 An application under rule 5.4B(2), 5.4C(2) or 5.4C(3)(b)(ii) for permission to obtain a copy of a document, even if made without notice, must be made under CPR Part 23 and the application notice must identify the document or class of document in respect of which permission is sought and the grounds relied upon.
4.4 An application under rule 5.4C(4) by a party or a person identified in a claim form must be made –

(1) under CPR Part 23; and
(2) to a Master or district judge, unless the court directs otherwise.

4.5 4.5 Rule 5.4B allows a person who is a party to proceedings to obtain copies of documents from court records. A person is a party to proceedings who has been named as a party on a statement of case irrespective of whether they have been served with that statement of case.

Supply of documents from court records—statements of case filed before 2nd October 2006

4A.1 Rule 5.4C(1A) provides that the rules of court relating to access by a non-party to statements of case in force immediately before 2nd October 2006 apply to statements of case filed before that date as if they had not been revoked. For ease of reference, those rules are set out in the following paragraphs as they applied to statements of case, along with the relevant supplementary provisions previously contained in this practice direction.
4A.2 A person who is not a party to proceedings may –

(1) unless the court orders otherwise, obtain from the records of the court a copy of a claim form, but not any documents filed with or attached to or intended by the claimant to be served with such claim form, subject to paragraph 4A.3 and to any order of the court under paragraph 4A.4; and
(2) if the court gives permission, obtain from the records of the court a copy of any other statement of case.

4A.3 A person may obtain a copy of a claim form under paragraph 4A.2(1) only if –

(1) where there is one defendant, the defendant has filed an acknowledgment of service or a defence;
(2) where there is more than one defendant, either –

(a) all the defendants have filed an acknowledgment of service or a defence;
(b) at least one defendant has filed an acknowledgment of service or a defence, and the court gives permission;

(3) the claim has been listed for a hearing; or
(4) judgment has been entered in the claim.

4A.4 The court may, on the application of a party or any person identified in the claim form –

(1) restrict the persons or classes of persons who may obtain a copy of the claim form;
(2) order that persons or classes of persons may only obtain a copy of the claim form if it is edited in accordance with the directions of the court; or
(3) make such other order as it thinks fit.

4A.5 A person wishing to obtain a copy of a document under paragraph 4A.2 must pay any prescribed fee and –

(a) if the court's permission is required, file an application notice in accordance with Part 23; or
(b) if permission is not required, file a written request for the document.

4A.6 An application for permission to obtain a copy of a statement of case, or for an order under paragraph 4A.4, may be made without notice, but the court may direct notice to be given to any person who would be affected by its decision.
4A.7 An application under paragraph 4A.3(2)(b) for permission to obtain a copy of a claim form must be made under Part 23.
4A.8 An application notice under paragraph 4A.2(2) or paragraph 4A.3(2)(b) must identify the document or class of document in respect of which permission is sought and the grounds relied upon.
4A.9 An application under paragraph 4A.4 by a party or a person identified in a claim form must be made –

(a) under Part 23; and
(b) to a Master or district judge, unless the court directs otherwise.

Documents for Filing at Court
5.1 The date on which a document was filed at court must be recorded on the document. This may be done by a seal or a receipt stamp.
5.2 Particulars of the date of delivery at a court office of any document for filing and the title of the proceedings in which the document is filed shall be entered in court records, on the court file or on a computer kept in the court office for the purpose. Except where a document has been delivered at the court office through the post, the time of delivery should also be recorded.
5.3 Filing by Facsimile

(1) Subject to paragraph (6) below, a party may file a document at court by sending it by facsimile ('fax').
(2) Where a party files a document by fax, he must not send a hard copy in addition.
(3) A party filing a document by fax should be aware that the document is not filed at court until it is delivered by the court's fax machine, whatever time it is shown to have been transmitted from the party's machine.
(4) The time of delivery of the faxed document will be recorded on it in accordance with paragraph 5.2.

(5) It remains the responsibility of the party to ensure that the document is delivered to the court in time.
(6) If a fax is delivered after 4 p.m. it will be treated as filed on the next day the court office is open.
(7) If a fax relates to a hearing, the date and time of the hearing should be prominently displayed.
(8) Fax should not be used to send letters or documents of a routine or non-urgent nature.
(9) Fax should not be used, except in an unavoidable emergency, to deliver:

(a) a document which attracts a fee
(b) omitted
(c) a document relating to a hearing less than two hours ahead
(d) trial bundles or skeleton arguments

(10) Where (9)(a) or (b) applies, the fax should give an explanation for the emergency and include an undertaking that the fee or money has been dispatched that day by post or will be paid at the court office counter the following business day.
(11) Where courts have several fax machines, each allocated to an individual section, fax messages should only be sent to the machine of the section for which the message is intended.

5.4 Where the Court orders any document to be lodged in Court, the document must, unless otherwise directed, be deposited in the office of that Court.
5.5 A document filed, lodged or held in any court office shall not be taken out of that office without the permission of the Court unless the document is to be sent to the office of another court (for example under CPR Part 30 (Transfer)), except in accordance with CPR rule 39.7 (impounded documents) or in accordance with paragraph 5.6 below.
5.6 (1) Where a document filed, lodged or held in a court office is required to be produced to any Court, Tribunal or arbitrator, the document may be produced by sending it by registered post (together with a Certificate as in paragraph 5.6(8)(b)) to the Court, Tribunal or arbitrator in accordance with the provisions of this paragraph.
(2) Any Court, Tribunal or arbitrator or any party requiring any document filed, lodged or held in any court office to be produced must apply to that court office by sending a completed request (as in paragraph 5.6 (8)(a)), stamped with the prescribed fee.
(3) On receipt of the request the court officer will submit the same to a Master in the Royal Courts of Justice or to a District Judge elsewhere, who may direct that the request be complied with. Before giving a direction the Master or District Judge may require to be satisfied that the request is made in good faith and that the document is required to be produced for the reasons stated. The Master or District Judge giving the direction may also direct that, before the document is sent, an official copy of it is made and filed in the court office at the expense of the party requiring the document to be produced.

(4) On the direction of the Master or District Judge the court officer shall send the document by registered post addressed to the Court, Tribunal or arbitrator, with:

(a) an envelope stamped and addressed for use in returning the document to the court office from which it was sent;
(b) a Certificate as in paragraph 5.6(8)(b);
(c) a covering letter describing the document, stating at whose request and for what purpose it is sent, referring to this paragraph of the Practice Direction and containing a request that the document be returned to the court office from which it was sent in the enclosed envelope as soon as the Court or Tribunal no longer requires it.

(5) It shall be the duty of the Court, Tribunal or arbitrator to whom the document was sent to keep it in safe custody, and to return it by registered post to the court office from which it was sent, as soon as the Court, Tribunal or arbitrator no longer requires it.
(6) In each court office a record shall be kept of each document sent and the date on which it was sent and the Court, Tribunal or arbitrator to whom it was sent and the date of its return. It shall be the duty of the court officer who has signed the certificate referred to in para 5.6(8)(b) below to ensure that the document is returned within a reasonable time and to make inquiries and report to the Master or District Judge who has given the direction under paragraph (3) above if the document is not returned, so that steps may be taken to secure its return.
(7) Notwithstanding the preceding paragraphs, the Master or District Judge may direct a court officer to attend the Court, Tribunal or arbitrator for the purpose of producing the document.
(8)

(a) I, of , an officer of the Court/Tribunal at /an arbitrator of /the Claimant /Defendant /Solicitor for the Claimant/ Defendant *[describing the Applicant so as to show that he is a proper person to make the request]* in the case of v. [19 No.] (REQUEST that the following document [or documents] be produced to the Court /Tribunal/arbitrator on the day of 19 [and following days] and I request that the said document [or documents] be sent by registered post to the proper officer of the Court/Tribunal/arbitrator for production to that Court/ Tribunal/arbitrator on that day.

(Signed).

Dated the day of 1999/2

(b) I, A.B., an officer of the Court of certify that the document sent herewith for production to the Court/Tribunal/arbitrator on the day of 1999/2 in the case of v. and marked 'A.B.' is the document requested on the day of 1999/2 and I

FURTHER CERTIFY that the said document has been filed in and is produced from the custody of the Court.

(Signed)

Dated the day of 1999/2 .

Enrolment of Deeds and other Documents

6.1 (1) Any deed or document which by virtue of any enactment is required or authorised to be enrolled in the Supreme Court may be enrolled in the Central Office of the High Court.

(2) Attention is drawn to the Enrolment of Deeds (Change of Name) Regulations 1994 which are reproduced in the Appendix to this Practice Direction.

6.2 The following paragraph of the Practice Direction describes the practice to be followed in any case in which a child's name is to be changed and to which the 1994 Regulations apply.

6.3 (1) Where a person has by any order of the High Court, County Court or Family Proceedings Court been given parental responsibility for a child and applies to the Central Office, Filing Department, for the enrolment of a Deed Poll to change the surname (family name) of a child who is under the age of 18 years (unless a child who is or has been married or has formed a civil partnership), the application must be supported by the production of the consent in writing of every other person having parental responsibility.

(2) In the absence of that consent, the application will be adjourned generally unless and until permission is given in the proceedings, in which the said order was made, to change the surname of the child and the permission is produced to the Central Office.

(3) Where an application is made to the Central Office by a person who has not been given parental responsibility for a child by any order of the High Court, County Court or Family Proceedings Court for the enrolment of a Deed Poll to change the surname of the child who is under the age of 18 years (unless the child is or has been married or has formed a civil partnership), permission of the Court to enrol the Deed will be granted if the consent in writing of every person having parental responsibility is produced or if the person (or, if more than one, persons) having parental responsibility is dead or overseas or despite the exercise of reasonable diligence it has not been possible to find him or her for other good reason.

(4) In cases of doubt the Senior Master or, in his absence, the Practice Master will refer the matter to the Master of the Rolls.

(5) In the absence of any of the conditions specified above the Senior Master or the Master of the Rolls, as the case may be, may refer the matter to the Official Solicitor for investigation and report.

Appendix

Regulations made by the Master of the Rolls, Sir Thomas Bingham M.R. on March 3, 1994 (S.I. 1994 No.604) under s.133(1) of the Supreme Court Act 1981.

1 (1) These regulations may be cited as the Enrolment of Deeds (Change of Name) Regulations 1994 and shall come into force on April 1, 1994.
(2) These Regulations shall govern the enrolment in the Central Office of the Supreme Court of deeds evidencing change of name (referred to in these Regulations as 'deeds poll').
2 (1) A person seeking to enrol a deed poll ('the applicant') must be a Commonwealth citizen as defined by section 37(1) of the British Nationality Act 1981.
(2) If the applicant is a British citizen, a British Dependent Territories citizen or a British Overseas citizen, he must be described as such in the deed poll, which must also specify the section of the British Nationality Act under which the relevant citizenship was acquired.
(3) In any other case, the applicant must be described as a Commonwealth citizen.
(4) The applicant must be described in the deed poll as single, married, widowed, divorced, a civil partner or former civil partner and, if a former civil partner, whether the civil partnership ended on death or dissolution.
3 (1) As proof of the citizenship named in the deed poll, the applicant must produce:

(a) a certificate of birth; or
(b) a certificate of citizenship by registration or naturalisation or otherwise; or
(c) some other document evidencing such citizenship.

(2) In addition to the documents set out in paragraph (1), an applicant who is married or a civil partner must:

(a) produce his certificate of marriage or civil partnership certificate; and
(b) show that the notice of his intention to apply for the enrolment of the deed poll had been given to his spouse or civil partner by delivery or by post to his spouse's or civil partner's last known address; and
(c) show that he has obtained the consent of his spouse or civil partner to the proposed change of name or that there is good reason why such consent should be dispensed with.

4 (1) The deed poll and the documents referred to in regulation 3 must be exhibited to a statutory declaration by a Commonwealth citizen who is a householder in the United Kingdom and who must declare that he is such in the statutory declaration.
(2) The statutory declaration must state the period, which should ordinarily not be less than 10 years, during which the householder has known the applicant and must identify the applicant as the person referred to in the documents exhibited to the statutory declaration.
(3) Where the period mentioned in paragraph (2) is stated to be less than 10 years, the Master of the Rolls may in his absolute discretion decide whether to permit the deed poll to be enrolled and may require the applicant to provide more information before so deciding.
5 If the applicant is resident outside the United Kingdom, he must provide evidence that such residence is not intended to be permanent and the applicant

may be required to produce a certificate by a solicitor as to the nature and probable duration of such residence.

6 The applicant must sign the deed poll in both his old and new names.

7 Upon enrolment the deed poll shall be advertised in the London Gazette by the clerk in charge for the time being of the Filing and Record Department at the Central Office of the Supreme Court.

8 (1) Subject to the following provisions of this regulation, these Regulations shall apply in relation to a deed poll evidencing the change of name of a child as if the child were the applicant.

(2) Paragraphs (3) to (8) shall not apply to a child who has attained the age of 16 and is or has been married or a civil partner.

(3) If the child is under the age of 16, the deed poll must be executed by a person having parental responsibility for him.

(4) If the child has attained the age of 16, the deed poll must, except in the case of a person mentioned in paragraph (2), be executed by a person having parental responsibility for the child and be endorsed with the child's consent signed in both his old and new names and duly witnessed.

(5) The application for enrolment must be supported:

(a) by a witness statement showing that the change of name is for the benefit of the child; and –

(i) that the application is submitted by all persons having parental responsibility for the child; or

(ii) that it is submitted by one person having parental responsibility for the child with the consent of every other person; or

(iii) that it is submitted by one person having parental responsibility for the child without the consent of every other such person, or by some other person whose name and capacity are given, for reasons set out in the affidavit; and

(b) by such other evidence, if any, as the Master of the Rolls may require in the particular circumstances of the case.

(6) Regulation 4(2) shall not apply but the statutory declaration mentioned in regulation 4(1) shall state how long the householder has known the deponent under paragraph (5)(a) and the child respectively.

(7) Regulation 6 shall not apply to a child who has not attained the age of 16.

(8) In this regulation 'parental responsibility' has the meaning given in section 3 of the Children Act 1989.

9 The Enrolment of Deeds (Change of Name) Regulations 1983 and the Enrolment of Deeds (Change of Name) (Amendment) Regulations 1990 are hereby revoked.

INDEX